MODERN AMERICAN
COMMUNES

MODERN AMERICAN COMMUNES

COMMUNES

A Dictionary

ROBERT P. SUTTON

GREENWOOD PRESS
Westport, Connecticut • London

POW
65
1-18-06

307.77
596 7m
2005

Library of Congress Cataloging-in-Publication Data

Sutton, Robert P.
    Modern American communes : a dictionary / Robert P. Sutton.
        p. cm.
    Includes bibliographical references and index.
    ISBN 0–313–32181–7 (alk. paper)
    1. Collective settlements—United States—History—20th century—Directories.
2. Utopias—United States—History—20th century—Directories. I. Title.
    HX653.S883   2005
    307.77'0973'03—dc22   2004025573

British Library Cataloging in Publication Data is available.

Library of Congress Catalog Card Number: 2004025573
ISBN: 0–313–32181–7

First published in 2005

Greenwood Press, 88 Post Road West, Westport, CT 06881
An imprint of Greenwood Publishing Group, Inc.
www.greenwood.com

Printed in the United States of America

The paper used in this book complies with the
Permanent Paper Standard issued by the National
Information Standards Organization (Z39.48–1984).

10 9 8 7 6 5 4 3 2 1

CONTENTS

LIST OF ENTRIES

GUIDE TO RELATED ENTRIES

THE GREAT DEPRESSION

Borsodi, Ralph

Catholic Worker Movement

Cohen, Joseph B.

Day, Dorothy

Divine, Father, and the Peace Mission
  Movement

Divine Light Mission

FERA (Federal Emergency Relief
  Administration)

Maverick, Maury

New Deal Cooperatives

Sunrise

HIPPIE COLONIES

Black Bear Ranch

Bryn Athyn

Cold Mountain Farm

Crashpads

Diggers

Drop City

The Family (Taos)

Grateful Dead

High Ridge Farm

Hog Farm

Kerista

Libre

Merry Pranksters

Millbrook

Morning Star East

Morning Star Ranch

MOVE

New Buffalo

Olompali Ranch

Reality Construction Company

Red Rockers

Renaissance Community/Brotherhood
  of the Spirit

Sunrise Hill

Table Mountain Ranch

Tolstoy Farm

Wheeler's Ranch

Nelson, Nelson O.

Paramahansa, Yogananda

Paramananda, Swami

Purnell, Benjamin F.

Riker, William E.

Russell, Charles Taze

Sandford, Frank

Sinclair, Upton

Skinner, B. F.

Smythe, William Ellsworth

Teed, Cyrus Read

Tingley, Katherine Augusta Westcott

Trungpa, Chogyam

Walters, James Donald (Swami Kriyananda)

Wayland, Julius A.

Whitehead, Ralph Radcliffe

Whitman, Walt

Whittaker, James

Willard, Cyrus Field

RELIGIOUS COMMUNITIES

Abode of the Message

The Alamo Christian Foundation

Amana

Amity Colony

Ananda Ashram

Ananda Ashrama

Ananda World Brotherhood Village

Arpin

Bethany Fellowship

Bethel Home

Branch Davidians (Davidian Seventh-Day Adventists)

Bruderhof

Burning Bush

Carmel

Catholic Worker Movement

Children of God (The Family)

Children of Light

Church of God and Saints of Christ

Church of the Savior

Clarion

The Colony

Davidian Seventh-Day Adventists

Divine, Father, and the Peace Mission Movement

Divine Light Mission

Ellicott City

Glendenning: The Levites/Order of Aaron

Gould Farm

Happyville

Havurat Shalom

Healthy-Happy-Holy Organization

The Himalayan Academy

Holy City

The House of David

Hutterite Brethren

International Society for Krishna Consciousness (ISKCON)

Jesus People USA

Kilgore: Zion's Order

Koinonia (Maryland)

Koinonia Farm

Krishna Venta

Kwan Um Zen School

Lama Foundation

The Land of Shalam

Lebaron

Lily Dale and Cassadaga

Lopez Island

The Lord's Farm

Love Israel Family

Mankind United

The Messianic Communities (Twelve Tribes)

Moonies (Unification Church)

New House of Israel

SECULAR COMMUNITIES

INTRODUCTION

Some students of utopian communalism claim that the nineteenth century was the heyday of the building of these communities and that the utopian impulse declined in the twentieth century. Nothing is farther from the historical reality, for in the twentieth century there was almost continuous experimentation with communal utopias. During the first decades of the last century, many of the utopian communities that were started in the 1880s and 1890s flourished. After a brief hiatus in the 1920s, the Great Depression gave rise to a new round of community building, much of it sponsored by the New Deal programs of the federal government. These communities, such as subsistence farm colonies or Greenbelt towns, lasted until the end of World War II, at which point they were disbanded. In the 1950s, the Fellowship of Intentional Communities (FIC), under the direction of Arthur Morgan, spearheaded the building of new "intentional communities." In the mid-1960s, the counterculture youth of the 1960s started hundreds of hippie colonies all across the country. As the hippie movement waned in the 1980s, utopian communalism was expressed in the creation of hundreds of new intentional cooperatives. As a testimony to the vitality of this latest growth of utopian communalism, the FIC (now known as the Fellowship for Intentional Community) in 2000 published a third edition of its *Communities Directory: A Guide to Intentional Communities and Cooperative Living* that listed more than 700 North American communities, along with articles about community living.

There is, therefore, a pressing need for an up-to-date dictionary as a guide to twentieth-century communal and utopian history. Published dictionaries either do not focus on this century or appeared well before the hippie movement was spent and the wave of intentional community building began. For example, Richard C. S. Trahair's *Utopias and Utopians: An Historical Dictionary,* which appeared in 1999, is a comprehensive treatment of communities from ancient Greece to modern Africa and Russia and, while touching on some twentieth-century American communal utopias, most were omitted. In 1980, Robert S. Fogarty's *Dictionary of American Communal and Utopian History,* a much welcomed coverage of what he called the "Paradise Planters," presented a thoroughly researched compilation of biographies of utopian leaders and sketches of communities. His dictionary, like that of Trahair, included valuable bibliographies. But Fogarty concentrated mostly on the nineteenth century and occasionally included biographies of twentieth-century individuals such as James Warren Jones, Swami Paramananda, or Cyrus Read Teed. And only 19 of the 55 communities included in the book were relevant to the twentieth century.

The entries in this dictionary are arranged alphabetically and, presented as such, it might appear that the twentieth-century communal experience lacked common features. But it had a number of distinct characteristics. There was a broad division of communities into those that were religious and those that were secular. Either way, they tended to show a tension between a dedication to common goals and persistent self-interest; and lofty communal ideals such as brotherhood and cooperation were challenged by chronic individualism. Most communities embraced equality and democratic leadership, but many were dominated by strong-willed leaders. Commitment to communal property was frequently undermined by economic opportunities available outside the colony. Many twentieth-century utopias wanted an emancipated role for women, but most kept them in traditional gender roles and subordinate to men. Utopians thought that children should be treated with understanding and compassion; but in some settlements they were viewed as nettlesome temptations for the parents to develop special love for their offspring rather than have unfettered attachment to the community. Except for the hippies and some intentional communities, most communal utopias claimed to be paradigms, or models, of a more perfect lifestyle that other Americans would want to emulate. The hippie groups, especially, showed some unique traits of their own. Compared to their predecessors, they were smaller, had looser communal economic arrangements, lower membership requirements, and a large turnover in communards. For an overview of twentieth-century American communalism see Timothy Miller's *The Quest for Utopia in Twentieth-Century America* (Syracuse, N.Y.: Syracuse University Press, 1998) and *The 60s Communes: Hippies and Beyond* (Syracuse, N.Y.: Syracuse University Press, 1999).

Miller sees the communal and utopian history of the twentieth century divided into distinct phases. The first phase included those religious communities that were carryovers from the previous century and whose presence represented a "continuing tradition" in the modern quest for utopia. Two outstanding examples of this tradition were the Amana Society, or the

Society of True Inspiration, and the Hutterites. Amana was founded in Iowa in 1854 and lasted as a cohesive religious society until the Great Depression forced it to abandon an 89-year commitment to community property. By far the largest of the religious communal experiments were the Hutterites. Established on the great plains of North Dakota in the 1870s by Russian immigrants, they grew to more than 350 colonies by the turn of the century. An explosion of growth, however, took place in the twentieth century and these communities of about 100 individuals collectively are the longest-lived communal movement in the United States.

Other, less known religious communal utopias include the Christian Commonwealth Colony in Georgia, the Salvation Army Colonies, the Olive Branch in Chicago, the New House of Israel in Texas, Shiloh: Church of the Living God in Maine, and the Women's Commonwealth in Washington, D.C., to mention a few. In the first decades of the century, new expressions of religious communalism, the evangelical and Pentecostal Christian colonies that stressed faith healing and speaking in tongues, appeared. John Alexander Dowie founded his theocratic Zion City on the shores of Lake Michigan north of Chicago. Thomas Gourley's plain, hard-working colony at Lopez Island off the shores of the state of Washington proscribed the taking of life in any form, even seafood. These two experiments were followed by the Burning Bush in Chicago, Pisgah Grande in southern California and Bethel Home, or the Jehovah's Witnesses, in lower Manhattan. Alongside the evangelical communities a number of Jewish utopian colonies appeared, such as Ellicott City, Arpin, Happyville, and Clarion.

During the Great Depression, both private individuals and the federal government offered communal living as a refuge from unemployment and eviction. In 1933, at Dayton, Ohio, Ralph Borsodi tried to create "Cooperative Production Units" to help the dispossessed. Then, in 1936, he built his School of Living as a private communal homestead near his home at Suffern, New York. The Quakers sponsored Penn-Craft and theologian Reinhold Niebuhr was involved in the Delta and Providence community. Maury Maverick's colony of old railroad cars at Diga near San Antonio was another example of a nongovernmental response to the Depression. Perhaps the most influential private venture in utopian communalism in the 1930s was the Catholic Worker movement under Dorothy Day, who organized relief centers in cities across the nation called Houses of Hospitality. Under the auspices of the New Deal, a number of land-colonization communities were organized by the Division of Subsistence Homesteads and the Resettlement Administration under the controversial Rexford G. Tugwell.

After World War II and into the 1950s, a third phase of community building appeared, encouraged by Arthur Morgan's Fellowship of Intentional Communities, located at Yellow Springs, Ohio. Morgan, president of Antioch College, promoted cooperative communities and an exchange of information and products among them. Indeed, the fellowship was the major force in the development of intentional communities until the end of the decade and responsible in large measure for the following, somewhat lesser known, experiments: Hidden Springs (New Jersey), Tanguy Homesteads (Pennsylvania), Tuolumne Co-operative Farms (California), Skyview Acres (New York), Canterbury (New Hampshire), May Valley (Washington), and The Vale (Ohio). But the two best known utopian FIC member communities were the interracial rural commune at Koinonia Farm in Georgia and Eberhard Arnold's Bruderhof (Society of Brothers).

The 1950s also saw the growth of non-Western communal living such as Trabuco College in southern California as a retreat of students, masters, and missionaries who meditated daily in silence and performed communal manual labor. Somewhat connected to the Eastern communal expression were the New Age colonies such as the Emissary Communities that emphasized spiritual seeking and regeneration, the Lemurian Fellowship, the Stelle Community, and the Children of Light colony. The last expression of communal living in the 1950s came from off-shoots of the Latter Day Saints. In 1956, Maurice Glendenning founded The Levites/Order of Aaron in a remote section of Utah and Marl V. Kilgore, once a member of Glendenning, led his followers to land close to Mansfield, Missouri, to build Kilgore: Zion's Order.

Intentional communities were a special type of communitarianism discussed at length by Timothy Miller in *The Quest for Utopia*. He specified seven criteria that intentional communities met.

1. They had a sense of common purpose and separation from the dominant society.
2. They had some form of self-denial and voluntary suppression of individual choice for the good of the group.
3. Community members lived in one geographic place, either in dormitories or in separate houses on the communal property.
4. They shared a sense of personal interaction much stronger than in suburban America.
5. They practiced a variety of economic sharing, ranging from a total community of goods to allowing a considerable amount of personal property ownership.
6. They had what he termed "real existence" even if they were small and lasted only a short period of time.
7. They had a "critical mass" that included at a minimum five unrelated individuals.

In the 1990s, Miller and a colleague at the University of Kansas, Deborah Altus, completed The 60s Communes Project, in which they canvassed the country compiling taped interviews with members of hundreds of hippie colonies and intentional communities. Eventually they collected over 500 interviews and an array of documents that included correspondence, newspapers, books, articles, videos and films, posters, and constitutions and bylaws. Relying on this information and other, more conventional historical sources such as published articles, Miller was able to complete *The 60s Communes: Hippies and Beyond,* his second book on the hippie colonies and the intentional communities of the last three decades of the twentieth century.

The hippie communes had distinctly sensational characteristics. They were bands of alienated young people who shared a sensational, counterculture, pleasure-seeking lifestyle that often involved drug use, nudity, and unconventional sexual practices. While they started with a small number of members, most suffered from almost immediate overcrowding by new people attracted to them by the colorful accounts that the mass print media gave them, such as articles in *Life, Time,* and *Newsweek.* Most of the hippie colonies encountered the hostility of their conventional neighbors and some were raided by police. Nevertheless, a number of the communes developed profitable projects such as producing books and films of their own.

Miller saw the year 1965 as the real beginning of hippie communalism with the building of Drop City in Colorado, since most of the hippie communes that followed it exhibited many of its characteristics. Offering radical alternatives to suburban America, Drop City was committed to personal freedom and expression, a "joy dance" of a daily life that embraced spontaneity, egalitarianism, sexual freedom, and drug use. Within a year they had organized a traveling exhibition of strobe-lights and psychedelic music that visited colleges and university urging students to "do their thing." They put out a newsletter and brochures. But by the summer of 1967, they were inundated with young people and within months the colony became a communal slum with inadequate food and sanitation facilities. By 1969, membership of Drop City, which at one time numbered in the hundreds, was reduced to about forty residents barely surviving in squalor.

At the same time that the hippie colonies began to appear, mainly in the Pacific Coast and Southwest, the intentional community movement that had started in the fifties with the FIC expanded all across the country. These communities continued to share the more conventional characteristics of their predecessors but some, like Twin Oaks, added a new emphasis on the behaviorism of B. F. Skinner. As Drop City was the model for its successors, the experiment at Twin Oaks, a colony modeled on B.F. Skinner's book *Walden Two,* was the prototype in many ways of the behaviorist intentional communities that came after it. This community was founded in 1967 by members of an unsuccessful Walden House cooperative in Washington, D.C., on 123 acres in rural Virginia. Adults lived in residential buildings built around a central courtyard. Work rules were made by a three-member planning board in a planner-manager system similar to the one described in the book. The colony was economically successful in the making and selling of rope hammocks, the manufacturing of tofu, and indexing of books. It stressed gender equality and members addressed each other as "co" instead of he or she. Twin Oaks also sponsored the East Wind colony in Missouri and Acorn in nearby Virginia.

Another variety of late-twentieth-century intentional community was the kind that followed Ralph Borsodi's emphasis on small-scale, self-sufficient, subsistence farming, although a few such communities adopted the unconventional customs of the hippie communities and used drugs and practiced nudity. In 1965, Borsodi purchased 37 acres and 5 buildings in rural Maryland and named the community the Heathcote Center. There, the residents attended classes on how to promote self-sufficiency and learned practical skills that helped them run their individual two-acre homesteads. Five less conventional subsistence-farm communities, modeled on Heathcote Center, were established in the Northeast. The first one was Sunrise Hill in Massachusetts, begun in the summer of 1966 by Gordon Yaswen. He and his communards wanted to build a communal "nest" where they would work together in the open and live in single houses. They had regular meetings in which they reached all decisions by consensus. However, there was no formal communal organization, and residents could keep their personal possessions or donate them to the colony. Bad weather and inadequate housing for the New England winter led to dissension and by February 1967, most members had moved away. Its successor was Cold Mountain Farm in New York. In late 1966, a group of political activists and anarchists came to a conference at Heathcote and afterwards decided to join Sunrise Hill. But by the time they were ready to move from their current residence in New York's Lower East Side, Sunrise Hill had collapsed. So, they formed their own community, Cold Mountain Farm, on a dilapidated 450-acre site near the town of Hobart, New York, with the goal of growing enough crops to send to friends still living in Manhattan. But these city-dwellers knew nothing about farming and their practice of nudity quickly caused local hostility. After a hepatitis epidemic hit the colony the local health authorities demanded that they install indoor plumbing and electricity. Most members refused the order and some left to join the Bryn Athyn community in Vermont. This colony was started in the summer of 1967 by Woody Ranson, a wealthy farmer, and attracted New Left radicals who used psychedelic drugs and practiced free love. But, as on Cold Mountain Farm, hepatitis devastated the communards, after which Ranson tried to impose a disciplined constitution that would restrict the drugs and sex and threw out those who would not comply. They moved to a house in Lyme, New Hampshire, where they continued their eclectic lifestyle before dispersing in less than a year. Back at Cold Mountain, Ransom renamed the group that remained the Rockbottom Farm, and under his leadership the colony continued on for several years as a serious colony of self-sufficient rural workers.

Still another type of intentional community was the sort that focused on a common center of religious and spiritual values. The best known of these communities included the Shiloh Youth Revival Centers, the Children of God, the Sojourners Community, the International Society for Krishna Consciousness (ISKCON), Ananda World Brotherhood Village, the Zen Center of Los Angeles, the Abode of the Message, and the most widely known of them all, Stephen Gaskin's Farm in rural Tennessee.

Shiloh was the largest of the Jesus movement communities and during the decade after it was started in 1968, it had built over 175 communal houses across the nation. John Higgins organized Shiloh in Costa Mesa, California, in a house called the House of Miracles where residents practiced poverty, hard work, and "loving Jesus." In the later Shiloh Centers, members farmed, fished, canned, repaired automobiles, and started other such businesses. A patriarchal commune, they kept women in traditional roles. The centers closed down in 1989, when the Internal Revenue Service foreclosed on them for back taxes.

In 1967, James Donald Walters, a disciple of Paramahansa Yogananda, the author of *Autobiography of a Yogi*, purchased 650 acres near Nevada City, California, and organized the Ananda World Brotherhood Village, a community of 100 residents committed to human spiritual brotherhood and living lives devoted to spiritualism, self-improvement, cooperation, respect for individuals, and a cheerful spirit of service to God. The village expanded to include preschool and secondary schools, a dairy farm, and an organic garden. It started the Expanding Light Retreat Center, offering classes on New Age and Indian topics and yoga.

ISKCON started in 1965 when Bhaktivedanta Swami Prabhupada, the leader of a Hindu sect stressing asceticism and devotion to the god Krishna, opened a mission in New York City as a "holy place of transcendental pastime." ISKCON soon opened other missions in American cities, the most important of which was in the Haight-Ashbury district of San Francisco. This commune had over 200 "devotees," who followed a daily routine of prayer, chanting, and study. They abjured meat, drugs, alcohol, coffee, tea, and tobacco. They were most noted for their preaching in the streets and in airports dressed in saffron robes. After the founder's death in 1977, ISKCON membership declined, and by the year 2000, there were just a handful of temples and a few rural communes.

In 1975, Pir Vilayt Kahn acquired part of the Shaker village at Mount Lebanon and invited adults from Europe and America to join the community. Most residents were educated, professional individuals such as physicians, teachers, engineers, computer experts, and psychologists. They believed in the wholeness of the mind and body and began each day with meditation, followed by cycles of work and more meditation. They organized a communal business called the Winged Heart Corporation that supervised a Reza Quality Bakery, a Mount Lebanon Natural Foods Company, a Winged Heart Energy System, a Springs Health Center, an Earth Light Apprentice Program, and an excavating service called Earthworks. Its community bookstore and school, the Omega Institute, offered instruction in Sufi beliefs and practices.

In 1971, Stephen Gaskin, a member of the faculty at San Francisco State College, led a following to 1,700 acres near Summertown, Tennessee, to create a commune dedicated to vegetarianism, pacifism, and saving the planet. Its 200 or so members started a Peace Corps called "Plenty" to help rebuild areas devastated by earthquakes and a mail-order clothing business to distribute items made in Central America. They were dedicated environmentalists and advocated protection of wetlands, research on global warming, and the use of wind-power energy devices. On a local level, they offered midwife services to area residents and in the South Bronx of New York City and other locations, they ran a free ambulance service. The Farm opened an Ecovillage Training Center that gave visitors instruction on organic gardening, solar power generation, and biological waste treatment.

Yet another type of intentional community was the social visionary kind—those groups committed to social reform and serving as paradigms, or models, that would inspire others to imitate them and enjoy the comfort and wisdom of communal life. Perhaps the best known of this genre were the Movement for a New Society (MNS) in Philadelphia, the Community for Creative Nonviolence (CCNV) in Washington, D.C., Arcosanti in Arizona, the Gesundheit Institute in West Virginia, and the largest and longest-lived of them all, Synanon in California.

MNS, a respectable commune advocating social reform, was started by A Quaker Action Group in 1970. Within a decade, a network of twenty MNS houses opened in the Philadelphia area and later communities were established in Minneapolis, Ann Arbor, Madison, Denver, Eugene, Seattle, and Durango, Colorado. Residents did not pool their assets but worked at part-time jobs in the city and paid for a share of the colony's expenses. While different houses varied in the issues they stressed, such as feminism or treatment of children, they were united by an overall commitment to spreading the idea of "decentralized socialism" and to developing new forms of human relationships.

The social visionary intentional community that received the widest national coverage by the television media was the CCNV, founded in 1970 by graduates of George Washington University. Their main activity was running a charity soup kitchen and a Hospitality House near the White House that offered medical assistance. The hunger strikes of one member, Mitch Snyder, were covered in the nightly news programs of the major television networks and partly as a result of the publicity, the federal government gave the CCNV a building to start another shelter. And, in 1986, the Reagan administration subsidized the project with a $4 million allocation. This house was run by 60 volunteers in 1990, the year Snyder committed suicide.

In 1970, Paolo Soleri, a student of Frank Lloyd Wright at Taliesin West, organized a community to integrate architecture and ecology as "archeology." He wanted to create a city of 5,000 residents who would use solar heat and practice environmentalism. At the turn of the century, however, there were only about 50 individuals at Arcosanti; they made bronze bells, bakery goods, and other items.

The Gesundheit Institute described itself in the 2000 edition of *Communities Directory* as "a group of healers, visionaries and clowns working to build a healing community based on humor, compassion, generosity, and enthusiastic hard work." Its organizer, a physician named Patch Adams, opened a hospital that refused payment for services and where Adams and four MDs worked with chiropractors and homeopaths. The institute became noted for its special emphasis on communicating with sick children. The movie *Patch Adams* was based on the institute.

Synanon opened in 1958 as a drug and alcohol rehabilitation center run by Charles Dederich, but in the late 1960s, it converted into an intentional community that admitted nonaddicts, who paid a nonrefundable admissions fee. The colony had communal kitchens, dormitories, and schools. It had encounter groups of mutual criticism known as "the game" that were held during the week. For two decades, Synanon expanded and organized other communities in California, but because of economic problems in the early 1990s, it filed for bankruptcy and closed all of its residences.

It is hoped that this historical dictionary, evenly divided between biographical and community entries, will be of interest to a diverse audience, as communal and utopian studies includes a wide spectrum of disciplines from anthropology, history, and politics to psychology and religion—to cite a few examples. For students and scholars, each entry has a list of sources to aid his or her research. The dictionary has an appendix listing the opening and closing of the communities and a selected bibliography.

THE DICTIONARY

A

ABBOTT, LEONARD. Leonard Abbott (1878–1953) was one of the prominent anarchists who, with Harry Kelly and Joseph Cohen, founded the utopian anarchist community the Ferrer Colony, near Stelton, New Jersey, in 1915. He was born in New England but grew up in England and attended the Uppingham School. For a while after he returned to the United States in 1898, he edited a radical anarchist magazine. In 1910, in New York City, Abbott helped form an anarchist organization called the Ferrer Association. He was instrumental in running the Ferrer Modern School, which emphasized unstructured, almost undisciplined, education until Elizabeth and Alexis Ferm arrived in 1920 and imposed adult authority and manual labor on the students. Because of internal divisions between the anarchists and the Communists, and because of troubles with neighbors deeply hostile to the colonists' radical views, he left the colony. Later, during the New Deal, Abbott became involved in the Works Progress Administration.

See Also Ferrer Colony

Sources:

Fogarty, Robert S. 1980. *Dictionary of American Communal History.* Westport, Conn.: Greenwood Press.

Miller, Timothy. 1999. *The 60s Communes: Hippies and Beyond.* Syracuse, N.Y.: Syracuse University Press.

Veysey, Laurence. *The Communal Experience: Anarchist and Mystical Countercultures in America.* New York: Harper and Row.

ABODE OF THE MESSAGE. The Abode is one of a number of intentional communities established by the Sufi Order, a mystical offshoot of Islam that first appeared in the West in 1910. The 1995 edition of *Communities Directory* stated that it was a "thriving spiritual community of 41 adults and 16 children living on 430 acres in the Berkshire Mountains." Pir Vilayt Kahn (*pir* meaning spiritual master), the son of the man who had brought Sufi to Europe, purchased a portion of the former Mount Lebanon Shaker Village in the winter of 1975 for $350,000. Within a year, there were 100 adults and 25 children from America, England, and Germany living there. One resident recalled in a tape-recorded interview with Timothy Miller, Professor of Religious Studies at the University of Kansas, that "there was a high level of educated people who came to the Abode...medical doctors, teachers, business people, engineers, computer people, and psychologists." The Abode, as a spiritual community, did not demand compliance with Sufi beliefs and a number of non-Sufis joined it. The central religious concept of the community was that "the whole of humanity is like one body, and any organ which is hurt or troubled can indirectly cause damage to the whole body." Each day began with meditation followed by work until noon and midday prayers, then more work until supper and evening meditation. On Sunday, the Abode has a religious "Sufi Universal Worship" service, in which members discuss peace and cooperation and books on the world's religions. The Abode has organized communal businesses under the direction of the "Winged Heart Corporation." These included a Reza Quality Bakery, a Mount Lebanon Natural Foods Company, a Winged Heart Energy System to install wood stoves, an excavating service named Earthworks, a Springs Health Center, and an Earth Light Apprentice Program. Members earn a salary for work performed in the community by way of these various businesses, while paying a monthly rent of $235. The Abode has a community bookstore and a school, the Omega Institute, to instruct adults in Sufi ideas and practices. For children up to the age of 12, they operate the Mountain Road Children's School; the older children attend the public schools. In the 1995 *Communities Directory*, the Abode described itself as a "retreat center for those who seek the opportunity to withdraw from the world for a period so they may commune with their innermost being."

Sources:

Communities Directory: A Guide to Cooperative Living. 1995. Langley, Washington: Fellowship for Intentional Community.

Miller, Timothy. 1999. *The 60s Communes: Hippies and Beyond.* Syracuse, N.Y.: Syracuse University Press.

———. 2000. "The 60s Communes Project." Lawrence, Kan.: University of Kansas Archives.

Popenoe, Cris, and Oliver Popenoe. 1984. *Seeds of Tomorrow: New Age Communities That Work.* San Francisco: Harper and Row.

THE ALAMO CHRISTIAN FOUNDATION. Soon after Tony Alamo (a converted Jew named Bernie Hoffman) and Susan Horn met in 1966, they started a communal home called the Alamo Christian Foundation in Saugus, California, north of Los Angeles. When the colony became overcrowded in 1977, it moved to Dyer, Arkansas, Susan Horn's hometown. There they started a number of profitable operations that included a restaurant, a trucking operation, a grocery store, and a concrete company. Things took a turn for the worse in 1982, when Susan died and for over two years, Tony would not inter the body. During that time he was indicted for criminal and civil violations of the law. He also launched a vicious attack on the Catholic Church and the Vatican, accusing the church of immorality, drug trafficking, and selling liquor on the black market. In 1990, the Internal Revenue Service confiscated most of the Alamo Foundation's property and four years later it convicted Tony on tax evasion and he was sentenced to five years in prison.

Sources:
Ellwood, Robert S., Jr. 1973. *One Way: The Jesus Movement and Its Meaning.* Englewood Cliffs, N.J.: Prentice-Hall.
Miller, Timothy. 1999. *The 60s Communes: Hippies and Beyond.* Syracuse, N.Y.: Syracuse University Press.

ALBERTSON, RALPH. Ralph Albertson (?–1945) was a young minister of an Indiana Congregational church who, after he read the Reverend George Herron's books on Christian Socialism that denounced private property, became a socialist reformer. He published articles in the Christian Socialist journal, *The Kingdom,* that argued for the creation of a utopian community as a workers' asylum. By 1896, he had converted 25 families to a project that ultimately counted 350 members. He was the leader of the group that in November of that year purchased 1,000 acres near Columbus, Georgia, and founded the Christian Commonwealth Colony. For three years, the colony flourished in its commitment to communal ownership of property, sharing all work, and taking communal meals in a refectory. But its open admission policy attracted a large number of hangers-on and caused Albertson's followers to live in base poverty. The winter of 1899 proved disastrous. Heavy snows and a drought destroyed the spring harvest. Food became scarce and Albertson's seven-year-old son died of starvation. Typhoid fever hit the colony and claimed Albertson as a victim. He was so debilitated from the attack that soon afterwards he left the Commonwealth.

Sources:
Albertson, Ralph. 1945. "The Christian Commonwealth in Georgia," *Georgia Historical Quarterly* 29 (June), 125–42.
Dombrowski, James. 1966. *The Early Days of Christian Socialism in America.* New York: Octagon Books, Inc.
Miller, Timothy. 1998. *The Quest for Utopia in Twentieth-Century America.* Syracuse, N.Y.: Syracuse University Press.
Oved, Yaacov. 1988. *Two Hundred Years of American Communes.* New Brunswick, N.J. and Oxford: Transaction.

Sutton, Robert P. 2003. *Communal Utopias and the American Experience: Religious Communities, 1732–2000.* Westport, Conn. and London: Praeger.

ALPHA FARM. This community is one of a number of communes established along the Pacific Northwest coast from San Francisco to British Columbia. In 1971, four Philadelphia youths published a brochure advocating the creation of a new social order in Oregon on 280 acres of land with a house and a barn. Thirteen communards moved there the following year. They adopted the name Alpha, one earlier used for the location. Some of the residents were Quakers and the colony's commitment to pacifism, egalitarianism, consensus, and simplicity reflected that sect's beliefs. They were openly friendly to outsiders and delivered mail to their rural neighbors. They ran a bookstore and restaurant in the nearby town of Mapleton. They championed protection of the environment against logging and herbicides, among other causes. Alpha Farm advertised itself in the 2000 edition of *Communities Directory* as a utopia of about 20 adults who live in an "extended-family style community."

See Also Black Bear Ranch; Olompali Ranch; Table Mountain Ranch

Sources:

Communities Directory: A Guide to Intentional Communities and to Cooperative Living. 2000. Rutledge, Missouri: Fellowship for Intentional Community.

Miller, Timothy. 1999. *The 60s Communes: Hippies and Beyond.* Syracuse, N.Y.: Syracuse University Press.

THE ALTRUIST COMMUNITY. In 1907, at the age of 77, Alcander Longley, who had created unsuccessful Fourierist colonies in Missouri at Reunion, Friendship, Principia, and Mutual Aid, founded the Altruist Community at Sulphur Springs about 22 miles south of St. Louis. There, on eight-and-a-half acres, he and a bedridden elderly woman, and several communards, lived in an old two-room house and raised chickens and vegetables. He also opened a headquarters for the colony in St. Louis. Longley's main commitment was to continue publishing manifestos on communal living and to print the *Altruist* magazine until 1917. Longley died in Chicago the following year.

See Also Longley, Alcander

Sources:

Fogarty, Robert S. 1990. *All Things New: American Communes and Utopian Movements 1860–1914.* Chicago: University of Chicago Press.

Grant, H. Roger. 1971. "Missouri's Utopian Communities." *Missouri Historical Review* 66 (Oct.): 20–48.

Miller, Timothy. 1998. *The Quest for Utopia in Twentieth-Century America.* Syracuse, N.Y.: Syracuse University Press.

Trahair, Richard C. S. 1999. *Utopias and Utopians: An Historical Dictionary.* Westport, Conn.: Greenwood Press.

AMANA. Amana was founded in 1854 in southeastern Iowa when some 800 German Pietists moved there from their original commune, called Ebenezer, located near Buffalo, New York. They named their religious utopia the Community of True Inspiration, and they developed in seven communal villages prosperous farming operations and industries. However, beginning in the first decades of the twentieth century, Amana went into economic decline. A catastrophic fire in 1923 severely accentuated the downward trend. Along with economic troubles, Amana experienced an erosion of communal commitment as members began to accumulate personal possessions and take jobs outside of the colony. The Great Depression forced it into bankruptcy. Faced with over $500,000 in debts, 75 percent of the adults voted to reorganize in the "Great Change." By May 1932, they had abolished their communal eating houses and homes and divided the society's assets among the members. From that time on, residents of Amana worked for wages in its farms and industries and lived as ordinary Americans. They did, though, continue their former religious life in the villages as the Amana Church Society.

Sources:

Barthel, Diane L. 1984. *Amana: From Pietist Sect to American Community.* Lincoln: University of Nebraska Press.

Miller, Timothy. 1998. *The Quest for Utopia in Twentieth-Century America.* Syracuse, N.Y.: Syracuse University Press.

Oved, Yaacov. 1988. *Two Hundred Years of American Communes.* New Brunswick, N.J. and Oxford: Transaction.

Rettig, Lawrence L. 1975. *Amana Today: A History of the Amana Colonies from 1932 to the Present.* Amana, Iowa: Amana Society.

Shambaugh, Bertha. 1971. *Amana: the Community of True Inspirations.* New York: B. Blom.

Sutton, Robert P. 2003. *Communal Utopias and the American Experience: Religious Communities, 1732–2000.* Westport, Conn. and London: Praeger.

THE AMERICAN WOMAN'S REPUBLIC. In 1908, Edward G. Lewis, publisher of the newspaper *Woman's National Daily,* organized the American Woman's League in support of women's suffrage. Members could join the league by selling 52 dollars' worth of its publications, and by 1910 there were more than 100,000 members. Two years later, Lewis reorganized the league, calling it the American Woman's Republic, as a communal movement where women could vote. Lewis's wife became the republic's president. In July 1913, the colonists moved to Rancho Atascadero, California, and started to build homes. During World War I, the community made money by selling dehydrated food products to the government. The members adopted a flag with six stars symbolizing the six states where women had the full franchise. The movement declined after the adoption of the Nineteenth Amendment in 1920.

Sources:

Meyer, Pauline. 1980. *Keep Your Face to the Sunshine: A Lost Chapter in the History of Woman Suffrage*. Edwardsville, Ill.: Alcott Press.
Miller, Timothy. 1998. *The Quest for Utopia in Twentieth-Century America*. Syracuse, N.Y.: Syracuse University Press.

AMITY COLONY. In 1898, the Salvation Army, under its new commander in America, Frederick Booth Tucker, founded a colony of 14 Chicago families on 640 acres at Fort Amity, Colorado, called the Amity Colony. The basic idea behind the experiment was that urban poverty could be eradicated by placing city families in self-sufficient farm communities. The inspiration for the colony was William Booth's book, *In Darkest England and the Way Out* (1890), where he argued that putting "waste labor" on "wasteland by means of waste capital" would result in economic and moral cooperation and create "a trinity of production." Although there were two other such farm colonies (at Romie, California, and Fort Herrick, Ohio), the one in California was by far the most successful. At the Amity Colony, each family was given 10 acres, farm machinery, and a horse. Their main crop was cantaloupe, planted under the supervision of a Salvation Army director living in the community. It reached its peak of development in 1903, when 450 residents were working there. But the alkaline soil proved too harsh for the crop and in 1909, the community suffered a severe financial loss. The Salvation Army shut down the Amity Colony the following year.

Sources:

Fogarty, Robert S. 1980. *Dictionary of American Communal and Utopian History*. Westport, Conn.: Greenwood Press.
Webb, Walter Prescott. 1931. *The Great Plains*. Boston: Ginn and Company.
Wisbey, Herbert, Jr. 1955. *Soldiers without Swords*. New York: Macmillan.

ANANDA ASHRAM. Dr. Ramamurti Misha established this spiritual community in 1964 at Monroe, New York. It continues into the twenty-first century as an educational center. It listed only 20 members in the 1990s and required a long period of residency before considering a person for membership.

Sources:

Communities Directory: A Guide to Cooperative Living. 1995. Langley, Washington: Fellowship for Intentional Community.
Communities: Journal of Cooperative Living. 1977. 24 (Jan.–Feb.): 46.
Miller, Timothy. 1999. *The 60s Communes: Hippies and Beyond*. Syracuse, N.Y.: Syracuse University Press.

ANANDA ASHRAMA. This community (1923–ongoing) was one of the Vedanta Society communes founded in the United States after Swami Vivekananda brought this Asian religion to America at the 1893 World's Parliament of Religions in Chicago. The Swami advocated social reform, charity work, inner peace, a spiritual rather than material reality, and tolerance of all religions. Swami Paramananda, one of the most effective disciples of Vivekananda, started a Vedanta center in Boston in 1912 after his arrival in the United States, and in 1923, he organized the Ananda Ashrama on 135 acres at La Crescenta, California, close to Pasadena. Paramananda, the youngest of 11 children of a Bengali family, was trained at a Ramakrishna monastery before he emigrated to New York City in 1906 at the age of 21. Within five year, the community had a Cloister, a Community House, and a Temple; eight nuns, one monk, and twenty-five residents tended goats and cows and cultivated a vegetable garden and orchard. They made incense sticks and wooden figures, clothes and scarves, and copper and pewter bowls, all of which they sold through ads in their magazine, the *Message of the East*. Days began with prayers and songs. Meals were vegetarian. Most evenings, Paramananda sat among his followers and conducted relaxation therapy, after which they all meditated and did yoga exercises. Paramananda thought that to be in an ashrama was "the greatest blessing, even though sometimes it may seem a discipline." "We learn in a community," he proclaimed, "to do things for one another." He said that individuals must surrender their egos in order to "remove all torment, all depression, all anger." In the summer of 1933, a fire destroyed some of the buildings and after this setback, the ashrama declined. Paramananda himself became discouraged and died of a heart attack in June 1940. Nevertheless, the community continued to survive, and according to Laurence Veysey, it became the "most long-lived communitarian venture founded during the twentieth century in the United States."

See Also Paramananda, Swami

Sources:

Miller, Timothy. 1998. *The Quest for Utopia in Twentieth-Century America*. Syracuse, N.Y.: Syracuse University Press.

Sutton, Robert P. 2003. *Communal Utopias and the American Experience: Religious Communities, 1732–2000*. Westport, Conn. and London: Praeger.

Veysey, Laurence. 1973. *The Communal Experience*. Chicago: University of Chicago Press.

ANANDA WORLD BROTHERHOOD VILLAGE. The village, otherwise known as Ananda Church of Self-Realization, Ananda Village, Ananda World Brotherhood Village, was founded in 1967 by James Donald Walters (b. 1926; spiritual name: Swami Kriyananda), a disciple of Paramahansa Yogananda (1893–1952), the author of *Autobiography of a Yogi* and the leader of the Self-Realization Fellowship (SRF). In 1967, Walters purchased 650 acres near Nevada City, California, to build a community based on the idea of spiritual brotherhood of all humankind and the creation of worldwide colonies dedicated to simple living and spiritualism. Difficulties in raising money hampered the growth of the village, a problem accentuated by the high number of dropouts from society that came there to live. In the summer of 1976, a fire destroyed all but one of the homes and 450 of the 650 acres of land. Even so, the following year the community still had about 100 residents, all of whom lived in community-owned houses in secluded parts of the village. Over the past 25 years, the village has prospered. Its preschool and secondary schools teach harmonious living and development of mind and body. It has businesses, a dairy farm, and a communal organic garden. It operates the Expanding Light Retreat Center, which offers classes on yoga, New Age and Indian subjects, and workshops. Daily life emphasizes an effort to communicate with the divine, including Morning Prayer at home and a communal period of meditation at noon and in the evening. Communal goals include self-improvement, cooperation, and respect for individuals. According to the 1995 *Communities Directory,* the village of 300 individuals on 750 acres of woods and meadows in the Sierra Nevada foothills had several branch branches, including one in Europe. They claimed to "seek a mood of friendship and harmony, together with a cheerful spirit of service to God...a balance is sought between spiritual guidance and self-motivation."

See Also Walters, James Donald; Paramahansa Yogananda

Sources:

Ball, John. 1982. *Ananda: Where Yoga Lives.* Bowling Green University: Popular Press.

Communities Directory: A Guide to Cooperative Living. 1995. Langley, Washington: Fellowship for Intentional Community.

Fogarty, Robert S. 1980. *Dictionary of American Communal History.* Westport, Conn.: Greenwood Press.

Miller, Timothy. 1999. *The 60s Communes: Hippies and Beyond.* Syracuse, N.Y.: Syracuse University Press.

Nordquist, Ted A. 1978. *Ananda Cooperative Village: A Study in the Beliefs, Values, and Attitudes of a New Age Religious Community.* Uppsala, Sweden: Bogströms Tryckeri.

Paramahansa Yognanda. 1946. *Autobiography of a Yogi.* Los Angeles: Self-Realization Fellowship.

Trahair, Richard C.S. 1999. *Utopias and Utopians: An Historical Dictionary.* Westport, Conn.: Greenwood Press.

ARCOSANTI. This environmental commune was founded in the Arizona desert in 1970 by Paolo Soleri, a student of Frank Lloyd Wright at Taliesin West. Soleri wanted to integrate architecture and ecology as "archeology." He envisioned Arcosanti becoming a commune of 5,000 residents who would practice a strict environmentalism, such as using solar heat and shunning automobiles. But progress has been slow as Soleri refuses to accept outside financial support. By 1999, the community had between 50 and 70 residents who worked in constructing new buildings and in manufacturing bronze bells and making bakery goods. Arcosanti also encourages tourists to visit the commune.

Sources:

Miller, Timothy. 1999. *The 60s Communes: Hippies and Beyond.* Syracuse, N.Y.: Syracuse University Press.

Soleri, Paolo. 1993. *Arcosanti: An Urban Laboratory?* 3rd ed. Scottsdale, Ariz.: Cosanti.

THE ARMY OF INDUSTRY. In 1914, Gerald Geraldson, a socialist living in Auburn, California, organized a utopian community on 100 acres of his father's fruit orchard outside of the town. Between 30 and 40 people, many of whom were out of work, shared food, clothing, housing, and recreation. As a condition of admission, a new member had to certify that he or she had no property and would abjure plans to make money. Sometimes called the "poor people's colony," it survived until 1920, when it dissolved. Two years later, Geraldson opened a settlement house on the East Side of New York City called the Brotherhood House.

Sources:

Fogarty, Robert S. 1980. *Dictionary of American Communal and Utopian History.* Westport, Conn.: Greenwood Press.

Hine, Robert V. 1983. *California's Utopian Colonies.* Berkeley: University of California Press.

Miller, Timothy. 1998. *The Quest for Utopia in Twentieth-Century America.* Syracuse, N.Y.: Syracuse University Press.

Wooster, Ernest S. 1924 *Communities of the Past and Present.* Newllano, La.: Llano Colonist.

ARNOLD, EBERHARD. Eberhard Arnold (1883–1935) was born in East Prussia into a Lutheran family. As a teenager, he went through a religious experience, left the Lutheran church, and dedicated himself to Christian socialism. He received a Ph.D. in 1909 and joined the German Youth Movement in its protest against traditional religions. After World War I, however, he and his wife, Emmy, left the movement and organized a religious commune at a rented farmhouse in Sannerz, Hesse, to prepare for the millennium. Although some historians claim that life at the farmhouse was unstructured and resembled the later hippie colonies in America, by the mid-1920s, a definite regimen and ideology had been developed. The community, called the Bruderhof, or Society of Brothers, believed in evangelism, pacifism, poverty, monogamous marriage, subordination of wife to husband, and communal reciprocity. They soon became interested in the communal Hutterites in North America and in 1930; Arnold stayed with the Hutterites for a year. While there, he joined the Hutterites and was ordained an elder and commissioned to spread Hutterite beliefs in Germany. With the Nazis' rise to power in 1932, the community was subjected to the military draft. Consequently, in 1936, following Arnold's death in November 1935, the Bruderhof moved to England.

See Also Bruderhof; Hutterite Brethren

Sources:

Miller, Timothy. 1998. *The Quest for Utopia in Twentieth-Century America*. Syracuse, N.Y.: Syracuse University Press.

Oved, Yaacov. 1996. *The Witness of the Brothers: A History of the Bruderhof*. New Brunswick, N.J.: Transaction.

Sutton, Robert P. 2003. *Communal Utopias and the American Experience: Religious Communities, 1732–2000*. Westport, Conn. and London: Praeger.

Trahair, Richard C.S. 1999. *Utopias and Utopians: An Historical Dictionary*. Westport, Conn.: Greenwood Press.

Zablocki, Benjamin. 1971. *The Joyful Community*. Chicago: University of Chicago Press.

ARPIN. This community was one of the longest-lived of the Jewish farm colonies founded in the first decades of the twentieth century. It was established in 1904 at Arpin, Wisconsin, an abandoned lumber company town located 150 miles northwest of Milwaukee by the Jewish community of that city for refugees from pogroms in Romania. The leader of Arpin, Adolph W. Rich, founded the Milwaukee Agricultural Society and purchased 720 acres. By December, seven families had joined the colony and lived in vacant company houses. Soon more than 80 people resided there. The community survived, and eventually prospered, by farming and selling firewood. In 1913, members opened a school and two years later a synagogue. By 1922, however, Arpin had declined severely because of the exodus of the children when they became adults. Just five families lived there. In 1940, there were only two families remaining. By 1958, everyone had departed.

Sources:

Miller, Timothy. 1998. *The Quest for Utopia in Twentieth-Century America*. Syracuse, N.Y.: Syracuse University Press.

Swichkow, Louis J. 1964–1965. "The Jewish Colony of Arpin, Wisconsin," *American Jewish Historical Quarterly* 54: 82–91.

B

BEAUX ARTS VILLAGE. In 1909, Alfred T. Renfro, one of a number of artists who worked in a building at the University of Washington, organized an arts and crafts colony with $16,500 of borrowed money. He, along with Frank Calvert and others, bought a 50-acre site across Lake Washington and within a dozen years the Beaux Arts Village had 15 houses and 78 residents. It was only part communal, however, since the houses were considered as homesites. Eventually, the village became a middle-class suburb of Seattle with attractive houses and a communal beach.

Sources:

Creese, Walter L. 1966. *The Search for Environment: The Garden City: Before and After*. New Haven: Yale University Press.

Miller, Timothy. 1998. *The Quest for Utopia in Twentieth-Century America*. Syracuse, N.Y.: Syracuse University Press.

BEILHART, JACOB. Beilhart (1867–1908) was the founder of the Spirit Fruit Society in Lisbon, Ohio. He was born on a farm in Columbiana County, Ohio. In 1884, he moved to Kansas, became a harness maker, joined the Seventh-Day Adventists, and distributed church literature in that state and in Colorado. He attended an Adventist college in California for a year and became an Adventist preacher. In 1890, he enrolled in the nursing program at the Seventh-Day Adventist Sanitarium in Battle Creek, Michigan. While there he met C. W. Post, the cereal manufacturer, and purchased stock in Post's sanitarium, La Vita Inn. Then, in 1899, he founded the Spirit Fruit Society with about a dozen members mainly from Chicago. After sexual scandals spread about free love at the community, he moved the colony to a 90-acre site in Lake County, Illinois. He believed in faith healing and free love. He died in 1908 from peritonitis following an operation for appendicitis.

See Also Spirit Fruit Society

Sources:

Fogarty, Robert S. 1980. *Dictionary of American Communal and Utopian History.* Westport, Conn.: Greenwood Press.

Murphy, James J. 1989. *The Reluctant Radical: Jacob Beilhart and the Spirit Fruit Society.* Lanham, Md.: University Press of America.

Trahair, Richard C.S. 1999. *Utopias and Utopians: An Historical Dictionary.* Westport, Conn.: Greenwood Press.

BELLANGEE, JAMES F. Bellangee (1844–1915) graduated from the University of Michigan in 1868 and was on the faculty of the University of Illinois until 1873, when he became a professor of mathematics at the State Normal School of Nebraska. He edited the tax journal *Opinion and Outlook.* In 1892, he was active in politics as the Populist Party's candidate for state auditor and in the presidential campaign he worked for the party. Two years later, with Ernest B. Gaston and others, he was one of the founders of the Fairhope colony. He also wrote articles for the *Arena* and the *Progressive Economist.* After he was defeated in 1905 in an election for colony treasurer, he never again sought office, although he lived at Fairhope until his death in 1915.

See Also Fairhope

Sources:

Fogarty, Robert S. 1980. *Dictionary of American Communal and Utopian History.* Westport, Conn.: Greenwood Press.

Sutton, Robert P. 2004. *Communal Utopias and the American Experience: Secular Communities, 1824–2000.* Westport, Conn. and London: Praeger.

Trahair, Richard C.S. 1999. *Utopias and Utopians: An Historical Dictionary.* Westport, Conn.: Greenwood Press.

BEREA. This experiment in utopian race relations began in 1866, when the Reverend Gregg Fee, an abolitionist missionary, founded a racially integrated school at Berea, Kentucky. Many of the teachers were graduates of Oberlin College, as was Berea's first president, Edward Henry Fairchild. Almost two-thirds of the student body was black until Fairchild's successor, William Goodell Frost, in 1889 increased white enrollments to the point that the ratio was reversed. In 1904, Congress passed the Day Law, which prohibited integrated education. In 1908, when the U.S. Supreme Court upheld the constitutionality of the statute, Berea sent its black students to other colleges. Frost founded an all-black college in 1910 called the Lincoln Institute.

Sources:
Sears, Richard. 1996. *A Utopian Experiment in Kentucky: Integration and Social Equality at Berea, 1886–1904.* Westport, Conn.: Greenwood Press.
Trahair, Richard C. S. 1999. *Utopias and Utopians: An Historical Dictionary.* Westport, Conn.: Greenwood Press.

BERG, DAVID. In 1968, David Berg (1919–1994) founded one of the most controversial of the Jesus movement communities in Los Angeles. Berg, a Christian and Missionary Alliance pastor, that year began a mission with teenagers in Huntington Beach, California. Within a year, more than 100 young people followed him around the United States preaching the impending millennium. They called themselves the Children of God and believed in a horrific apocalypse inflicted by a God furious at a sinful world. They finally settled at a Texas ranch and in a run-down section of Los Angeles. They relied on outside donations to survive. In 1971, Berg created the Children of God community and soon he claimed to have 2,348 followers in 134 colonies in 41 countries. In 1976, Berg initiated "flirty fishing," or having women use sex to gain new converts, a controversial practice later terminated. During the 1990s, most of the Children returned to the United States, formed new communities, and adopted a new name, The Family.

See Also Children of God (The Family)

Sources:
Miller, Timothy. 1999. *The 60s Communes: Hippies and Beyond.* Syracuse, N.Y.: Syracuse University Press.
Van Zandt, David E. 1991. *Living in the Children of God.* Princeton, N.J.: Princeton University Press.

BETHANY FELLOWSHIP. Founded in Minneapolis in 1945, Bethany Fellowship was an independent Christian community that focused on evangelism and missionary work. Its founder, Theodore A. Hegre, pastor of the Lutheran Free Church in that city, persuaded some of his followers to sell their homes and put the money into a communal fund to support Christian evangelists. They bought 60 acres in Bloomington, a Minneapolis suburb, and began a missionary training school. By the end of the twentieth century, they had trained hundreds of missionaries, who proselytized in foreign countries. The fellowship publishes evangelical literature.

Sources:
Bloesch, Donald B. 1964. *Centers of Christian Renewal.* Philadelphia: United Church Press.
Miller, Timothy. 1998. *The Quest for Utopia in Twentieth-Century America.* Syracuse, N.Y.: Syracuse University Press.
Pratney, Winkie. 1977. *A Handbook for Followers of Jesus.* Minneapolis: Bethany Fellowship.

BETHEL HOME. This community, founded in 1904 by Charles Taze Russell and Joseph Franklin Rutherford, was one of the largest early-twentieth-century conservative Pentecostal communities. It is usually called simply Bethel and its communal headquarters in Brooklyn is now called the Jehovah's Witnesses, or the Watchtower Bible and Tract Society. Another communal site was the Watchtower Farm, which raised products for the Bethel commune. The two colonies, and several additional residential communities, contained more than 2,000 members, all of whom predicted the coming of a millennium in 1914. In 1909, they incorporated as the People's Pulpit Association and purchased more land and buildings. By 1970, Bethel Home had 1,449 members and an additional 500 or more at Watchtower Farm. Daily life was highly structured at all Jehovah's Witness communities. Members rose at 6:30, ate communally, and had communal Bible study sessions and prayer. There was a dress code and tobacco was prohibited. Through such regimentation the organization, according to Timothy Miller, produced "the hundreds of millions of books, magazines, and tracts that the rank and file of the movement annually use 'in service,' in their ongoing program of door-to-door canvassing for which they are so well known."

See Also Russell, Charles Taze

Sources:

Harrison, Barbara Gruzzuti. 1978. *Vision of Glory: A History and a Memory of Jehovah's Witnesses.* New York: Simon and Schuster.

Miller, Timothy. 1998. *The Quest for Utopia in Twentieth-Century America.* Syracuse, N.Y.: Syracuse University Press.

Penton, M. James. 1985. *Apocalypse Delayed: the Story of Jehovah's Witnesses.* Toronto: University of Toronto Press.

Stroup, Herbert H. 1945. *The Jehovah's Witnesses.* New York: Columbia University Press.

BLACK BEAR RANCH. Black Bear Ranch was organized in 1968 by Richard Marley and others on an isolated 80-acre site that was at one time a booming gold mine at Forks of Salmar, California. That year, the abandoned property had so degenerated in value that it sold for just $22,500. Marley and his group were able to raise a down payment and later pay off the balance of the loan. Their aim was to create, in Marley's words, a "mountain fortress in the spirit of Che Guevara, where city activists would be able to come up, hide out, practice riflery and pistol shooting, have hand grenade practice, whatever." Black Bear Ranch had cabins for members and a community center where meals were served. In the beginning, the ranch proscribed all private property, even clothing. They agreed that to avoid "coupling," individuals could have sex with another person for only two nights. Since the colony was isolated—it was located in the national forests, hours by automobile from San Francisco—by necessity, it was extraordinary self-reliant. Members stored firewood for the winter, gathered a stockpile of food each fall, and had medical supplies to take care of illnesses and veterinary needs. They operated a sawmill and some residents found jobs in fighting forest fires. They educated their children at the commune. Timothy Miller reported that by 2000, a second generation had replaced the original settlers and that the ranch is "thriving."

Sources:

January Thaw: People at Blue Mt. Ranch Write about Living Together in the Mountains. 1974. New York: Times Change.

Miller, Timothy. 1999. *The 60s Communes: Hippies and Beyond.* Syracuse, N.Y.: Syracuse University Press.

BLACK MOUNTAIN COLLEGE. This experiment in communal higher education was begun in 1933, when John A. Rice, formerly a professor at Rollins College, Florida, opened a college at the rented facilities of the Baptist Blue Ridge Assembly camp in Lake Eden, North Carolina. The college was so poor at first that the faculty received no salary, only room and board. Students and faculty were devoted communards and shared all individual assets. Operation of the school was totally communal, with students attending faculty meetings and sitting on administrative committees. Faculty and students both worked in running the physical plant. They opened a dairy farm and lumbering operation. They shared a communal social life of music and dancing. Distinguished visitors such as John Dewey and Aldous Huxley spent time at Black Mountain College. In 1941, the community opened a new campus nearby and it became a nationally famous center of art and literature. Most of the graduates of Black Mountain College went on to earn professional degrees or to become renowned artists. Still, the community never became economically prosperous and poverty plagued it until it finally closed in 1956.

See Also Commonwealth College

Sources:

Duberman, Martin. *Black Mountain: An Experiment in Community.* 1973. Garden City, N.Y.: Doubleday/Anchor.

Fielding, Dawson. 1987. *The Black Mountain Book.* Cambridge, Mass.: MIT Press.

Lane, Mervin, ed. 1990. *Black Mountain College: Sprouted Seeds—An Anthology of Personal Accounts.* Knoxville: University of Tennessee Press.

Miller, Timothy. 1998. *The Quest for Utopia in Twentieth-Century America.* Syracuse, N.Y.: Syracuse University Press.

THE BOHEMIAN COOPERATIVE FARMING COMPANY. In the spring of 1913, immigrants from Bohemia purchased 5,300 acres near Maryland, Tennessee, to build a model cooperative agrarian society. They grew corn and potatoes by working seven days a week and taking time off for only Christmas and New Year's Day. Because most members could not speak

English, they had little contact with outsiders. They lived in a communal village and worked the land in common. All personal assets were held communally. After a year-long fight over leadership, they divided the land in half and created a second village. But that measure solved nothing and dissension escalated into armed conflict. In 1916, the two communities dissolved.

Sources:

Fogarty, Robert S. 1980. *Dictionary of American Communal and Utopian History.* Westport, Conn.: Greenwood Press.

Miller, Timothy. 1998. *The Quest for Utopia in Twentieth-Century America.* Syracuse, N.Y.: Syracuse University Press.

BORLAND, WILFRED. Borland was born in 1860 and, until crippled by an accident in 1889, was a railway fireman. After the accident, he wrote for labor magazines. In 1897, Borland became editor of the Socialist Party's periodical, the *Social Democrat,* and served on the group's colonization committee. In 1898, he became a member of the Burley Colony and was editor of the community's journal, *The Cooperator.* Two years later, he resigned from the colony and took a job in government service.

See Also Burley Colony (Cooperative Brotherhood)

Sources:

Fogarty, Robert S. 1980. *Dictionary of American Communal and Utopian History.* Westport, Conn.: Greenwood Press.

LeWarne, Charles P. 1975. *Utopias on Puget Sound, 1885–1915.* Seattle: University of Washington Press.

BORSODI, RALPH. During the Great Depression, Ralph Borsodi (1886–1977) advocated subsistence communal farming for families as a way to escape poverty. He and his wife began such a community on a seven-acre rental property near Suffern, New York, and in 1933 he published his utopian ideas in *Flight from the City.* In the book, he advocated "creative living on the land" and claimed that "domestic production" would "not only annihilate the undesirable and nonessential factory ... it would release men and women from their present thralldom to the factory." Later that year, city officials of Dayton, Ohio, invited him to build a "Cooperative Productive Unity" of buildings to house between 350 to 500 families. In this community, the families would work cooperatively to produce food, clothing, and other basics of life. But Borsodi suggested instead building "Liberty Homesteads" that would include 2,000 families living on leased farms. Dayton officials agreed with the idea and purchased a 160-acre farm on which to construct the commune, called the Dayton Homesteads project. However, Borsodi soon came into conflict with city officials and a Dayton weekly newspaper editor charged him with mismanagement, hypocrisy, and, most importantly, inviting black families to join the community. In 1934, Harold L.

Ickes, Roosevelt's Secretary of the Interior and supervisor of the Division of Subsistence Homesteads, federalized the project and removed Borsodi from power. By the winter of 1936, the Liberty Homesteads community had dissolved. That same year, Borsodi opened the School of Living near his Suffern home. It was a cluster of 16 homesteads with a common area called Bayard Lane. Homesteaders, living on two-acre plots, were taught skills useful to running the homestead. Borsodi had residents accept low wages as a trade-off for continuous employment. In 1940, a conflict arose when some residents claimed that he diverted community funds for his own research. He resigned as director and wrote two books, *Prosperity and Security* (1940) and *Inflation Is Coming* (1943). In 1950, he moved to Florida and founded Melbourne University and the Melbourne Homestead Village. He largely abandoned interest in utopian communalism and concentrated on his research and writings on economic theories. After World War II, however, Borsodi's plan was revived by Mildred Loomis in her new School of Living near Brooksville, Ohio. Borsodi died in 1977 at Exeter, New York.

See Also Melbourne Village; School of Living

Sources:

Borsodi, Ralph. 1929. *This Ugly Civilization*. New York: Simon and Schuster.
———. 1933. *Flight from the City*. New York: Harper and Row.
———. 1935. "Wanted: A School of Living," *Progressive Education* 12 (Jan.): 21.
Dorn, Jacob H. 1969. "Subsistence Homesteading in Dayton, Ohio, 1933–1935," *Ohio History* 78: 27.
Fogarty Robert S. 1980. *Dictionary of American Communal and Utopian History*. Westport, Conn.: Greenwood Press.
Miller, Timothy. 1998. *The Quest for Utopia in Twentieth-Century America*. Syracuse, N.Y.: Syracuse University Press.

BRANCH DAVIDIANS (DAVIDIAN SEVENTH-DAY ADVENTISTS).

David Koresh (1960–1993), leader of this communal society, claimed to be the Lamb who would unleash punishment on mankind and elevate the sect to heaven. The Branch Davidians believed that they were once a part of the Seventh-Day Adventist church, although this church denies any connection. They lived communally on 377 acres west of Waco, Texas. With Koresh as a patriarch, they raised their own food, ran a school for the children, and printed their own scrip money. They had daily religious education classes for adults and daily religious services. In February 1993, for reasons still unclear, the federal government laid siege to the commune; the siege ended on April 19 when government agents stormed the headquarters. Koresh and 74 members of the sect, including 21 children, died in the conflagration. Historians consider the Branch Dravidians as similar to other modern dystopian utopias such as the Peoples Temple (Jonestown).

See Also Koresh, David (Vernon Howell); Peoples Temple

Sources:

King, Martin. 1993. *Preacher of Death: The Shocking Inside Story of David Koresh and the Waco Siege.* New York: Signet.
Miller, Timothy. 1998. *The Quest for Utopia in Twentieth-Century America.* Syracuse, N.Y.: Syracuse University Press.
Tabor, James D., and Eugene V. Gallagher. 1995. *Why Waco? Cults and the Battle for Religious Freedom in America.* Berkeley: University of California Press.
Trahair, Richard C. S. 1999. *Utopias and Utopians: An Historical Dictionary.* Westport, Conn.: Greenwood Press.

BRAY, R. E. R. E. Bray (1862–after 1918) moved to Kansas in 1889, became a newspaper reporter, and joined the Populist Party. He led a delegation at the 1892 Populist state convention that nominated "Sockless" Jerry Simpson for Congress. After the election, he moved to Oklahoma and began publishing *Coming Events* and worked for Oklahoma City newspapers. Between 1900 and 1913, he had jobs as a reporter for other newspapers in New York and Illinois. In 1914, he joined the Llano del Rio communal utopia founded by Job Harriman near Los Angeles. Two years later, he organized a satellite colony, Llano del Rio of Nevada, and began publishing its newspaper, *The Cooperative Colonist,* which promoted utopian socialist ideas. In 1917, he became involved in a contest with some members of the colony who then went to court to get him removed as the community's director. In October 1918, he sold his shares of stock in the venture to the dissidents and moved to Washington, D.C.

See Also Harriman, Job; Llano del Rio/Newllano

Sources:

Fogarty, Robert S. 1980. *Dictionary of American Communal and Utopian History.* Westport, Conn.: Greenwood Press.
Shepperson, Wilbur. 1966. *Retreat to Nevada: A Socialist Colony of World War I.* Reno: University of Nevada Press.
Sutton, Robert P. 2004. *Communal Utopias and the American Experience: Secular Communities, 1824–2000.* Westport, Conn. and London: Praeger.

BRUDERHOF. This group, known as the Society of Brothers, was founded in 1920 when German socialist Eberhard Arnold, his wife, Emmy, and a handful of followers started a farm commune in Sannerz, Hesse. This unstructured colony was somewhat similar to the hippie communities of the 1960s. In 1926, they moved to a farm in southern Germany in the Rhön mountains, called the Rhön Bruderhof and began a more structured communal life. They concentrated on reading about the early Anabaptists and the communal Hutterites. In 1930, Arnold visited the Hutterite colonies in North Dakota and Canada and was ordained an elder in their society. After returning to Germany, Arnold and his followers adopted many Hutterite communal rules. In 1933, the Society moved to Liechtenstein in order to avoid the military draft imposed in Germany by the Nazis. In 1935, Arnold died following complications from surgery. But, fearing that they were still not safe from the Nazis, the next year the group members went to a new colony, or *hof,* in Wheathill, England. When war broke out between England and Germany, the 350 Bruderhofs immigrated to Paraguay and built three *hofs* on a 20,000-acre ranch. In 1953, a group of their leaders visited the American Hutterites and later organized the first American Bruderhof, Woodcrest, at Rifton, New York. By 1956, there were nine Bruderhof colonies in the United States with a membership of more than 1,500, counting those still living in Paraguay. Later, members of the Macedonia Cooperative Community joined the Bruderhof as did members of the Forest River Hutterite colony. In the 1960s, more than 600 members left the Society of Brothers after one of Arnold's sons, Heine Arnold, assumed leadership. Others departed for various reasons. In the 1980s, some of the defectors began publishing a newsletter entitled *KIT* or "Keep in Touch." Relations between the Bruderhof and the American Hutterites became tense when the Forest River Hutterites exiled those of their colony who would not affiliate with the Bruderhof. And, in the 1990s, a doctrinal controversy developed between the Schmiedeleut Hutterites and the Bruderhofs. Even so, the Society of Brothers has continued to grow and to expand its missionary work in Nigeria.

See Also Arnold, Eberhard; Hutterite Brethren; Macedonia Cooperative Community

Sources:

Arnold, Emmy. 1963. *Torches Together: The Beginning and Early Years of the Bruder-hof Commune.* Rifton, N.Y.: Plough.

Bohlken-Zumpe, Elizabeth. 1993. *Torches Extinguished: Memories of a Communal Bruderhof Childhood in Paraguay, Europe, and the USA.* 2d ed. San Francisco: Carrier Pigeon.

Miller, Timothy. 1998. *The Quest for Utopia in Twentieth-Century America.* Syracuse, N.Y.: Syracuse University Press.

Mow, Merrill. 1989. *Torches Rekindled: The Bruderhof's Struggle for Renewal.* 3d rev. ed. Rifton, H.Y.: Plough.

Oved, Yaacov. 1996. *The Witness of the Brothers: A History of the Bruderhof.* New Brunswick, N.J.: Transaction.

Sutton, Robert P. 2003. *Communal Utopias and the American Experience: Religious Communities, 1732–2000.* Westport, Conn. and London: Praeger.

Trahair, Richard C. S. 1999. *Utopias and Utopians: An Historical Dictionary.* Westport, Conn.: Greenwood Press.

BRYN ATHYN. In the summer of 1967, Woody Ransom, a wealthy farmer, started Bryn Athyn, an eclectic community in Vermont made up of New Left radicals dedicated to psychedelic drugs and free love. The following summer, some members of the defunct Cold Mountain Farm came to the colony. In

1969, a hepatitis epidemic hit the community and for unexplained reason, Ransom decided to make a radical change and impose a more disciplined community renamed Rockbottom Farm. Most of the Bryn Athyn colony moved to a nearby town, Lyme, New Hampshire, and lived in a donated house. Soon, though, they abandoned communal living entirely.

See Also Cold Mountain Farm

Sources:

Houriet, Robert. 1971. *Getting Back Together.* New York: Avon.
Miller, Timothy. 1998. *The Quest for Utopia in Twentieth-Century America.* Syracuse, N.Y.: Syracuse University Press.
Whitworth, John McKelvie. 1975. *God's Blueprints: A Sociological Study of Three Utopian Sects.* London: Routledge and Kegan Paul.

BURLEY COLONY (COOPERATIVE BROTHERHOOD). The Burley Colony was one of a number of utopian socialist communities founded in the state of Washington in the 1890s. In the spring of 1898, Cyrus Field Willard, a scion of a wealthy Boston family and close friend of Edward Bellamy, purchased land on Puget Sound to build a cooperative community near the Home Colony, founded the previous year. Within a year, 120 colonists had arrived. One thousand nonresident members also contributed to the colony. The communards erected houses, began a logging business, and published a journal, *The Cooperator.* The early years were prosperous and picturesque. Until 1901, they had a general assembly that controlled a communal treasury. After that time, they allowed each family or individual to keep the profits of their own work. Families lived in private homes and single members in a large building called the "hotel." Burley's economy centered on lumbering, a sawmill, a cigar factory, and growing vegetables. On Tuesday and Wednesday evenings, they had symposiums that sometimes included outside lecturers. On Saturday night, they enjoyed dances with music by a communal dance band. On Sunday evenings, they held religious services under the direction of two Unitarian ministers. *The Cooperator* bragged that they had "better educational facilities than any village of the same size in the state." But after 1905, an internal dispute broke out between the followers of Alonzo A. Wardall, who wanted to return to the communal economy in place before 1901, and those who opposed the change. Finally, in 1912, the two factions went to court and asked that Burley be dissolved, but it took over 11 years for the dissolution to be finalized.

See Also Borland, Wilfred; Equality; Freeland; Home Colony; Willard, Cyrus Field

Sources:

LeWarne, Charles P. 1975. *Utopias on Puget Sound, 1885–1915.* Seattle: University of Washington Press.
Miller, Timothy. 1998. *The Quest for Utopia in Twentieth-Century America.* Syracuse, N.Y.: Syracuse University Press.

Sutton, Robert P. 2004. *Communal Utopias and the American Experienced: Secular Communities, 1824–2000.* Westport, Conn. and London: Praeger.

Trahair, Richard C. S. 1999. *Utopias and Utopians: An Historical Dictionary.* Westport, Conn.: Greenwood Press.

BURNING BUSH. Burning Bush was a Pentecostal utopia started in 1912 in Waukesha, Wisconsin, when Duke M. Farson, a wealthy Chicago stockbroker, became the head, or "angel," of the Metropolitan Church Association. The association was made up of Methodists who resented the formal service used by the main church. Farson changed their name to Society of the Burning Bush, or Burning Bush, and in 1913 purchased a 1,520-acre plantation in east Texas near Bullard. Members of the sect were extremely evangelical and believed in salvation through God's grace. They engaged in services that involved trances, faith healing, and speaking in tongues. The next year, Farson and his 375 followers, a combination of farmworkers and professionals, arrived at the Texas plantation by train. They constructed a tabernacle, houses, and dormitories. All possessions were communally owned, although in fact Farson's personal fortune paid the colony's expenses. Even so, because of financial difficulties, members of Burning Bush had to find work outside the community. But when Farson lost his bond buisness, the colony could not pay its debts and in April 1919, the sheriff auctioned the land and property for $1,000.

Sources:

Fogarty, Robert S. 1980. *Dictionary of American Communal History.* Westport, Conn.: Greenwood Press.

Miller, Timothy. 1998. *The Quest for Utopia in Twentieth-Century America.* Syracuse, N.Y.: Syracuse University Press.

BYRDCLIFFE. Byrdcliffe (1902–1976) was a communal settlement of artists near Woodstock, New York, that was begun in 1902 by a wealthy Englishman, Ralph Radcliffe Whitehead. Educated at Oxford, he became a dedicated follower of John Ruskin's utopian ideas and had tried, unsuccessfully, to build communal utopias in Italy before coming to the United States in the mid-1890s. In 1899 Whitehead, along with novelist Hervey White, then at Hull-House in Chicago, laid plans for an artist-craftsperson colony in western Oregon, but the plan was never implemented. At this time, they were joined by painter Bolton Coit Brown, who located land near the town of Woodstock, in upstate New York, where the artist purchased 1,200 acres of land and named the colony Byrdcliffe, a combination of the middle names of Whitehead and his wife, Jayne Byrd Whitehead. Construction of 29 communal buildings was started in 1902, with Whitehead personally financing over $500,000 for the work. In 1903, Whitehead issued an invitation for "true craftsmen" to join the colony. He advertised that it would run by "cooperation" and combine groups of artists to produce "many things which would be impossible as individuals." He also planned to have a communal school for the children that was to be "more rational" than the public schools. Colonists arrived that summer, and a summer art school began to take shape involving painting, woodworking, drawing, weaving, and metalwork. The atmosphere was carefree, exciting, and bohemian and colony members hiked mountain trails, danced, sang, and made love. A number of celebrities eventually visited the colony, such as Heywood Broun, John Dewey, Clarence Darrow, Will Durant, and Bob Dylan. But Byrdcliffe was never an economic success because its main money-making product, huge oak William Morris–style furniture, was out of fashion and the colony could not realize a profit on these items. Financial troubles appeared, along with disagreements between Whitehead and some of his associates. For example, Bolton Coit Brown left the colony after only a few months. The problem was Whitehead's autocratic style of leadership, and some complained that he acted like a feudal baron. By 1912, most of the residents had departed to live in nearby towns. But those who remained stayed on into the 1930s doing craft work. Whitehead died in 1929 and his widow turned over management of Byrdcliffe to her son Peter. Between that year and 1976, when Peter died, much of the acreage had to be sold to keep up maintenance of the buildings and pay taxes. By then, title to what remained of Byrdcliffe was transferred to the Woodstock Guild of Craftsmen. Today it rents studio buildings at $500 a season to raise money to preserve the structures with the hope that another artist colony will again be started there.

See Also Whitehead, Ralph Radcliffe

Sources:

Brown, Bolton. 1937. "Early Days at Woodstock," *Woodstock Historical Society Publications* 13 (Aug.–Sept.): 3–14.

Davidson, Carla. 2003. "Remembering Byrdcliffe…" *American Heritage* (July): 22–25.

Evers, Alf. 1987. *Woodstock: History of an American Town.* Woodstock: Overlook Press.

Miller, Timothy. 1998. *The Quest for Utopia in Twentieth-Century America.* Syracuse, N.Y.: Syracuse University Press.

Smith, Anita M. 1959. *Woodstock: History and Hearsay.* Saugerties, N.Y.: Catskill Mountains Publishing Corp.

C

CARMEL. This Jewish agricultural commune was sponsored by Michael Heilprin and the Hebrew Emigrant Aid Society (HEAS) as one of three such utopian communities in southern New Jersey (the others being Alliance and Woodbine). The colony was founded in 1889 on a 185-acre farm and named the Industrial Co-operation in Combination with Consumer-Patrons. The families cooperatively farmed the land and manufactured items such as jellies, canned goods, and ready-to-wear clothing. An elected governing board assigned work duties and paid individuals piecework salaries. The colony had a library and main communal building for lectures and band concerts. Carmel ran its own school for the children, supported with HEAS money. Although morale was high and the residents were hard-working, Carmel gained a reputation as a refuge for atheists and anarchists. Consequently, during the 1920s, membership declined steadily. By 1932, it was abandoned and the factories were closed. A few single-family farms remained on the original site.

See Also Alliance, Woodbine

Sources:

Bartelt, Pearl W. "American Jewish Agricultural Colonies." 1997. In *America's Communal Utopias,* Donald E. Pitzer, ed., 352–74. Chapel Hill and London: University of North Carolina Press.

Brandes, Joseph. 1972. *Immigration to Freedom: Jewish Communities in Rural New Jersey since 1882.* Philadelphia: University of Pennsylvania Press.

Eisenberg, Ellen. 1995. *Jewish Agricultural Societies in New Jersey 1882–1920.* Syracuse, N.Y.: Syracuse University Press.

Herscher, Uri D. 1981. *Jewish Agricultural Utopias in America, 1880–1910.* Detroit, Mich.: Wayne State University Press.

Sutton, Robert P. 2003. *Communal Utopias and the American Experience: Religious Communities, 1732–2000.* Westport, Conn. and London: Praeger.

CATHOLIC WORKER MOVEMENT. In 1933, Dorothy Day started the Catholic Worker movement in New York City as an anti-Communist alternative for helping the poor deal with the hardships of the Great Depression. Its two essential communal features were urban Houses of Hospitality in New York City and subsistence farms. Its monthly penny newspaper, *The Catholic Worker,* brought national attention to Day's experiments. Soon similar Houses of Hospitality stretched across the country to San Francisco. Although they varied in size, the mother house in New York City, St. Joseph's, served food to 1,200 individuals daily and the one in St. Louis provided 2,600 meals annually and dispatched meals to more than 700 homes. In addition to food, the Houses provided sleeping rooms for city transients. Many Houses organized "worker groups" that held discussions of Christian ethics and Social Gospel ideas. Others helped to organize labor unions and promoted rent strikes. Some did charity work, visiting hospitals and bringing food to the desperate. None of the Houses had formal bylaws, constitutions, and officers. But they all operated on three principles: voluntary poverty (where members made do with simple food, clothing, and shelter), and distribution of food and clothes. The absence of rules and formal work assignment, however, often resulted in disputes over who should do what. Until 1936, the Catholic Church approved of Day's communalism. But that year, when she opposed its stand against the Child Labor Amendment, its hierarchy attacked Day's radical political views as "subversive teaching." As the schism increased, internal division surfaced inside the Houses over Day's fight with the church. Beginning on Staten Island in 1936, Day founded about a dozen subsistence farm communities near Boston, Pittsburgh, Minneapolis, Detroit, Cleveland, Chicago, St. Louis, and San Francisco. But their success was mixed. Many attracted urban poor who were totally unfamiliar with farmwork. Some farms allowed indolents to stay as guests. In other colonies, conflicts erupted between those who were willing to do farmwork and intellectuals who only wanted to organize discussion groups. Most farms shut down after World War II; and those that remained became small truck farms within easy reach of New York City that were able to sell vegetables to its markets.

See Also Day, Dorothy

Sources:
Miller, Timothy. 1998. *The Quest for Utopia in Twentieth-Century America.* Syracuse, N.Y.: Syracuse University Press.

Piehl, Mel. 1982. *Breaking Bread: The* Catholic Worker *and the Origin of Catholic Radicalism in America.* Philadelphia: Temple University Press.

Riegle, Rosalie Troester. 1993. *Voices from the* Catholic Worker. Philadelphia: Temple University Press.

Roberts, Nancy L. 1984. *Dorothy Day and the* Catholic Worker. Albany, N.Y.: State University of New York Press.

Sutton, Robert P. 2003. *Communal Utopias and the American Experience: Religious Communities, 1732–2000.* Westport, Conn. and London: Praeger.

CELO COMMUNITY. The 2000 edition of *Communities Directory: A Guide to Intentional Communities and Cooperative Living* listed Celo Community as "a land trust with 1,200 acres occupied by some 40 households." At that time there were "about 30 families waiting to become trial members." In 1936, Arthur Morgan, who in 1920 became president of Antioch College in Yellow Springs, Ohio, founded this community in North Carolina based on the idea of land stewardship. Under this system, individuals owned their homes but not the land, which was held by the community. Residents could not take out a bank mortgage to purchase their property, called "holdings," but they were permitted to use it as collateral to borrow from the community. Although it grew slowly at first, during World War II Morgan gathered new members from among conscientious objectors confined in the Civilian Public Service camps. Celo was underwritten by philanthropist William Regnery of Chicago as a alternative model to New Deal federalism (which he vehemently opposed), hoping to demonstrate that if individuals lived in small villages and engaged in communal subsistence farming the republic could be saved, not by welfare state paternalism. Celo was governed by a board of directors, the first of whom were Regnery, Morgan, and the executive secretary of the American Friends Service Committee, Clarence Pickett. It had a number of cooperative activities, including a food store, retail crafts store, and a Cabin Fever University. They ran cottage industries and a summer camp. Some members were employed by the county government and school districts. Celo opened a medical clinic that treated both residents and outsiders, at a nominal charge. Its Arthur Morgan School, opened in 1962, taught only junior high students from within and without the community, and ran a summer family camp.

By the 1950s, Celo had become a community inhabited mostly by Quakers and pacifists; or as it advertised in *Intentional Communities: 1959 Yearbook of the Fellowship of Intentional Communities,* of "like-minded people, striving for honesty in all human relations, with resulting mutual trust...." During the last quarter of the twentieth century, Celo population stabilized at about 35 families.

See Also Morgan, Arthur; Macedonia Cooperative Community

Sources:

Communities Directory: A Guide to Intentional Communities and Cooperative Living. 2000. Rutledge, Mo.: Fellowship for Intentional Community.

Fogarty, Robert S. 1980. *Dictionary of American Communal and Utopian History.* Westport, Conn.: Greenwood Press.

Hicks, George Leon. 1969. "Ideology and Change in an American Utopian Community." Ph.D. diss., University of Illinois.

Intentional Communities: 1959 Yearbook of the Fellowship of Intentional Communities.
     1959. Yellow Springs, Ohio: Fellowship of Intentional Communities.
Miller, Timothy. 1998. *The Quest for Utopia in Twentieth-Century America.* Syracuse,
     N.Y.: Syracuse University Press.
Willeford, Lynn Murray. 1993. "Cleo, North Carolina: A Community for Individual-
     ists," *New Age Journal* (May/June).

CERRO GORDO. Along with the Arcosanti community in the Arizona desert, Cerro Gordo is an ecovillage commune. It was begun near Cottage Grove, Oregon, in 1973 on 1,158 acres. Most of the land was preserved in its natural state, but homes and business stores for about 2,500 residents were planned in selected spots, although by 2000 only a few buildings had been completed. Numerous problems accounted for the slow progress. The community had to comply with Oregon's restrictive land-use laws, and banks were reluctant to grant loans for the unconventional buildings that the colony proposed, such as non-freestanding homes. Further antagoniz- ing the development of the colony were reports of financial mismanage- ment by its leaders, some of whom were sued in court for fraud. In 2000, it advertised itself in the *Communities Directory* as a "symbiosis of village, farm, and forest" with homes, businesses, and community facilities. They engaged in communal organic agriculture and the manufacturing of Equinox bicycle trailers. They cut enough lumber from their Forestry Cooperative to build their homes and they planned a lakeview lodge for vis- itors. All homes and business are individually owned, but everyone is a member of a Community Cooperative that owns everything else in Cerro Gordo. They aim "to create a life-enhancing community which reintegrates the human community and our inner selves with the larger community of the biosphere."

See Also Arcosanti

Sources:

Cerro Gordo: Plans, Progress and Process. 1985. Cottage Grove, Ore.: Town Forum.
Communities Directory: A Guide to Intentional Communities and Cooperative Living.
     2000. Rutledge, Missouri: Fellowship for Intentional Community.
Miller, Timothy. 1999. *The 60s Communes: Hippies and Beyond.* Syracuse, N.Y.: Syra-
     cuse University Press.

CHEESEBOARD. This community was organized in San Francisco in 1967 as an eight-member small business that sold imported and domestic cheese. Since then it has grown to become a cooperative of 21 individuals, most of whom work 26 hours weekly. However, all such assignments and hours are made collectively in group discussions. Most internal conflicts are resolved by consensus and it survives as a profitable business in the twenty- first century.

Sources:
Jackall, Robert, and Mary M. Levin. 1984. *Worker Cooperatives in America*. Berkeley: University of California Press.
Trahair, Richard C. S. 1999. *Utopias and Utopians: An Historical Dictionary*. Westport, Conn.: Greenwood Press.

CHILDREN OF GOD (THE FAMILY). This community was one of a number of religious utopias that came out of the Jesus movement of the 1960s. It began in Huntington Beach, California, in 1968 when David Berg (1917–1994), a pastor in the Christian and Missionary Alliance church, started a mission among teenagers in the city's coffee houses. His followers, who by 1972 numbered 2,348 among 134 communities in 41 countries, were doomsday millennialists. They created two main communities—one on a Texas ranch and the other in a mission building in Los Angeles. After 1972, Berg lived in England and communicated with his followers in a series of "Mo" letters that had instructions on health, child care, and sex. In 1976, the Children of God began the practice of "flirty fishing," or having the women, many of them married and living in one of the communes, have sex with men in order to gain new converts. Later, they stopped recruiting by such methods. Parents of some of the community members formed one of the first anticult organizations, Free the Children of God (FREECOG). In the 1990s, they adopted the name The Family.

See Also Berg, David

Sources:
Lewis, James R., and J. Gordon Melton, eds. 1994. *Sex, Slander, and Salvation: Investigating the Family/Children of God*. Stanford, Calif.: Center for Academic Publication.
Miller, Timothy. 1999. *The 60s Communes: Hippies and Beyond*. Syracuse, N.Y.: Syracuse University Press.
Pritchett, W. Douglas. 1985. *The Children of God/Family of Love: An Annotated Bibliography*. New York: Garland.
Shupe, Anson D., Jr., and David G. Bromley. 1980. *The New Vigilantes: Deprogrammers, Anti-Cultists, and the New Religions*. Beverly Hills, Calif.: Sage.
Van Zandt, David E. 1991. *Living in the Children of God*. Princeton, N.J.: Princeton University Press.
Wallis, Roy. 1979. *Salvation and Protest: Studies of Social and Religious Movement*. London: Frances Pinter.

CHILDREN OF LIGHT. This community is a New Age religious experiment (along with the Emmissary and Lemurian communities) constructed in 1963 in the Arizona desert near Dateland, Arizona. It had previously existed in British Columbia since 1948, when Grace Agnes Carlson, who called herself Elect Gold, formed a Pentecostal community of about a dozen individuals in a farmhouse close to the town of Keremos. They believed in an imminent millennium. Elect Gold claimed that God had ordered them to purchase the Arizona property. On 80 acres, they constructed homes and planted trees and vegetables. When the Gila River flooded in 1993, officials tried unsuccessfully to relocate the community. By the late 1990s, only seven members still lived at the site.

See Also The Emissary Communities; Sunrise Ranch

Source:
Miller, Timothy. 1998. *The Quest for Utopia in Twentieth-Century America.* Syracuse, N.Y.: Syracuse University Press.

CHRISTENSEN, JOHN B. Christensen (1874–1930) was born in Kansas City, took a degree at the University of Missouri School of Law in 1895, and practiced law in that state. He moved to Dallas, Texas, in 1914 and then to Glen Rose, where he discovered a Danish farm communal utopia, Danevang (Danish Meadow). In January 1928, he started his own colony on 12,000 acres near Fort Worth named Kristenstaet, after himself. He sold land to resident families at $40 an acre, payable in 20 years at 6 percent. They were allowed to purchase as much land as they needed. The colony prospered until the hard times of the Great Depression caused it to decline and disband.

See Also Kristenstaet

Sources:
Fischer, Ernest. 1980. *Marxists and Utopias in Texas.* Burnet, Tex.: Eakin Press.
Trahair, Richard C.S. 1999. *Utopias and Utopians: An Historical Dictionary.* Westport, Conn.: Greenwood Press.

CHURCH OF GOD AND SAINTS OF CHRIST. In 1901, William Saunders Crowdy (1847–1908) founded a black Jewish communal society at Belleville, Virginia, after he had spent years as a revivalist preacher in Midwestern cities urging a return to Jewish orthodoxy among American blacks. He preached that African Americans were descended from the 10 lost tribes of Israel. The church celebrated the Saturday Sabbath and the Passover with a Seder meal. Crowdy maintained that Jesus, while not divine, advocated racial equality, and church members expected the Messiah to come in the future. His successor, William Henry Plummer, moved the headquarters of the church to a 1,000-acre site near the city of Portsmouth, Virginia. The community had a school for orphans and a home for widows as well as communal apartments, dining hall, print shop, music hall, and a general store. Most members of the church were not communal and lived outside the colony location. In the 1940s, the church abandoned the communal organization of the headquarters, although in the 1990s, plans were made to construct communal homes for the elderly at the colony. Robert S. Fogarty wrote of William Crowdy that although he "deserves study," the "bare facts of his life are not known."

Sources:

Armao, Rosemary, and Greg Schneider. 1988. "Black Jews Step Out of the Shadows," *Virginia-Pilot* (Norfolk) (Apr. 1): 1, 6–7.

Fogarty, Robert S. 1980. *Dictionary of American Communal and Utopian History.* Westport, Conn.: Greenwood Press.

Miller, Timothy. 1998. *The Quest for Utopia in Twentieth-Century America.* Syracuse, N.Y.: Syracuse University Press.

Wynia, Elly. 1994. *The Church of God and Saints of Christ: The Rise of Black Jews.* New York: Garland Publishing.

CHURCH OF THE SAVIOR. In 1946, Gordon Cosby, a Baptist preacher, founded the Church of the Savior at Alexandria, Virginia, as a means to funnel religious commitment to solve social problems. The following year, he moved to Washington, D.C., eventually relocating to a 175-acre farm in Maryland. Members carried on outreach projects such as sponsoring community centers, providing help for the homeless, and advocating pacifism. Members followed a daily routine of prayer and Bible study. They were committed to spirituality and social service. A core group of members lived communally but most followers did not.

Sources:

Miller, Timothy. 1998. *The Quest for Utopia in Twentieth-Century America.* Syracuse, N.Y.: Syracuse University Press.

O'Connor, Elizabeth. 1963. *Call to Commitment: The Story of the Church of the Savior, Washington, D.C.* New York: Harper and Row.

CLARION. This community was the last in a string of Jewish intentional communities founded during the early decades of the twentieth century. Located in central Utah, it was established under the leadership of Benjamin Brown, a Russian immigrant and farm laborer. In 1909, he laid grandiose plans to build a western colony, because of the cheap price of land there, that eventually would have 1,000 families. But in 1911, only a dozen diverse colonists, all men, followed him to the 6,085-acre site near the town of Gunnison. They put up living quarters and dining buildings with assistance from the Mormons. The first year was full of problems, the most serious of which were the lack of water and the meager harvest. They refused to be discouraged. Some members even wrote embellished accounts of the colony's success, predicting a prosperous future where the residents would move beyond agriculture to can and process the crops. They predicted that a town built on agriculture, manufacturing, and mining would develop. However, Brown only avoided a complete disaster after the first year by raising money in the East. But the water problem proved intractable and when the next harvest was equally disappointing internal dissention began to break out. In 1912, the group abandoned communal living and each family received 40 acres, not enough to support a family. There were arguments over what should be taught at the colony school and whether Yiddish or Hebrew would be studied. Nevertheless, additional families arrived over the next two years. In 1915, Brown, totally frustrated, resigned. Creditors and the state of Utah, from which they had mortgaged the land, foreclosed. After a public auction to satisfy these demands, the residents departed.

Sources:

Goldberg, Robert A. 1986. *Back to the Soil: The Jewish Farmers of Clarion, Utah, and Their World*. Salt Lake City: University of Utah Press.

Miller, Timothy. 1998. *The Quest for Utopia in Twentieth-Century America*. Syracuse, N.Y.: Syracuse University Press.

COHEN, JOSEPH B. Joseph B. Cohen (1881–1953) was one of the leaders of the Ferrer Colony (1915–1946) and the founder of Sunrise (1933–1936). He was born in Russia and, while studying to become a rabbi at the Mir seminary, he became a follower of radical anti-Czarist groups and was arrested. He immigrated to Philadelphia in 1903, worked in a cigar factory, and converted to anarchism. He was a cofounder of the Radical Library in the city. In 1916, he joined the Ferrer Colony, located close to New York City at Stelton, New Jersey. Because of the colony's radical beliefs, Cohen and others often were engaged in confrontational discussions with their neighbors during World War I. He also was deeply involved in the Ferrer Modern School and its unstructured curriculum on anarchism and socialism. Between 1925 and 1932, he devoted all his time to being editor of the Jewish left-wing newspaper, the *Freie Arbeiter Stimme*. In 1933, he purchased a 9,000-acre farm near Saginaw, Michigan, and organized Sunrise, which quickly grew to more than 300 residents by the end of the first year, many of them Jewish anarchists. Because of internal dissention over his leadership of the colony, Cohen decided to relocate. In 1938, he and 19 families moved to 640 acres on the Rappahannock River in Virginia. Due to continuing bickering and economic problems, Sunrise lasted only until the fall of that year, when the members voted to dissolve. Cohen then lived at the Home Colony, near Tacoma, Washington, until 1946, when he left to edit the anarchist magazine *Der Freier Gedank* in Mexico and France. He died in New York City in 1952.

See Also Ferrer Colony; Sunrise

Sources:

Cohen, Joseph J. 1975. *In Quest of Heaven: The Story of the Sunrise Co-operative Farm Community*. New York: Sunrise History Publishing Committee, 1957; reprint, Philadelphia: Porcupine Press

Fogarty, Robert S. 1980. *Dictionary of American Communal and Utopian History*. Westport, Conn.: Greenwood Press.

Miller, Timothy. 1998. *The Quest for Utopia in Twentieth Century-America*. Syracuse, N.Y.: Syracuse University Press.

Oved, Yaacov. 1988. *Two Hundred Years of American Communes*. New Brunswick, N.J., and Oxford: Transaction.

Sutton, Robert P. 2004. *Communal Utopias and the American Experience: Secular Communities, 1824–2000.* Westport, Conn. and London: Praeger.
Veysey, Laurence. 1973. *The Communal Experience: Anarchist and Mystical Counter-cultures in America.* New York: Harper and Row.

COLD MOUNTAIN FARM. In 1966, a group of anarchists, political activists, and pacifists living on New York's Lower East Side attended the School of Living conference at Heathcote, Maryland, and planned to move to Sunrise Hill. But Sunrise Hill disbanded by Christmas and in 1967, the New Yorkers and several Sunrise Hill residents built a new community, Cold Mountain Farm, at a dilapidated 450-acre farm not far from Hobart, New York. Their main goal was to serve as a source of free food for their friends living in New York City. Enthusiasm for communal life quickly declined, as it had at Sunrise, for a number of reasons. These urbanites could not farm, the practice of nudity caused neighbors to condemn them as hippies, and a hepatitis epidemic struck. When the local health authorities demanded that they install electricity, refrigeration, and indoor plumbing, most members abandoned the farm. Some of them regrouped and went to the Bryn Athyn community in Vermont.

See Also Bryn Athyn; Sunrise Hill

Sources:
Gardner, Joyce. 1970. *Cold Mountain Farm: An Attempt at Community.* n.p.
Miller, Timothy. 1999. *The 60s Communes: Hippies and Beyond.* Syracuse, N.Y.: Syracuse University Press.

THE COLONY. This independent Christian community was founded by Brother John Korenchan, a former Catholic, and 18 celibate followers from Seattle. In 1940, they moved to Hawkins Bay, California, to begin a communal farm on 16 acres. By the mid-1970s, the Colony still had only a dozen members. They believed that a Power can motivate individuals to follow a life of the spirit that includes living by the teachings of Christ. When Korenchan died in 1982, leadership of the commune was assumed, without controversy, by Agnes Vanderhoof. Some historians consider the Colony as one of the most enduring and stable intentional communities.

Source:
Miller, Timothy. 1998. *The Quest for Utopia in Twentieth-Century America.* Syracuse, N.Y.: Syracuse University Press.

COLORADO CO-OPERATIVE COMPANY. E. L. Gallatin (1828–1900) founded the Colorado Co-operative Company in 1894 to reclaim desert land in southwest Colorado at Tabegauche Park by constructing irrigation ditches. It was organized after the failure of the overly ambitious Topolobampo Colony, a cooperative venture in Mexico that was intended to become a major Pacific Ocean port. A number of members of the Mexican colony responded to advertisements in *The Altrurian* about a massive irrigation project involving 20,000 acres where work would be done communally, although the land itself would be privately owned. Members could join by purchasing shares at $100 each, which would give them voting and water rights. They moved to a community site in southeastern Colorado called Tabegauche Park in the fall of 1894 and constructed a communal town called Piñon. By 1900, it had 50 buildings and 200 members. The colonists completed the irrigation ditch by 1904. In 1910, they renamed the colony Nucla Town Improvement Company. Since the colony by then was no longer communal, a number of members joined the Newllano colony in Louisiana. What remained in Colorado was a community of private citizens who owned the irrigation ditch and cooperatively used the water supply.

See Also Llano del Rio/Newllano

Sources:

Fogarty, Robert S. 1980. *Dictionary of American Communal and Utopian History.* Westport, Conn.: Greenwood Press.

Julihu, C. E. 1899. "Pinon—A New Brook Farm of the West," *National Magazine* (October).

Mercer, Duane D. 1967. "The Colorado Co-operative Company, 1894–1904," *Colorado Magazine* 44 (fall): 293–306.

Miller, Timothy. 1998. *The Quest for Utopia in Twentieth-Century America.* Syracuse, N.Y.: Syracuse University Press.

Peterson, Ellen Z. 1957. *The Spell of the Tabegauche.* Denver: Sage Books.

Sutton, Robert P. 2004. *Communal Utopias and the American Experience: Secular Communities, 1824–2000.* Westport, Conn. and London: Praeger.

Trahair, Richard C. S. 1999. *Utopias and Utopians: An Historical Dictionary.* Westport, Conn.: Greenwood Press.

COMMONWEALTH COLLEGE. This was one of the most significant communal experiments dedicated solely to education. In 1923, the noted educator William E. Zeuch and socialist publisher Kate O'Hare organized Commonwealth College at the Newllano Colony in order to train labor leaders. Disagreements soon broke out over how to run the college and the next year the members moved, under Zeuch's leadership, to 80 acres (eventually 320) near Mena, Arkansas, in the Ozark Mountains. The basic tenet of the community was that competition should be replaced with cooperation. The faculty was not paid salaries and had to live communally with the students; both groups had to work up to 24 hours each week in agriculture. Classes for the 55 students were held in the morning and manual labor was done in the afternoon. Everyone studied together and ate communally. They built a spacious guest house for visitors. A number of prominent Americans were trustees of the college, including Upton Sinclair and Roger Baldwin. Orval Faubus and Kenneth Patchen were students, and singer Lee Hays was on the faculty. No black Americans were admitted. Even so, their southern neighbors soon condemned the campus as being run by radicals and subsidized by the Industrial Workers of the World (or Wobblies) and Communists. After Zeuch was replaced in 1931 by Lucien Koch, and in 1935 succeeded by Richard Whitten, Commonwealth College became openly connected with the Communist Party. Consequently, the Arkansas legislature introduced a sedition bill aimed at the college in 1937 and three years later it was found guilty of the crime of not displaying the American flag. That year, all its assets were liquidated to pay creditors and the court-levied fine for failure to display the flag.

See Also Black Mountain College; Llano del Rio/Newllano

Sources:
Koch, Raymond, and Charlotte Koch. 1972. *Educational Commune: The Story of Commonwealth College*. New York: Schocken.
Miller, Timothy. 1998. *The Quest for Utopia in Twentieth-Century America*. Syracuse, N.Y.: Syracuse University Press.

COMMUNITY FOR CREATIVE NONVIOLENCE (CCNV). In 1970, some graduates of George Washington University opened the Community for Creative Nonviolence (CCNV), a communal home in Washington, D.C., dedicated to social change. Six members initially joined the home and they focused on anti-Vietnam war activities. The next year, however, they turned to running a soup kitchen near the White House and in 1973 they opened the Hospitality House as a haven for the homeless that provided medical facilities. One of its members, Mitch Snyder, attracted wide public attention when he went on hunger strikes on behalf of the homeless. As a result of one of these strikes in 1984, the federal government gave the CCNV the use of a building to run a shelter. When, in 1986, another such episode dramatized the fact that the government had never allocated enough funds to use the building, the Reagan administration allocated $4 million to subsidize the project. By the time of Snyder's death by suicide in July 1990, 60 volunteers were running the shelter.

Source:
Miller, Timothy. 1999. *The 60s Communes: Hippies and Beyond*. Syracuse, N.Y.: Syracuse University Press.

COPELAND, WILBUR F. Copeland (1869–after 1936) and his wife founded the Straight Edge Industrial Settlement in New York City as a communal experiment in practical Christianity. Copeland was the son of a Methodist minister and, after graduating from Ohio Wesleyan University in 1889, he began missionary work in the city's rescue houses. He also was employed for a brief time by Funk and Wagnall's publishing house. In 1898, while working for the Methodist Church in Manhattan, he organized a group of individuals interested in opening a cooperative settlement, among them the philanthropist Ernest H. Crosby. Copeland was also supported by Edward Everett Hale, author and reformer, and Unitarian minister M. R. Heber Newton. He called the community A School of Methods for the Application of the Teaching of Jesus to Business and Society. Copeland was a follower of Edward Bellamy and Laurence Gronlund and thought that the community members should be active in society as urban missionaries rather than remaining an isolated colony. He believed in cooperation instead of communalism. Copeland also founded cooperative farms on Staten Island and a similar colony in Alpine, New Jersey. The latter community became a worker's residence during the Great Depression.

See Also Straight Edge Industrial Settlement

Sources:

Fogarty, Robert S. 1980. *Dictionary of American Communal History.* Westport, Conn.: Greenwood Pres.
——. 1990. *All Things New: American Communes and Utopian Movements 1860–1914.* Chicago: University of Chicago Press.
Miller, Timothy. 1998. *The Quest for Utopia in Twentieth-Century America.* Syracuse, N.Y.: Syracuse University Press.
Trahair, Richard C. S. 1999. *Utopias and Utopians: An Historical Dictionary.* Westport, Conn.: Greenwood Press.

CRASHPADS. These hippie communes were examples of a number of free-life communities founded in the mid-1960s modeled on Drop City, such as the Hog Farm, the Diggers, Morning Star Ranch, and Wheeler's Ranch. Some contemporaries did not see the literally thousands of urban crashpads, often just apartments or places where anyone could stay, as communes, per se, in the beginning. Many, though, developed a communal association as they lived together, usually a dozen or so individuals, and practiced cooperative sharing. While many crashpads where chaotic and infested with hepatitis and gonorrhea, others were well organized with regular communal meals and designated areas for sleeping. Some places engaged in social service work, such as Galahad's Pad in New York City's East Village. This pad, run by Ronald Johnson, was created in an abandoned tenement building converted into apartments that housed up to 30 persons. Johnson prohibited drugs. Galahad ran well until one of their members was murdered there in October 1967. Other crashpads included Sylvia Anderson's Haight-Ashbury apartment and the Family in Bronx Park, New York.

See Also Diggers; Drop City; Hog Farm; Morning Star Ranch; Wheeler's Ranch

Sources:

Barnes, Carolyn, ed. 1968. *The Hippie Scene.* New York: Scholastic Book Services.
Miller, Timothy. 1999. *The 60s Communes: Hippies and Beyond.* Syracuse, N.Y.: Syracuse University Press.

Stevens, Jay. 1987. *Storming Heaven: LSD and the American Dream.* New York: Harper and Row.

CREFFIELD, FRANZ EDMUND. Creffield (?–1906) was born in Germany and came to Portland, Oregon, in 1903 where he joined the Salvation Army and was sent on a mission to the town of Corvallis. Once there he broke from the Army and declared that he was "Joshua," the second Jesus Christ. He soon attracted a number of female followers, who gathered in afternoon meetings in their homes while their husbands were absent at work. Known as the "Holy Rollers," they practiced nudity and some women became Creffield's wives. A Corvallis businessman, Victor Hurt, whose wife and two daughters were followers of Joshua, offered the use of his home for meetings, but this arrangement lasted only a short time. Creffield then moved his people to a location outside of Corvallis near the Willamette River. But when a photograph of the naked group surfaced in the town, he was tarred and feathered by its good citizens. Dauntless, he returned to Corvallis and had an affair with a married woman there. Her husband moved to have him arrested for adultery. Joshua fled, to be found three months later hiding naked under Hurt's home. He was arrested and given a two-year term in the penitentiary. The prophet was released after a year and purchased land at Waldport, Oregon, were he gathered his followers. But on May 7, 1906, George Mitchell, the brother of one of Creffield's female followers, shot and killed him. His sister, shortly afterward, killed her brother in a railroad station in Seattle. She was sentenced to a mental hospital. After Joshua's death his followers abandoned communal living.

Sources:

Beam, Maurice. 1964. *Cults of America.* New York: MacFadden-Bartell.
Miller, Timothy. 1998. *The Quest for Utopia in Twentieth-Century America.* Syracuse, N.Y.: Syracuse University Press.

D

DAVIDIAN SEVENTH-DAY ADVENTISTS. In 1934, Victor Houteff, a Bulgarian immigrant to Los Angeles in 1907, founded the Davidian Seventh-Day Adventists. In 1918, he had joined the Adventists, a millennialist Pentecostal movement having its origins in the teachings of William Miller (1782–1849). But by 1929, Houteff dissented from many of its beliefs and organized a communal church called the Shepherd's Rod, later the Davidian Seventh-Day Adventists, centered on the belief that the Israeli Kingdom of David was going to be restored in Palestine coinciding with the return of Christ. With a dozen followers, Houteff purchased 189 acres near Waco, Texas, and by 1940 64 Davidians were living in the compound, called Mt. Carmel. They spent much of their time printing literature on their theology and dispatching missionaries to convert new believers. But after Houteff's death, when his wife, Florence, took over, a schism developed, led by Benjamin and Lois Roden and called The Branch. Mrs. Houteff relocated most of the community to another site east of Waco on 941 acres of land. After she announced that the Kingdom in Palestine was going to be established on April 22, 1959, more than 900 individuals were living at the colony. However, when that day passed without the event occurring, only 50 Davidians stayed on at Mt. Carmel. After this failed prophecy, Mrs. Houteff left the colony and Benjamin Roden took over the leadership until his death in 1978, whereupon he was succeeded by Lois Roden. In 1981, Vernon Howell joined the community and soon became the designated successor to Mrs. Roden. He took over in 1988 and assumed the name of David Koresh—David for King David and Koresh, the Hebrew name for the biblical Persian king Cyrus. On April 19, 1993, the federal government injected gas into the compound and the ensuing conflagration destroyed most of the colony.

See Also Branch Davidians; Koresh, David

Sources:

Miller, Timothy. 1998. *The Quest for Utopia in Twentieth-Century America.* Syracuse, N.Y.: Syracuse University Press.

Tabor, James D., and Eugene V. Gallagher. 1995. *Why Waco? Cults and the Battle for Religious Freedom in America.* Berkeley: University of California Press.

Trahair, Richard C. S. 1999. *Utopias and Utopians: An Historical Dictionary.* Westport, Conn.: Greenwood Press.

Wright, Stuart A., ed. 1995. *Armageddon in Waco: Critical Perspectives on the Branch Davidian Conflict*Chicago: University of Chicago Press.

DAY, DOROTHY. Dorothy Day (1897–1980) was born in New York City and as a youth participated in the bohemian lifestyle of Greenwich Village until she converted to Catholicism in 1928. After seeing the devastating effect of the Great Depression on the city's poor, she wrote articles published in *Commonweal* and *America* that described desperate families driven to rent strikes to avoid eviction. She warned of the increasing popularity of the Communist Party among these people. In early 1932, she met Peter Maurin, a French radical and eccentric, who persuaded her to begin a newspaper that would give national attention to the need to confront these problems. They pushed for a "Three-Point-Program" that included rural communal farms, urban Houses of Hospitality, and vigorous discussion of social problems. On May 1, 1933, the first issue of the monthly *Catholic Worker* appeared. Later that year, the first House of Hospitality opened, St. Joseph's House, on East Third Street. Soon the House, after relocating to a larger building nearby, had an average of 150 "guests," and by the late 1930s over 1,000 people daily were served food there. In April 1936, Day began the first subsistence communal farm with the purchase of land in Staten Island and soon a dozen more farms were established. Day died in 1980 at the Maryhouse, in New York City, where she had lived the last years of her life. Today the *Catholic Worker,* Houses of Hospitality, and the rural farms continue as vital parts of the continuing Catholic Worker Movement.

See Also Catholic Worker Movement

Sources:

Day, Dorothy. 1952. *The Long Loneliness: An Autobiography.* New York: Harper.

Miller, Timothy. 1998. *The Quest for Utopia in Twentieth-Century America.* Syracuse, N.Y.: Syracuse University Press.

Riegle, Rosalie Troester. 1993. *Voices from the* Catholic Worker. Philadelphia: Temple University Press.

Roberts, Nancy L. 1984. *Dorothy Day and the* Catholic Worker. Albany, N.Y.: State University of New York Press.

Sutton, Robert P. 2003. *Communal Utopias and the American Experience: Religious Communities, 1732–2000.* Westport, Conn. and London: Praeger.

DELTA AND PROVIDENCE. This colony was one of a number of private resettlement communities that appeared during the Great Depression of the 1930s. Several prominent religious figures, including such men as Reinhold Niebuhr and Episcopal bishop William Scarlett, organized a program to assist southern black tenant farmers. They purchased 2,138 acres close to Hillhouse, Mississippi, and then 2,880 more acres near Cruger, Mississippi. They named the first farm of 24 interracial families the Delta Cooperative Farm and concentrated on running a sawmill and farming. The second one, Providence Farm, was developed as a dairy farm. Both colonies prospered and were financially supported by northern white liberals. Delta Cooperative was sold after World War II and Providence Farm was dissolved in 1956 because of the racial tensions that followed the Supreme Court desegregation decision in *Brown v. Board of Education.*

Sources:

Eddy, Sherwood. 1937. *A Door of Opportunity, or an American Adventure in Cooperation and Sharecroppers.* New York: Association Press.

Miller, Timothy. 1998. *The Quest for Utopia in Twentieth-Century America.* Syracuse, N.Y.: Syracuse University Press.

Sutton, Robert P. 2004. *Communal Utopias and the American Experience: Secular Communities, 1824–2000.* Westport, Conn. and London: Praeger.

THE DES MOINES UNIVERSITY OF LAWSONOMY (DMUL).

Alfred W. Lawson was a minor-league baseball player, aviation pioneer, economist, and author of *Direct Credits for Everybody* and other books. He also was the founder of an integrated system of physics, economics, physiology, and philosophy called Lawsonomy, the study of which he promoted at the Des Moines University of Lawsonomy (DMUL). In 1943, he purchased 14 acres and six buildings of the then closed down Des Moines University and about 100 members joined the DMUL. Instead of a traditional curriculum, he had students just memorize his published books. They lived communally, without contact with outsiders, and grew their own food in gardens on the campus. They took part in physical fitness programs Lawson prescribed. But Iowa residents increasingly resented the DMUL, seeing it as something like a prison camp. After violence between the students and their neighbors broke out in October 1944, Lawson ordered that no one could enter the campus. Over the next 10 years, enrollments steadily declined and the property was sold in 1954, to be replaced within a year by a shopping center.

Sources:

Henry, Lyell D., Jr. 1991. *Zig-Zag-and-Swirl: Alfred W. Lawson's Quest for Greatness.* Iowa City: University of Iowa Press.

Lawson, Alfred W. 1935–1939. Three volumes. *Lawsonomy.* Detroit: Humanity Publishing Company.

Miller, Timothy. 1998. *The Quest for Utopia in Twentieth-Century America.* Syracuse, N.Y.: Syracuse University Press.

DIGA. In 1932, Maury Maverick, tax collector of Bexar County, Texas, built one of the most structured utopian communities on a 35-acre site near the edge of San Antonio donated to him by the Humble Oil Company. He gathered abandoned railroad cars to house members of Diga, a reverse acronym for Agricultural and Industrial Democracy. It was opened to World War I veterans in the beginning and then to unemployed heads of families. Maverick organized it as a military camp with "divisions" and governing "officers," who reported to him on regular basis. He imposed a strict discipline, prohibiting any criticism of the rules. No resident could leave Diga without his permission. He placed left-wing magazines in the colony library and opened a kindergarten, retail businesses, and a medical clinic. He even tried to start a lecture series. But the 171 colonists were not intellectuals, only unemployed men concerned about food and health care. And when the New Deal began to offer federal relief from Depression miseries they turned to it rather than Maverick's draconian communalism.

See Also Maverick, Maury

Sources:

Miller, Timothy. 1998. *The Quest for Utopia in Twentieth-Century America.* Syracuse, N.Y.: Syracuse University Press.

Sutton, Robert P. 2004. *Communal Utopias and the American Experience: Secular Communities, 1824–2000.* Westport, Conn. and London: Praeger.

DIGGERS. Historian Timothy Miller called the Diggers "the communal shock troops of the early hip era." It was a communal commitment to "do your own thing," a hippie paradigm imitated by hundreds of other youth communes across the country. Founded in the Haight-Ashbury section of San Francisco in 1966, the Diggers comprised a diverse mixture of 35 communal houses where members performed as theatrical troupes. Some did "life acting," in which they just acted out their fantasies the best way they could. Others practiced "garbage yoga," in which the women daily scavenged for leftovers and then distributed it as free food in Golden Gate Park. The Diggers opened stores where people could pick up free whatever item they wished. Several houses pulled together communally to become Haight-Ashbury community centers. The Diggers rejected traditional religious ideas and approached religion as something spiritual, such as the idea of karma yoga (without the meditation), service, and doing good works. During the following decade, other communes appeared in cities modeled on the "free thinking" of the Diggers. Miller concluded that the "communitarian Digger way had a powerful impact on those who would found communes, both in the city and in the countryside."

See Also Morning Star Ranch; Olompali Ranch; Wheeler's Ranch

Sources:

Miller, Timothy. 1999. *The 60s Communes: Hippies and Beyond.* Syracuse, N.Y.: Syracuse University Press.

Smith, David E. 1971. *Love Need Care: A History of San Francisco's Haight-Ashbury Free Medical Clinic and Its Pioneer Role in Treating Drug-Abuse Problems.* Boston: Little, Brown.

DIVINE, FATHER, AND THE PEACE MISSION MOVEMENT.

George Baker (1879–1965), later known as Father Divine, was born in Rockville, Maryland, and became an itinerant preacher to African Americans, first in his native state and then throughout the South. Baker claimed to be God's spokesman and announced that the spirit of God was within everyone. He ended up in Harlem in 1915 after southern black ministers condemned his evangelical message. In 1919, he moved to the prosperous Long Island suburb of Sayville, where he first called himself "Major J. Divine," and continued to evangelize, now emphasizing communal sharing and the need to help the poor and unfortunate. He avoided an emphasis on salvation and damnation. He operated a communal residence for some of his followers and used it as both a church and an employment agency. Still, his congregation remained small, between 20 to 40 adults. After 1927, when he started to publish his sermons, his following rapidly increased. So much so that the predominantly white residents of Sayville feared that Major Divine was building a "Negro colony" in their town and had him arrested as a public nuisance. In 1933, Divine relocated his church to Harlem, where he founded the Divine Peace Mission Movement Cooperatives. Throughout the 1930s, Divine acquired property, usually in ghetto slums, and soon there were 150 communal centers for more than 10,000 followers. The residents of the centers obeyed Divine's commands on cleanliness and prohibition of tobacco, alcohol, and cosmetics. Divine encouraged his followers to practice celibacy. The missions provided food both for residents and for visitors and operated restaurants, grocery stores, barber shops, and laundries. Frequently, the centers gave outlandish banquets for hundreds of people as a gesture of God's love and human fellowship. Sometimes Father Divine attended and preached a sermon, and in his absence someone would read one of them. Divine's message was always the same: help the downtrodden and bring them closer to God. Encouraged by the success of the urban communes, he started a rural resettlement community in 1935 on fertile farmland in upstate New York called Promised Land. The experiment was racially integrated. It soon was a highly profitable truck farm selling its produce at a substantial profit. In 1940, he led a campaign to get Congress to end racial injustice and segregation and was able to send in a petition with 250,000 signatures. His "Righteous Government Platform" demanded a federal civil rights act against racial segregation in the schools, public facilities, and all-white suburbs. In the 1960s, Father Divine's health declined and his assistants took over the running of the Peace Missions. But without his charismatic presence, the movement lost its support and became involved in administrative battles among the assistants. Nevertheless, his second wife (Divine claimed that it was a celibate marriage), Edna Rose Ritchings, a Caucasian, kept the Peace Mission and communal residences active through the 1990s as "Second Mother Divine," with headquarters in Philadelphia.

See Also Peace Mission

Sources:

Fogarty, Robert S. 1980. *Dictionary of American Communal and Utopia History.* Westport, Conn.: Greenwood Press.

Miller, Timothy. 1998. *The Quest for Utopia in Twentieth-Century America.* Syracuse, N.Y.: Syracuse University Press.

Sutton, Robert P. 2003. *Communal Utopias and the American Experience: Religious Communities, 1732–2000.* Westport, Conn. and London: Praeger.

Watts, Jill. 1992. *God, Harlem, U.S.A.: The Father Divine Story.* Berkeley: University of California Press.

Weisbrot, Robert. 1983. *Father Divine and the Struggle for Racial Equality.* Urbana: University of Illinois Press.

DIVINE LIGHT MISSION. This community was one of a number of Sikh communities organized in America in the 1970s. Lead by Guru Maharaj Ji, it practiced a Radhasoami form of orthodox Sikhism that emphasized yoga and direct communion with the Word through divine sounds and divine light. With its headquarters at Denver, Colorado, and a staff of 125, the mission established ashrams, or communal colonies, in 55 countries. These communities practiced spiritual exercises in a daily regimen of instruction, meditation, and work. They were vegetarians and lived a life of poverty and chastity. In the 1980s, as Maharaj Ji slowly dissolved most of the ashrams and resigned his responsibilities as leader of the Divine Light Mission to become a lecturer, the communal aspect of the movement disappeared.

Sources:

Cameron, Charles, ed. 1973. *Who Is Guru Maharaj Ji?* New York: Bantam.

Downton, James V., Jr. 1979. *Sacred Journeys: The Conversion of Young Americans to Divine Light Mission.* New York: Columbia University Press.

Miller, Timothy. 1999. *The 60s Communes: Hippies and Beyond.* Syracuse, N.Y.: Syracuse University Press.

DOWIE, JOHN ALEXANDER. In 1900, John Alexander Dowie (1847–1907) founded the Christian Catholic Church at Zion City just north of Chicago on Lake Michigan, the first of a number of Pentecostal communes that emphasized faith healing and Christian living. Dowie was born in Edinburgh, Scotland, the son of a poor local preacher. He lived with his parents when they went to Australia in 1860, where he worked in a wholesale dry goods firm. In 1867, he attended the University of Edinburgh and three years later returned to Australia, where he became a pastor of a Congregational church and was known as a religious eccentric. In Melbourne, he was arrested for nonpayment of debts because he refused to answer to anyone but

God. Dowie was a social reformer who demanded temperance laws and free education. He also become known as a faith healer and in 1882 opened a healing tabernacle in the city. In 1888, he moved to San Francisco and eventually to Chicago where, in 1893, he opened Zion's Tabernacle. Three years later, he organized the Christian Catholic Church. Zion City, with 8,000 residents, was an austere theocracy where Dowie owned all the property and prohibited tobacco, alcohol, swearing, gambling, fighting, spitting, riding of bicycles on sidewalks, and the eating of pork. He forbade dancing, theatrical productions, and drugstores. He controlled the city's manufacturing plants, banks, and schools. He appointed inspectors called "parish officers," who regularly inspected moral conduct. He arranged all marriages. In 1904, he went on a worldwide mission that took him to Ireland and Mexico, where he planned to build a second Zion City. In his absence, an opposition party formed under Wilbur Glenn Voliva, a city official, and they deposed him on the charge of using communal funds for personal reasons. He died at Zion City in 1907.

See Also Zion City

Sources:

Cook, Philip L. 1996. *Zion City, Illinois: Twentieth Century Utopia.* Syracuse, N.Y.: Syracuse University Press.

Fogarty, Robert. 1980. *Dictionary of American Communal and Utopian History.* Westport, Conn.: Greenwood Press.

Miller, Timothy. 1998. *The Quest for Utopia in Twentieth-Century America.* Syracuse: Syracuse University Press.

Sutton, Robert P. 2003. *Communal Utopias and the American Experience: Religious Communities, 1732–2000.* Westport, Conn. and London: Praeger.

Trahair, Richard C. S. 1999. *Utopias and Utopians: An Historical Dictionary.* Westport, Conn.: Greenwood Press.

DROP CITY. Drop City began a new era in the history of American communalism, the counterculture "hippie" movement. In May 1965, three young artists purchased six acres of pasture near the town of Trinidad, in southern Colorado. The commune held out the promise of radical alternatives to mainstream American culture and morality—a communal dedication to freedom, mysticism, and artistic expression. One of the members later recalled that they danced "the joydance" of spontaneity, cooperation, egalitarianism, sexual freedom, and drugs. They constructed geodesic domed buildings, using old telephone poles and scrap lumber from a local lumberyard, and covered them with stucco, tarpaper, and bottle caps. Its members, calling themselves "Droppers," traveled to colleges and universities with messages called "droppings" that urged students to "do their thing." They accented the messages with strobe lights and psychedelic music. They produced *The Drop City Document,* a film that demonstrated how similar communities could spring up on cheap land. They printed a newsletter and brochures. Their publicity resulted in new arrivals in the summer of 1967, mostly thrill-seeking teenagers from Haight-Ashbury, who caused overcrowding and sanitation problems. Within months, Drop City became a communal slum. There was not enough money to feed the expanded population, which by late 1967, included transients. By 1969, only one of the original Droppers lived at the community. Newspaper reporters described an increasingly grim life for the 40 or so people at Drop City. By 1970, it was mainly a commune of "motorcycle and speed freaks" living in squalor. Three years later, the original Droppers returned, shut down the buildings, and put up "Keep Out" signs. A neighbor bought the six acres in 1978.

Sources:

Gardner, Hugh. 1978. *The Children of Prosperity: Thirteen Modern American Communes.* New York: St. Martin's Press.

Miller, Timothy. 1999. *The 60s Communes: Hippies and Beyond.* Syracuse, N.Y.: Syracuse University Press.

Sutton, Robert P. 2004. *Communal Utopias and the American Experience: Secular Communities, 1824–2000.* Westport, Conn. and London: Praeger.

DRUMMOND ISLAND. In 1905, Maggie Walz, a temperance advocate, organized this ethnic community of Finnish immigrants on Drummond Island in Lake Huron. As managing editor of the first Finnish newspaper in the United States, the *Suometar,* she laid plans for a cooperative community and a temperance utopia in order "to take the man from the saloon," as she put it. She purchased land on the island and organized four settlements that soon had 900 residents working in the lumber business and on sugar beet farms. For a while it seemed to prosper. But its location was too isolated and in 1914, a group of the colony's socialists rejected Walz's rule. Soon afterwards, communal aspects of the settlement were abandoned.

Sources:

Miller, Timothy. 1998. *The Quest for Utopia in Twentieth-Century America.* Syracuse, N.Y.: Syracuse University Press.

Ross, Carl, and K. Marianne Wargelin Brown, eds. 1986. *Women Who Dared: The History of Finnish American Women.* St. Paul: Immigration History Research Center, University of Minnesota.

DURHAM AND DELHI. Durham, a subsistence farm colony, was sponsored by the state of California in 1917 when it appropriated money to establish two homestead colonies. The first one was Durham, located on 6,239 acres near Chico. Directed by the state's Land Settlement Board and headed by Elwood Mead, an irrigation expert, it had 100 families the first year. Mead set aside acres for a community recreational center and gave each family a small plot to farm. The residents cooperatively constructed all of the homes and buildings and installed an irrigation system. They had a dairy farm and planted orchards. Durham was so successful economically that in 1921 the

Land Settlement Board started a second colony, Delhi, on 400 acres in the San Joaquin Valley. But the agricultural depression of the 1920s hampered its development and by the time of the Great Depression, Delhi was an admitted failure.

Sources:

Conkin, Paul K. 1959. *Tomorrow a New World: The New Deal Community Program.* Ithaca, N.Y.: Cornell University Press.
Miller, Timothy. 1998. *The Quest for Utopia in Twentieth-Century America.* Syracuse, N.Y.: Syracuse University Press.

E

EGGLESTON, C. V. Eggleston (1855–?) was born in Oklahoma and was president of the Eggleston-King Pigeon Company in 1915 when, along with Job Harriman, he became a promoter of the Llano del Rio colony in the Antelope Valley, California. He advertised the commune in a radical Los Angeles newspaper, *The Western Comrade,* and was its fiscal agent. The following year, he organized another cooperative colony in at Fallon, Nevada, called the Nevada Colony. In March 1916, he started publishing *The Cooperative Colonist* to promote an experiment that soon had 200 members. In 1917, he planned the resettlement of 100 Llanoites to an abandoned mill town in Vernon Parish, Louisiana, and called this community Newllano. By 1930, it housed 500 colonists who paid an admission fee of $2,000. This last venture was less communal than the other two communities since houses, automobiles, and furniture were privately owned. It went into bankruptcy in 1936.

See Also Harriman, Job; Llano del Rio/Newllano; Nevada Colony

Sources:

Fogarty, Robert. 1980. *Dictionary of American Communal and Utopian History.* Westport, Conn.: Greenwood Press.

Miller, Timothy. 1998. *The Quest for Utopia in Twentieth-Century America.* Syracuse, N.Y.: Syracuse University Press.

Sutton, Robert P. 2004. *Communal Utopias and the American Experience: Secular Communities, 1824–2000.* Westport, Conn. and London: Praeger.

ELLICOTT CITY. This was the first twentieth-century Jewish farm community and was located at Ellicott City, Maryland, 10 miles west of Baltimore. In 1900, Baltimore Jews purchased 351 acres and moved to the site the following year. But they encountered financial difficulties from the beginning and their first report, published in 1908, listed only ten families living there. Nothing more is known about the colony and historians surmise it gradually abandoned communal living and became a suburb of Baltimore.

Source:
Miller, Timothy. 1998. *The Quest for Utopia in Twentieth-Century America.* Syracuse, N.Y.: Syracuse University Press.

THE EMISSARY COMMUNITIES. In 1930, Lloyd Meeker started to organize one of the largest New Age religious movements with the backing of British aristocrat Lord Martin Cecil. Its first communal utopia began in 1945 as Sunrise Ranch in Loveland, Colorado. Three years later, another community, called the Hundred, was started on land owned by Martin Cecil in British Columbia. These two communities were the core of the Emissary movement and they support dozens of other centers in the United States, usually made up of a couple of families. All satellite centers share characteristics of Sunrise Ranch and the Hundred. They stress aligning bodily and mental energy for New Age healing and conduct seminars on personal growth, creativity, and spirituality. They also publish inspirational books and audio and video tapes.

See Also Children of Light; Sunrise Ranch

Source:
Miller, Timothy. 1998. *The Quest for Utopia in Twentieth-Century America.* Syracuse, N.Y.: Syracuse University Press.

EQUALITY. Equality was the second of four utopian communities founded in the Puget Sound area in the last years of the nineteenth century. Ed Pelton, a Populist politician from Maine, who had become discouraged by the defeat of William Jennings Bryan in the 1896 presidential election, turned to communal socialism as a viable alternative to the economic crisis he saw facing the nation. He conceived a plan to build enough utopian socialist colonies in a given state so as to gain control of the legislature and pass a socialist agenda into law. He targeted the state of Washington. In 1897, he purchased 600 acres of land near Samish Bay, accessible by boats at high tide. By year's end, 15 settlers had arrived. They were a diverse lot of machinists, carpenters, tailors, blacksmiths, engineers, teachers and preachers. They named the colony Equality after the novel published that year by Edward Bellamy. Soon they had an apartment house, barn, workshops, and cabins. Their newspaper, the *Industrial Freedom,* described daily life. They sold produce (vegetables, oats, and barley) in Seattle and Tacoma. They ran a sawmill and developed a fishing industry (salmon and herring) with a sloop called *Progress.* Cottage industries developed (coopering, blacksmithing, furniture manufacturing, and the making of shoes and cereal coffee) in which men and women worked eight hours each day at jobs assigned to them by elected foremen. Everyone ate in a communal dining hall. By the summer of 1898, they had a two-story schoolhouse. Cultural life included evening concerts by the communal orchestra, dancing, and group singing. One historian, Charles LaWarne, claims that Equality's social life was "the most fully developed communitarian experiment in the Pacific Northwest." But problems eventually appeared. In February 1901, Pelton died from injuries suffered when he was struck by a falling tree; there was no one to replace him. By then, a number of drifters had joined Equality, people with no sympathy for its long-range goal to socialize the state. A couple of efforts were made to revive the community, one in 1903 and another in 1905, but to no avail. Factionalism intensified and, finally, in spring of 1907 the group decided to dissolve because of "irreconcilable differences."

See Also Burley Colony (Communal Brotherhood); Freeland; Home Colony

Sources:

LeWarne, Charles P. 1975. *Utopias on Puget Sound, 1885–1915*. Seattle and London: University of Washington Press

Oved, Yaacov. 1988. *Two Hundred Years of American Communes*. New Brunswick, N.J. and Oxford: Transaction.

Sutton, Robert P. 2004. *Communal Utopias and the American Experience: Secular Communities, 1824–2000*. Westport, Conn. and London: Praeger.

ESALEN INSTITUTE. This communal retreat was founded in 1962 by two graduates of Stanford University, Michael Murphy and Richard Price, and used psychedelic drugs, hypnosis, group therapy, and sex. It combined these approaches to self-knowledge with vegetarianism, Sufism, yoga, and theories drawn from astrology, psychology, and psychiatry. Most members of Esalen were middle-class white males. Outsiders considered them "flower people," even though a number of prominent individuals have visited the community and expert therapists gave lectures there. Most of the membership is transient and historians see it more as a utopian center of self-fulfillment than a permanent intentional community.

Sources:

McCord, William. 1989. *Voyages to Utopia: From Monastery to Commune, the Search for the Perfect Society in Modern Times*. New York: W.W. Norton.

Trahair, Richard C. S. 1999. *Utopias and Utopians: An Historical Dictionary*. Westport, Conn.: Greenwood Press.

F

FAIRHOPE. Fairhope (also named the Fairhope Industrial Association and, later, the Fairhope Single Tax Corporation) was founded in 1895 on 132 acres across the bay from Mobile, Alabama, by Ernest B. Gaston, an associate editor of the Des Moines *Tribune,* and three other families. The utopian experiment was subsidized by Marie Howland (1835–1921) and Joseph Fels (1854–1914). The colony was organized under the principles of Henry George's single-tax ideas, according to which the only taxes would be on unimproved land. Individual ownership of homes and businesses was allowed, but all public utilities were owned communally. Within a year, there were about 600 residents living at Fairhope on 1,600 acres. When it was incorporated as a town in 1908, 60 percent of the property was owned by the corporation and 40 percent was held privately. Residents became members of the community by purchasing land for $200, later $100, payable in monthly installments of $5. Colonists had to construct their houses, fence their land, and find jobs. The colony had cooperative stores, a restaurant, three hotels, a lumber mill, a corn and rice mill, a brickyard, a print shop, and a 12,000-volume library. Fairhope operated a profitable steamship line to Mobile. It gained a reputation as a community of intellectuals largely due to its various clubs and societies. In 1896, the colony opened an "organic school," in which students would be developed both mentally and spiritually, without any examinations. In 1954, the colony was absorbed into the town of Fairhope, although the "colony people," according to Paul Gaston, grandson of the founder, still adhere to "the virtues of George's philosophy" as the Fairhope Single Tax Corporation.

See Also Bellangee, James F.

Sources:

Alyea, Paul E., and Blanche Alyea. 1956. *Fairhope, 1894–1954: The Story of a Single Tax Colony.* Birmingham, Ala.: University of Alabama Press.

Fogarty, Robert S. 1980. *Dictionary of American Communal and Utopian History.* Westport, Conn.: Greenwood Press.

Gaston, Paul M. 1993. *Man and Mission: E. B. Gaston and the Origins of the Fairhope Single Tax Colony.* Montgomery, Ala.: The Black Belt Press.

———. 1984. *The Women of Fair Hope.* Athens: University of Alabama Press.

Miller, Timothy. 1998. *Quest for Utopia in Twentieth Century-America.* Syracuse, N.Y.: Syracuse University Press.

Sutton, Robert P. 2004. *Communal Utopias and the American Experienced: Secular Communities, 1824–2000.* Westport, Conn. and London: Praeger.

Trahair, Richard C. S. 1999. *Utopias and Utopians: An Historical Dictionary.* Westport, Conn.: Greenwood Press.

THE FAMILY (TAOS). This biracial colony was the largest of the group-marriage communes founded in the 1960s. Its 50 residents were packed into a small two-bedroom adobe house and a bus near the city of Taos, New Mexico. It was first organized in Berkeley in 1967, relocated to Arizona, and then moved to New Mexico. The communards called each other "Lord" and "Lady." They slept on multiperson mattresses on the floor and had continuously changing sexual partners. A wealthy outsider's subsidy allowed them to open a natural-foods store and a medical clinic and to publish a newspaper called the *Fountain of Light.* It lasted for two years and then some of the members moved to Detroit.

Sources:

Kanter, Rosabeth Moss. 1972. *Commitment and Community: Communes and Utopias in Sociological Prospective.* Cambridge, Mass.: Harvard University Press.

Katz, Elia. 1971. *Armed Love.* New York: Bantam.

Miller, Timothy. 1999. *The 60s Communes: Hippies and Beyond.* Syracuse, N.Y.: Syracuse University Press.

THE FARM. In 1971, Stephen Gaskin (1935–) and a following of hippies from Haight-Ashbury in San Francisco founded a utopian community at Summertown, Tennessee, on 1,700 acres of wooded land. By 1980, membership had peaked at 1,400 residents. In the beginning, conditions were primitive and members lived in school buses and did laundry in a creek. They were vegetarians and abjured not only meat but also milk, eggs, and anything made from animals. Their main crop, raised by organic farming, was soybeans, which they made into tofu, or soy milk, as well as other commercial products. The colony used wind generators and solar power for energy. They did not condone artificial birth control and encouraged childbearing assisted by colony doctors, nurses, and midwives, who offered their services to Farm mothers as well as to women from the county. Farm members opposed abortion. The Farm has embraced a number of lofty projects, all designed, they think, to save the planet. These have included the "hippie Peace Corps," called Plenty, rebuilding worldwide communities devastated by earthquakes, and a mail-order business in the Central American clothing operation. They started a free ambulance service in the South Bronx of New York City and other localities. The Farm is active in a variety of environmental causes, such as protection of wetlands, research on global warming, and wind-power energy systems. During the 1970s, it established satellite Farms. But the deep agricultural recession late in that decade severely hurt The Farm's economy and it became bogged down in millions of dollars in debt. This setback, plus long absences of Gaskin from the community in the 1980s, caused changes. Membership declined and there was a drop in community morale. In 2000, there were between 150 to 200 residents at The Farm still practicing vegetarianism and pacifism and serving with the Plenty in various international relief projects. They operated an Ecovillage Training Center that offered instruction to visitors on such things as organic gardening, alternative building styles, solar power generation, and biological waste treatment. The Farm is now a cooperative association of nuclear families and friends where members own private property and have private incomes, part of which they turn over to the community as rent.

See Also Gaskin, Stephen

Sources:

Miller, Timothy. 1999. *The 60s Communes: Hippies and Beyond.* Syracuse, N.Y.: Syracuse University Press.

Popenoe, Cris, and Oliver Popenoe. 1984. *Seeds of Tomorrow New Age Communities That Work.* San Francisco: Harper and Row.

Sutton, Robert P. 2004. *Communal Utopias and the American Experience: Secular Communities, 1824–2000.* Westport, Conn. and London: Praeger.

Trahair, Richard C. S. 1999. *Utopias and Utopians: An Historical Dictionary.* Westport, Conn.: Greenwood Press.

FELLOWSHIP FARM (PUENTE, CA). In 1912, a Los Angeles dentist named Kate D. Buck contacted George Elmer Littlefield and asked him to come to California to build a replica of the Fellowship Farm at Westwood, Massachusetts, on a 75-acre location near Santa Barbara called Puente. It was to be a communal alternative for the oppressive congestion of urban life in Los Angeles. That winter, 12 families joined the community. As in Westwood, each adult received an acre to cultivate and had to help farm communal land. The colony grew to 60 members, some of whom were eccentric. They often walked the streets of Los Angeles preaching about cooperative living. While at the farm, some practiced nudism. However, the one-acre plot of land proved inadequate to make a living and members gradually left the colony. In 1927, a utility company purchased the property.

See Also Fellowship Farm (Westwood, MA); Littlefield, George Elmer

Sources:

Fogarty, Robert S. 1990. *All Things New: American Communes and Utopian Movements 1860–1914.* Chicago: University of Chicago Press.

Hine, Robert V. 1983. *California's Utopian Colonies.* Berkeley: University of California Press.

Miller, Timot. 1998. *The Quest for Utopia in Twentieth-Century America.* Syracuse: Syracuse University Press.

Trahair, Richard C. S. 1999. *Utopias and Utopians: An Historical Dictionary.* Westport, Conn.: Greenwood Press.

FELLOWSHIP FARM (WESTWOOD, MA). In 1908, George Elmer Littlefield (c. 1862–1930), and 40 associates purchased a 70-acre farm near Westwood, Massachusetts, to put into practice the utopian ideas of Edward Bellamy, whom Littlefield had met in Boston. Littlefield was an idealistic, reform-minded Unitarian minister who resigned his pulpit to devote his energies to organizing a "cooperative church" dedicated to cooperative work. The motto of the community at Westwood was to "Get an acre and live on it...get honest. Get busy." It had a 30-acre common that was farmed communally and each person worked one acre of his or her own. Littlefield turned a radical reform magazine that he had been publishing, called the *Ariel,* into the communal journal. He was the editor until he left the colony in 1912 to found another cooperative farm in California. But Fellowship Farm was never a full communal society because some members lived there only during the summer while others traveled to jobs in Boston. Those who stayed at the colony built attractive frame houses and seemed quite content with their routine of gardening and raising poultry, according to a 1912 article published in *Technical World.* There is some disagreement as to how long the experiment lasted. One historian claims it dissolved within a year, another that it lasted until 1918, and still another that it continued into the 1920s. What historians do agree upon, however, is that it spawned a number of satellite cooperative farms founded by Littlefield in or near Norwood, Massachusetts, Independence and Kansas City, Missouri, and Los Angeles.

See Also Fellowship Farm (Puente, CA); Littlefield, George Elmer

Sources:

Fogarty, Robert V. 1990. *All Things New: American Communes and Utopian Movements 1860–1914.* Chicago: University of Chicago Press.

Miller, Timothy. 1998. *The Quest for Utopia in Twentieth-Century America.* Syracuse: Syracuse University Press.

Trahair, Richard C. S. 1999. *Utopias and Utopians: An Historical Dictionary.* Westport, Conn.: Greenwood Press.

FELLOWSHIP FOR INTENTIONAL COMMUNITIES (FIC). The Fellowship for Intentional Communities (FIC) had its orgin in 1940, when

Arthur Morgan founded Community Service, Inc., while serving as president of Antioch College, Yellow Springs, Ohio, to promote the building of communal utopias. After World War II, it was reorganized as the InterCommunity Exchange under Art Wiser to facilitate communication among the utopian communities. Then it became the FIC under the leadership of Wiser. There were at least 10 communities founded under the auspices of the FIC. Hidden Springs was formed in the late 1940s near Neshanic Station, New Jersey, to promote spirituality and cooperative living. Communal activities of its dozen or so members included gardening and a worship service. Meals, however, were taken as families. They promoted racial integration modeled on the Koinonia Farm; but like the Georgia community, Hidden Springs encountered racial prejudice from its neighbors and it dissolved in the late 1950s. Tanguy Homesteads was founded on 100 acres near West Chester, Pennsylvania, in 1945 by Dan Wilson, a Pennsylvania insurance agent, and included as members conscientious objectors to the war. It was a community of eclectic residents who made all decisions by consensus. It had a community building, a swimming pond, and community work days. In 2000, it described itself in the *Communities Directory* as an intentional community "open to all races and religions" dedicated to developing low-cost housing for families on two-acre plots of leased land. The families paid a $30 monthly assessment fee that went for upkeep on community land and buildings. Near Modesto, California, the Tuolumne Cooperative Farms was created on 155 acres in 1945 by four families to develop field crops, livestock, and an orchard. A community fund provided financial aid to families based on size and everyone participated in communal meals and worship. Skyview Acres was a colony of mostly Quaker pacifists that began in 1948 on 161 acres at Pomona, New York. Organized like Tanguy Homesteads, it embraced racial integration and mutual support in living a rural communal life. It initially had 45 residents, but they never were able to develop a sense of mutual cooperation and disbanded in the 1960s. Episcopalians founded Parishfield in 1948, near Brighton, Michigan, on 38 acres. It was conceived as a communal training community for members of that faith. The three families who lived there in the 1950s adopted communal property and a commitment to a spiritual life. But by the end of the decade, it had mostly abandoned any features of an intentional community. Kingwood was another Quaker colony created in 1949 on 24 acres near Frenchtown, New Jersey. They had a communal fund that was formed largely from income from farming. In 1959, the year Kingwood closed, it had seven adults and two children. Most of them joined the American Bruderhof. Quest was founded in 1950 in Royal Oak, Michigan, as a small rural cooperative committed to Methodism and raising chickens. Its five families were only part-time residents who lived in two duplex houses. Canterbury appeared the next year as a largely Quaker colony that purchased the Canterbury Shaker Village at Concord, New Hampshire. The three resident families formed a cooperative business named the Community Builders that did remodeling jobs. By 1960, just two families were living there. May Valley was a racially integrated land-trust cooperative founded in 1957 near Renton, Washington on 37 wooded acres. It mixed communal and private ownership in the beginning, but in 1973 it abandoned all cooperative aspects of living and became a homeowner's association that offered housing at a low rate in the 1990s of a one time payment of $95 per bedroom. The Vale was a Community Service, Inc.-related community that appeared only eight miles from Yellow Springs, Ohio, the Community Service headquarters. The son of Arthur Morgan, Griscom Morgan, was its founder and the leader of the dozen mostly Quaker families who moved to its 40-acre site in 1959. They practiced sharing, mutuality, and decisions by mutual agreement. David and Betty Dellinger and three couples purchased 20 acres and buildings in 1947 near Glen Gardner, New Jersey, to begin a communal publishing operation called the Libertarian Press. Eventually 18 residents joined the colony. It became a focal point of the opposition to the war in Vietnam in the 1960s and David Dellinger was one of the Chicago Seven who was arrested for disrupting the 1968 Democratic Party convention in that city. In the 1950s, the community changed its name to St. Francis Acres and announced that God owned the land and that they were God's trustees. The colony's main income came from gardening and raising livestock. They realized other income from books published by the Libertarian Press. It dissolved in 1968 largely because of external criticism and threats due to its position on the Vietnam War. The FIC itself continues today in a new incarnation. When the Bruderhof withdrew from the FIC, the latter's membership declined and the group dissolved in 1961. It was revived in 1986 as the Fellowship for Intentional Community and in the 1990s published three editions of *Communities Directory: A Guide to Cooperative Living.*

See Also Bruderhof; Koinonia Farm; Morgan, Arthur

Sources:

Best, James S. 1978. *Another Way of Life: Experiencing Intentional Community.* Wallingford, Pa.: Pendle Hill Pamphlet.

Communities Directory: A Guide to Intentional Communities and Cooperative Living. 2000. Rutledge, Missouri: Fellowship for Intentional Community.

Dellinger, David. 1993. *From Yale to Jail: The Life Story of a Moral Dissenter.* New York: Pantheon.

Hine, Robert V. 1983. *California's Utopian Colonies.* Berkeley: University of California Press.

Lee, Dallas. 1971. *The Cotton Patch Evidence.* New York: Harper and Row.

Miller, Timothy. 1998. *The Quest for Utopia in Twentieth-Century America.* Syracuse, N.Y.: Syracuse University Press.

FELS, JOSEPH. Joseph Fels (1854–1914) was a single-tax crusader and wealthy soap manufacturer who financed single-tax utopias in the 1890s and during the first decade of the twentieth century. Fels was born in Halifax County, Virginia, of German-Jewish immigrants who later moved to Yanceyville, North Carolina, then later to Richmond and Baltimore. As a teenager, he joined his father in manufacturing hand soap. As an adult, he developed the technique of making soap from naptha, and his Fels-Naptha plant shipped products around the world. He gave thousands of dollars to the Fairhope Colony and to other utopian communities in the United States, England, Canada, and Australia. He died in London.

See Also Fairhope

Sources:
Dudden, Arthur Power. 1971. *Joseph Fels and the Single-Tax Movement.* Philadelphia: Temple University Press.
Trahair, Richard C.S. 1999. *Utopias and Utopians: An Historical Dictionary.* Westport, Conn.: Greenwood Press.

FERA (FEDERAL EMERGENCY RELIEF ADMINISTRATION) HOMESTEADS. In response to the Great Depression, the federal government, under Harry Hopkins, head of the Federal Emergency Relief Administration (FERA), created a subsection of FERA called the Division of Rural Rehabilitation and Stranded Populations (DRRSP) to construct four farm cooperatives at Woodlake (Texas), Dyess Colony (Arkansas), Pine Mountain Valley (Georgia), and Cherry Lake Farm (Florida). In the summer of 1933, Hopkins had Lawrence Westbrook, a Texas state senator, and David Williams, an architect, construct a cooperative farm for unemployed farmers in southeast Texas. By September, they had built 100 two-story homes, each on three acres, in a 1,200-acre site called Woodlake. When finished in June 1935, it was the first completely constructed New Deal colony. Every family had, in addition to the home, a garage, a chicken house, and an orchard and paid the government an annual rent of $180 in poultry and crops. Each adult also had to help farm 1,200 communal acres and work in colony handcraft shops. Woodlake was closed down in 1943. In 1934, FERA built Dyess Colony, the largest farm cooperative, as a 17,500-acre cotton farm in Arkansas. It was subdivided into 500 20-acre homesteads and had community buildings consisting of an administrative center, barns, seed house, cotton gin, store, hospital, and school. The colony never made a profit, however, and lost $750,000 before it was closed down in 1939. Pine Mountain Valley was located on 12,651 acres near Warm Springs, Georgia in 1933. It was built for indigent farm families and had a hatchery, a grape cannery, a sawmill, and a dairy and egg freezing plant. Other buildings included seven barracks structures, a warehouse, barns, a school, an auditorium, and a church. Unfortunately, the farmsteads were too small, between 10 and 40 acres, to support the 300 families who moved there. The cannery, though, allowed to community to survive until 1943. Cherry Lake Farm was constructed for 132 families who were on relief in Tampa, Miami, and Jacksonville. Located on

12,420 sandy acres in northern Florida and built at a cost of $2 million, it had an administrative building that was used as a community center and ran a poultry business and gristmill. It went into bankruptcy in 1939.

See Also New Deal Cooperatives

Sources:

Conkin, Paul K. 1959. *Tomorrow a New World: The New Deal Community Program.* Ithaca, N.Y.: Cornell University Press.

Miller, Timothy Miller. 1998. *The Quest for Utopia in Twentieth-Century America.* Syracuse, N.Y.: Syracuse University Press.

Sutton, Robert P. 2004. *Communal Utopias and the American Experience: Secular Communities, 1824–2000.* Westport, Conn. and London: Praeger.

FERM, ELIZABETH BYRNE. Elizabeth Byrne Ferm (1857–1944) was a native of Galva, Illinois, but moved to New York City when she married at the age of 20. After she left her abusive husband, she lived with her mother in Brooklyn and developed an interest in children's education. She graduated in 1899 from the Training School for Kindergartners connected with All Souls Episcopal Church. While attending theosophy meetings, she met Swedish immigrant Alexis Ferm, whom she married in 1898. Between 1901 and 1913, the couple crusaded for the creation of free schools in New York City that would substitute the development of the child's personality for the intellectual indoctrination that they found so repressive in the public schools there. In 1920, they joined the Ferrer Colony utopia where Joseph Cohen had them run the colony's Modern School near Stelton, New Jersey. Here they emphasized manual training, craft work, and physical activities and the uniting of schoolwork and daily living. Each child was allowed to advance at his or her own pace. In 1925, following a dispute with some parents who wanted their children to have a more practical vocational training, they resigned.

See Also Cohen, Joseph B.; Ferrer Colony

Sources:

Ferm, Mary Elizabeth (Byrne). 1949. *Freedom in Education.* New York: Lear.

Fogarty, Robert S. 1980. *Dictionary of American Communal and Utopian History.* Westport, Conn.: Greenwood Press.

Miller, Timothy. 1998. *The Quest for Utopia in Twentieth-Century America.* Syracuse, N.Y.: Syracuse University Press.

Sutton, Robert P. 2004. *Communal Utopias and the American Experience: Secular Communities, 1824–2000.* Westport, Conn. and London: Praeger.

Trahair, Richard C. S. 1999. *Utopias and Utopians: An Historical Dictionary.* Westport, Conn.: Greenwood Press.

FERRER COLONY. Ferrer Colony was founded in 1915 by anarchists, led by Joseph Cohen, Leonard Abbott, and Harry Kelly, on 143 acres near Stelton, New Jersey, close to the main line of the Pennsylvania Railroad with easy access to New York City. Colonists purchased lots in the colony, from one to two acres, for $150 per acre, on which they built their own homes. Community land was used for a school, a water system, and a culture center. At its peak in the 1920s, it had 90 houses and more than 200 residents. Daily life included discussion of political issues, folk dancing, communal dinners, and evening lectures. The residents ran a cooperative store. Its Modern School was famous for its pioneering innovations in instruction of children. During the 1920s, a schism developed between the anarchists and the communists, but the colony managed to remain intact until during World War II, when the army built Camp Kilmer right next to Ferrer. This event prompted a number of the colonists to leave and sell their homes for a profit to the soldiers. By 1946, the Ferrer Colony had disappeared.

See Also Abbott, Leonard; Cohen, Joseph B.; Kelly, Harry

Sources:

Fogarty, Robert S. 1980. *Dictionary of American Communal and Utopian History.* Westport, Conn.: Greenwood Press.

Miller, Timothy. 1998. *The Quest for Utopia in Twentieth-Century America.* Syracuse, N.Y.: Syracuse University Press.

Trahair, Richard C. S. 1999. *Utopias and Utopians: An Historical Dictionary.* Westport, Conn.: Greenwood Press.

Veysey, Laurence. 1973. *The Communal Experience: Anarchist and Mystical Countercultures in America.* New York: Harper & Row, Publishers.

FREEDOM COLONY. This cooperative community was similar to Ruskin and was started in 1898 at Fulton, Kansas, by the General Labor Exchange Organization of Independence, Missouri. The exchange admitted 14 families to the community of 60 acres. It had a sawmill, some light industry, and farmland. Eventually, 30 individuals joined Freedom Colony, one of whom was Carl Browne, an artist, who planned to build an airplane factory to provide jobs. No plant was ever built, although Brown ran unsuccessfully for Congress. Eugene V. Debs, Social Democratic Party candidate for president, visited the colony. Membership steadily declined after 1900 and when a fire razed most of the buildings in 1905, the community dissolved.

Sources:

Fogarty, Robert S. 1980. *Dictionary of American Communal and Utopian History.* Westport, Conn.: Greenwood Press.

Miller, Timothy. 1998. *The Quest for Utopia in Twentieth-Century America.* Syracuse, N.Y.: Syracuse University Press.

FREEDOM HILL. The anarchist J. William Lloyd founded this small colony at Roscoe, California, sometime between 1908 and 1913. Lloyd was born in 1857 in New Jersey and died sometime after 1914. In 1900, he became the editor of the radical newspaper the *Free Comrade*. Some of Lloyd's ideas influenced Leonard Abbott and the building of the Ferrer Colony. He also was associated with George Littlefield and the Fellowship Farm community and one of his utopian novels was published by that colony's press. At Freedom Hill, Lloyd opened a print shop and had LeRoy Henry, a physician, run the press. Henry printed segments of Jacob Beilhart's writings, such as *Spirit Fruit* and *Spirit Voice*.

See Also Beilhart, Jacob; Ferrer Colony; Littlefield, George Elmer; Spirit Fruit Society

Sources:

Fogarty, Robert S. 1980. *Dictionary of American Communal and Utopian History.* Westport, Conn.: Greenwood Press.

Miller, Timothy. 1998. *The Quest for Utopia in Twentieth-Century America.* Syracuse, N.Y.: Syracuse University Press.

FREELAND. This was the last of the cooperative colonies founded in the Puget Sound area. It is not to be confused with the second colony called Freeland, when Equality adopted that name in 1904. In 1899, George Washington Daniels purchased land for the utopia on Whidby Island and organized the Free Land Association. It had a central cooperative store that gave dividends to residents with which they could buy land, usually five-acre tracts. Most settlers were former members of Equality who had become disgruntled with the running of that colony. Freeland had a community boat for transportation to the mainland, a newspaper called the *Whidby Islander,* a school, and social organizations that brought socialist lecturers to the island. There was no central political organization and the community held together for ideological reasons, not common property ownership. It ended its cooperative phase about 1906 and became just another island village on Puget Sound.

See Also Burley Colony (Cooperative Brotherhood); Equality; Home Colony

Sources:

Fogarty, Robert S. 1980. *Dictionary of American Communal and Utopian History.* Westport, Conn.: Greenwood Press.

LeWarne, Charles P. 1975. *Utopias on Puget Sound, 1885–1915.* Seattle: University of Washington Press.

Miller, Timothy. 1998. *The Quest for Utopia in Twentieth-Century America.* Syracuse, N.Y.: Syracuse University Press.

G

GASKIN, STEPHEN. Stephen Gaskin (1935–) is the charismatic leader of
The Farm. While a graduate student and later a faculty member at San Francisco State University, he developed a hippie philosophy that was a combination of spirituality and religious tenets—an amalgam of Christianity, karma,
mysticism, and human psychology. He taught his philosophy in the form of
classes on "Group Experiments in Unified Field Theory," which by 1969 had
grown so large that they had to use an auditorium known as the "Family
Dog." Gaskin said that he was a "spiritual teacher" of eternal truths that
would result in "enlightenment," or a "permanent high." This was not a
drug-induced high, but rather a euphoria that came about because of a new
sensitivity to the beauty of the universe. Gaskin preached that humans can
experience a lasting sense of peace and communication with each other
through this enlightenment because it would release an "energy of the universe" in the individual. He later explained his ideas in a number of pamphlets printed at The Farm's Book Publishing Company. In 1971, after an
extended speaking tour throughout the United States, he founded The Farm
community on 2,000 acres near Summertown, Tennessee. He denied that he
played a leadership role except in the spiritual aspects of life at The Farm, but
historians believe that he was the paramount director of the nonspiritual
aspects of communal life there. In 1990, he purchased 100 acres of adjacent
land to found a retirement commune for senior hippies called Racinante, the
name of Don Quixote's horse. In 1994, he started the Ecovillage Training
Center to disseminate information and resources on organic gardening, alternative building styles, biological waste treatment methods, solar heating and
cooling, and other related topics.

See Also The Farm

Sources:

Miller, Timothy. 1999. *The 60s Communes: Hippies and Beyond.* Syracuse, N.Y.: Syracuse University Press.

Popenoe, Cris, and Oliver Popenoe. 1984. *Seeds of Tomorrow: New Age Communities That Work.* San Francisco: Harper and Row.

Sutton, Robert P. 2004. *Communal Utopias and the American Experience: Secular Communities, 1824–2000.* Westport, Conn. and London: Praeger.

GESUNDHEIT INSTITUTE. In 2000, Gesundheit Institute advertised itself in the *Communities Directory* as being "a group of healers, visionaries and clowns working to build a healing community based on humor, compassion, generosity, and enthusiastic hard work." It is still working toward its ultimate goal of constructing a 40-bed, free hospital on the 310 acres near Hillsboro, West Virginia, that Patch Adams purchased in 1971. Adams received an M.D. degree and had started a residency at Georgetown University Hospital when he and some friends decided to try a new way to practice medicine. They started to build a hospital that would not accept payment of any kind for services and would work with chiropractors and homeopaths. Adams and his five colleagues stressed humor as a means of communicating with patients, especially children. The movie *Patch Adams* was based on their story. At the beginning of the twenty-first century, Adams moved to Arlington, Virginia, where he opened a medical practice to raise money to subsidize the building of the free hospital.

Sources:

Adams, Patch, with Maureen Mylander. 1993. *Gesundheit! Bringing Good Health to You, the Medical System, and Society through Physician Service, Complementary Therapies, Humor, and Joy.* Rochester, Vt.: Healing Arts.

Communities Directory: A Guide to Intentional Communities and Cooperative Living. 2000. Rutledge, Mo.: Fellowship for Intentional Community.

Miller, Timothy. 1999. *The 60s Communes: Hippies and Beyond.* Syracuse, N.Y.: Syracuse University Press.

GILMAN, CHARLOTTE PERKINS STETSON. Gilman (1860–1935) was born into a poor family in Hartford, Connecticut. She married artist Charles Walter Stetson (1858–1911) in 1884, had one child, and divorced him in 1894. In 1900, she married her cousin George Gilman. By then she had read Edward Bellamy's *Looking Backward* and joined the Fabians and the Nationalist movement. In 1898, she published her popular *Women and Economics,* in which she advocated economic equality between the sexes. In 1915, she wrote her fictional account of a communal utopia, *Herland,* where healthy, intelligent women have children by parthenogenesis. She was editor of the social reform magazine the *Forerunner.* She worked for feminist and social causes including universal suffrage, better education, executive jobs, elimination of housekeeping drudgery, better health care for children, and world peace. She committed suicide in 1935.

Sources:

Kessler, Carol Farley. 1995. *Charlotte Perkins Gilman: Her Progress toward Utopia with Selected Writings.* Syracuse, N.Y.: Syracuse University Press.

Trahair, Richard, C.S. 1999. *Utopias and Utopians: An Historical Dictionary.* Westport, Conn.: Greenwood Press.

GLENDENNING: THE LEVITES/ORDER OF AARON. Soon after a chiropractor, Maurice Glendenning, joined the Mormon Church in the 1930s, he began having divine revelations. In 1942, he left the Church of the Latter Day Saints to found a commune in western Utah called the Order of Aaron, whose members called themselves Levites. After trying communal life in various locations in that remote part of the state, in 1956 they settled permanently at EskDale. In 1998, about 100 residents lived by farming and dairy operations. Glendenning's successor, Robert J. Conrad, has established small, noncommunal colonies throughout the West.

See Also Kilgore: Zion's Order

Sources:

Baer, Hans A. 1988. *Recreating Utopia in the Desert: A Sectarian Challenge to Modern Mormonism.* Albany: State University of New York Press.

Miller, Timothy. 1998. *The Quest for Utopia in Twentieth-Century America.* Syracuse, N.Y.: Syracuse University Press.

GORDA MOUNTAIN. Gorda Mountain was one of the first open land communes of the 1960s hippie era. In 1962, Amelia Newell, operator of an art gallery in the small town of Gorda Mountain, near Big Sur, California, issued an open invitation to everyone to come and live on her property. Gorda Mountain soon gained a reputation as a refuge for derelicts and drug traders, whose numbers swelled to 200 by the summer of 1967. Accounts of visitors to Gorda depicted a depressing assortment of hippies living in caves and tents, without sanitation facilities or adequate water. Local hostility to the commune was vicious. Neighbors severed the water line to the place in order to get health officials to condemn it as a public hazard. A gun-carrying gas station owner would not serve anyone who lived at Gorda. Because of such harassment and the decrepit living conditions, the community dissolved in 1968.

Sources:

Miller, Timothy. 1999. *The 60s Communes: Hippies and Beyond.* Syracuse, N.Y.: Syracuse University Press.

Gustaitis, Rasa. 1969. *Turning On.* London: Weidenfeld and Nicolson.

Yablonsky, Lewis. 1968. *The Hippie Trip.* New York: Pegasus.

GOTTLIEB, LOU. Lou Gottlieb (1937–1996) was the founder and leader of the Morning Star Ranch commune and an apostle of open land communal living. A former Communist and a musician in a folk band, he became an advocate of Indian mysticism and LSD at his vacation home in Occidental, Sonoma County, California. In 1966, he invited hippies to come there to live. In July 1967, when about 200 individuals were living on 32 acres, the police arrested him for violating health codes. Because of public nudity and open drug use at the colony, the FBI raided it in October 1969, but the raid did not close down the ranch. However, after county officials bulldozed the houses and buildings four times, the residents moved out and by 1973 the place was abandoned. In July 1996, shortly after Gottlieb's death, a casual memorial service was held at site of the ranch.

See Also Morning Star Ranch

Sources:

Fogarty, Robert S. 1980. *Dictionary of American Communal and Utopian History.* Westport, Conn.: Greenwood Press.

Gardner, Hugh. 1978. *The Children of Prosperity: Thirteen Modern American Communes.* New York: St. Martin's.

Miller, Timothy. 1999. *The 60s Communes: Hippies and Beyond.* Syracuse, N.Y.: Syracuse University Press.

GOULD FARM. In 1913, William Gould and his wife, Agnes, founded this religious service community at Great Barrington, Massachusetts, after they had experimented with a variety of summer camp relief programs. The community helped alcoholics, sex offenders, the mentally ill, and the physically handicapped. The staff lived communally and Gould stressed spiritual development that included worship services. When he died in 1925, Agnes continued the leadership for the next 40 years. In 1989, a staff of 35 individuals ran the farm and 40 "guests" were being treated there.

Sources:

McKee, Rose. 1963. *"Brother Will" and the Founding of Gould Farm.* Great Barrington, Mass.: William J. Gould Associates.

Miller, Timothy. 1998. *The Quest for Utopia in Twentieth-Century America.* Syracuse, N.Y.: Syracuse University Press.

GRATEFUL DEAD. In 1964, this communal rock-and-roll band was formed in a Victorian mansion in the Haight-Ashbury district of San Francisco. Led by Jerry Garcia, they pooled all expenses and money made from band concerts. Garcia's wife, Carolyn Adams, served as the manager of the "family." After 1966, some members left the commune to live privately, although the Grateful Dead continued its communal life. A group of hippie fans called the Deadheads followed the band around the country on its bus tours.

Sources:

Brandelius, Jerilyn Lee. 1989. *Grateful Dead Family Album*. New York: Warner.
Miller, Timothy. 1999. *The 60s Communes: Hippies and Beyond*. Syracuse, N.Y.: Syracuse University Press.
Scully, Rock, with David Dalton. 1996. *Living with the Dead: Twenty Years on the Bus with Garcia and the Grateful Dead*. Boston: Little, Brown.

H

HAPGOOD, WILLIAM POWERS. Hapgood (1872–1960) was born in Alton, Illinois, of a wealthy family and was educated at Harvard University. In 1917, he turned his 100-employee canning business, the Columbia Conserve Company, into a workers' cooperative run by a council. It adopted profit-sharing, whereby all the employees received an equal share of the profits. The council determined wages, hours, and other aspects of labor in the factory. The company became a model of a worker's cooperative utopia. During the Great Depression, the company began to decline and in 1943 it was dissolved by a court order. Hapgood died in Indianapolis.

Source:
Fogarty, Robert S. 1980. *Dictionary of American Communal and Utopian History.* Westport, Conn.: Greenwood Press.

HAPPYVILLE. In 1905, this colony was a Jewish farm commune in South Carolina founded by Charles Weintraub and Morris Latterman on a 2,200-acre plantation near Aiken. Within a year, 25 families, mostly Russian immigrants, lived there. Bad weather, however, retarded the community's development and by 1908 most colonists returned to New York and New Jersey. Weintraub tried unsuccessfully to recruit new settlers but gave up and moved to Atlanta. Happyville was sold to outsiders later that year.

Source:
Miller, Timothy. 1998. *The Quest for Utopia in Twentieth-Century America.* Syracuse, N.Y.: Syracuse University Press.

HARRIMAN, JOB. Job Harriman (1861–1925), the founder of Llano del Rio, was an Indiana farm boy until he left home to attend Butler College (then called North Western Christian University) in Indianapolis. He wanted to become a minister but left school without graduating. He then studied law at Colorado College, Colorado Springs, and was admitted to the Indiana bar in 1885. The following year, he moved to San Francisco and became a leading socialist attorney, a member of that city's Nationalist Club, and an associate of the Altrurians, a Christian socialist colony in Sonoma County, California. He soon became a leader in the Socialist Labor Party and was that party's nominee for governor in 1898. In 1900, he was a candidate for the vice presidency of the United States along with Eugene V. Debs. In 1911 and 1913, he ran unsuccessfully for mayor of Los Angeles. Discouraged with the growing unpopularity of the Socialist Party of America, he turned to economic cooperatives rather than politics as the solution for America's problems. In 1914, he purchased several thousand acres of arid land 45 miles north of Los Angeles that had once been the site of a temperance colony. He called his community Llano del Rio and it practiced lofty principles of cooperation spelled out in the colony's "Declaration of Principles." In 1918, internal dissention and the lack of an adequate water supply caused Harriman to relocate the colony to a place near Stables, in Vernon Beach, Louisiana. Harriman lived at the community, called Newllano, for four years, until health problems forced him to move back to California.

See Also Llano del Rio/Newllano

Sources:

Fogarty, Robert S. 1980. *Dictionary of American Communal and Utopian History.* Westport. Conn.: Greenwood Press.

Hine, Robert V. 1983. *California's Utopian Colonies.* Berkeley: University of California Press.

Miller, Timothy. 1998. *The Quest for Utopia in Twentieth-Century America.* Syracuse, N.Y.: Syracuse University Press.

Oved, Yaacov. 1987. *Two Hundred Years of American Communes.* New Brunswick, N.J. and Oxford: Transaction.

Sutton, Robert P. 2004. *Communal Utopias and the American Experience: Secular Utopias, 1824-2000.* Westport, Conn. and London: Praeger.

HAVURAT SHALOM. This Jewish utopia was among the first such communities created in the 1960s to have a close fellowship that eliminated all sexual distinctions in Judaism and supported liberal political agendas. It had 38 members living in a communal house in Somerville, Massachusetts. Members wore their hair long and used psychedelic drugs. Their Sabbath services adopted Quaker silent meditation and group singing and dancing. They published *The Jewish Catalog,* which described their lifestyle and gave direction on creating a new havurot, or fellowship group. Several other fellowship groups were subsequently founded in New York, Washington, D.C., and San

Francisco and about a dozen such fellowship houses appeared near college campuses.

Sources:

Bubis, Gerald B., and Alan Lert. 1983. *Synagogue Havurot: A Comparative Study.* Washington, D.C.: Center for Jewish Community Studies and University Press of America.

Miller, Timothy. 1999. *The 60s Communes: Hippies and Beyond.* Syracuse, N.Y.: Syracuse University Press.

Siegel, Richard, Michael Strassfield, and Sharon Strassfield, eds. 1973. *The Jewish Catalog.* Philadelphia: Jewish Publication Society of America.

HEALTHY-HAPPY-HOLY ORGANIZATION. This community was rooted in the traditions of Sikhism that went back 500 years to a Hindu offshoot sect in the Punjab, located between the border of India and Pakistan. In 1969, the founder of the Healthy-Happy-Holy Organization, Yogi Bhajan, immigrated to the United States to begin a mission of spreading Sikhism to Americans. One of his converts gave him 12 acres near Santa Fe, New Mexico, and there the yogi established Maharaj Ashram. It grew to 50 members during the next two years. The colonists meditated on the meaning of the name of God and practiced Kundalini yoga and breathing exercises. Over the next 30 years, the Healthy-Happy-Holy Organization, or 3HO, as it called itself, built another ashram near Española, New Mexico, and then about 100 smaller communities throughout the country. They earn money by selling specialty foods, health foods, and operating vegetarian restaurants.

Sources:

Gardner, Hugh. 1978. *The Children of Prosperity: Thirteen Modern American Communes.* New York: St. Martin's.

Miller, Timothy. 1999. *The 60s Communes: Hippies and Beyond.* Syracuse, N.Y.: Syracuse University Press.

HEARD, GERALD. Gerald Heard (1890–1971) was born in London and died in Los Angeles. He attended Sherborne and Cambridge Universities. During the 1920s, he was associated with Sir Horace Plunkett and the planning of Irish agricultural cooperatives. Heard published books on architecture and human evolution as well as detective stories. In 1938, he moved to Hollywood, California, and became involved with the Eastern religious community, the Vedanta Society, under the leadership of Swami Prabhavananda. He was convinced that America was headed for an apocalypse and that this calamity could only be avoided by the leadership of a new generation of spiritual individuals trained in meditation, self-discipline, and humility. In 1942, he purchase a 382-acre ranch 60 miles south of Los Angeles and founded Trabuco College ("college" was used in the sense of "collegium," or community). The members of this ascetic and celibate community led lives of self-mortification, meditation, and manual labor. Aldous Huxley stayed for a while at Trabuco, where he wrote *The Perennial Philosophy*. Abruptly, Heard announced in 1947 that God had determined that the community should dissolve, and in 1949 he deeded it to the Vedanta Society. Heard returned to live in Los Angeles until his death.

See Also Trabuco College

Sources:

Fogarty, Robert S. 1980. *Dictionary of American Communal and Utopian History*. Westport, Conn.: Greenwood Press.

Miller, Timothy. 1998. *The Quest for Utopia in Twentieth-Century America*. Syracuse, N.Y.: Syracuse University Press.

Veysey, Laurence. 1973. *The Communal Experience: Anarchists and Mystical Counter-cultures in America*. New York: Harper & Row, Publishers.

HEAVEN CITY. This communal utopia was founded by Albert J. Moore (1893–1963) of Chicago in 1923 near Harvard, Illinois. He wanted to build a refuge for a series of worldwide calamities that he predicted would occur annually, beginning with a money panic that year. The 130-acre colony soon had 36 residents. Each family lived in a private home but everyone ate and worked communally. They opened a school run on the Montessori Method and published a newspaper, *The Harvard Herald*. By the mid 1930s, Heaven City had 75 residents. At that time, Moore moved the colony to Mukwonago, Wisconsin, where they continued their communal life and operated a motel with a restaurant and bar. After Moore died, Heaven City went into a slow decline and the motel was sold to outsiders who still operated it in the 1990s.

Source:

Miller, Timothy. 1998. *The Quest for Utopia in Twentieth-Century America*. Syracuse, N.Y.: Syracuse University Press.

HELICON HALL COLONY. Upton Sinclair (1878–1968) founded this utopian socialist community in 1906 with royalties from his book *The Jungle*. He named the colony after the mythical home of ancient Greek muses and organized it at a former boys' school in Englewood on the New Jersey Palisades. Helicon Hall was more bohemian than communal and attracted a number of famous visitors from New York City. Within six months, 46 adults and 15 children lived there. The colonists lived comfortably and hired personal servants who waited on them at lavish evening dinners, after which they sat in front of a large fireplace and engaged in intellectual conversation. A fire totally destroyed their single building on March 16, 1907, and the community never recovered. Sinclair was forced to sell the property to residential developers in 1908.

See Also Sinclair, Upton

Sources:

Fogarty, Robert S. 1980. *Dictionary of American Communal and Utopian History*. Westport, Conn.: Greenwood Press.

Miller, Timothy. 1998. *The Quest for Utopia in Twentieth-Century America*. Syracuse, N.Y.: Syracuse University Press.

Sinclair, Upton. 1962. *The Autobiography of Upton Sinclair*. New York: Harcourt, Brace, and World.

Trahair, Richard C. S. 1999. *Utopias and Utopians: An Historical Dictionary*. Westport, Conn.: Greenwood Press.

HIGH RIDGE FARM. Like Table Mountain Ranch, High Ridge Farm was a spin-off from San Francisco's counterculture. In 1968, Richard Fairfield, a seminary student from Boston, and friends decided to organize a communal utopia as an escape from the congestion of city life. They purchased a 17-acre farm in southwestern Oregon, accessible from a state highway by a dirt road. It was a community without planning or regulations where a member felt free to do what he or she wanted to do. Within a few years, about 30 people lived there, in addition to a number of constantly arriving visitors. They paid their bills from savings that members donated to the farm and also purchased supplies using food stamps. They built a storeroom, goat shed, sauna, and outhouse. They cultivated a communal garden and canned vegetables. Children slept in a farmhouse with an adult supervisor and the adults lived in an A-frame house. Sexual behavior was promiscuous. In the 1970s, they began to have encounter sessions that involved holding and hugging and confessional discussions. During that decade, they started construction of a communal hall with facilities for washing, bathing, and storage and with living and eating quarters.

See Also Table Mountain Ranch

Sources:

Gardner, Hugh. 1978. *The Children of Prosperity: Thirteen Modern American Communes*. New York: St. Martin's.

Sundancer, Elaine [Elaine Zablocki]. 1973. *Celery Wine: The Story of a Country Commune*. Yellow Springs, Ohio: Community Publications Cooperative.

Sutton, Robert P. 2004. *Communal Utopias and the American Experience: Secular Communities, 1824–2000*. Westport, Conn. and London: Praeger.

HIMALAYAN ACADEMY. The Himalayan Academy was one of the open land communities created before 1965 in the states of California, Washington, and New York. Bob Hanson, born and raised in the Lake Tahoe area, converted to Hinduism while traveling in Ceylon in the 1940s. In 1957, he organized the Krishna Temple, later known as the Christian Yoga Church, in San Francisco under his name of Master Subramuniya. In the beginning, only older women joined the church but in the 1960s, younger members of both sexes became followers. In 1962, the "Monks" and "Nuns," living communally and committed to celibacy and poverty, moved to Virginia City, Nevada, where they opened the Himalayan Academy in an abandoned building that they restored. The academy started the *Ponderosa Press,* a financially successful venture that focused on yoga instruction. They also printed materials on contracts from outsiders, especially gambling casinos. By 1967, they had abandoned their earlier practice of having the monks shave their heads and wear flowing robes and the academy members looked just like any other citizen of Virginia City. That same year, Master Subramuniya and a few members found a new place for the community on the island of Kauai in Hawaii. They purchased a 50-one acre tract on which they constructed a temple and relocated the headquarters of the Himalayan Academy. There, in 1979, the Master began publishing the periodical *Hinduism Today,* which has become a world-famous journal.

Sources:

Fairfield, Richard [Dick]. 1972. *Communes USA: A Personal Tour.* Baltimore: Penguin.
———. 1971. *The Modern Utopian Communes: U.S.A.* San Francisco: Alternatives Foundation.
Miller, Timothy. 1999. *The 60s Communes: Hippies and Beyond.* Syracuse, N.Y.: Syracuse University Press.

HINDS, WILLIAM ALFRED B. Hinds (1833–1919) was born in Belchertown, Massachusetts, and died in Sherill, New York, a town located two miles north of what would became the Oneida Community. In 1846, while working as a store clerk in Putney, Vermont, he joined the community of Perfectionists organized on a nearby farm by John Humphrey Noyes. He was with the colony when in 1847 the 87 men, women, and children moved to New York state and organized the "Oneida Association." As a member of the Oneida Community, Hinds was editor of its newspaper, *The Circular.* He entered Yale University in 1867 to study botany and graduated in 1870. Then he began a personal investigation of utopian communities throughout United States and published *American Communities and Co-operative Colonies* (1875) based on his visits to these groups. In 1881, when the Oneida Community dissolved and became a joint-stock corporation, he was elected to the board of directors and in 1903, he became its president for the rest of his life.

Sources:

Fogarty, Robert S. 1980. *Dictionary of American Communal and Utopian History.* Westport, Conn.: Greenwood Press.
Hinds, William A. 1908. *American Communities and Co-operative Colonies.* Chicago: Kerr, 3d ed.
Klaw, Spencer. 1993. *Without Sin: The Life and Death of the Oneida Community.* New York: Penguin Books.
Parker, Robert A. 1935. *A Yankee Saint: John Humphrey Noyes and the Oneida Community.* New York: G. P. Putnam's Sons.

HOEDADS. In 1970, this 300-member cooperative community located in Eugene, Oregon, was founded by Jerry Rust under a contract from the U.S. Departments of Agriculture and Interior to spread conservationist reforms and practice reforestation. The colony hoped to change local attitudes about the uses of herbicides and pesticides. It was organized into worker crews who lived communally and worked collectively in tree-planting projects. All the crews assembled to decide whether or not to accept a new contract offer. They also met together on cooperative policies to vote on issues.

Sources:

Hartzell, Hal, Jr. 1987. *Birth of a Cooperative: Hoedads Inc., a Worker Owned Cooperative Forest Labor Camp.* Eugene, Ore.: Hugolosi.

Jackall, Robert, and Henry M. Levin. 1984. *Worker Cooperatives in America.* Berkeley: University of California Press.

Trahair, Richard C. S. 1999. *Utopias and Utopians: An Historical Dictionary.* Westport, Conn.: Greenwood Press.

HOG FARM. Hugh Romney, the founder and leading personality of Hog Farm, was given the name Wavy Gravy in 1969 and is called by that appellation today. Romney was living in New York City and California in the early 1960s; he was active in theater and teaching improvisation to actors at Columbia Pictures in Hollywood. In 1965, he and some companions were given a rent-free farm in Sunland, California, in return for taking care of the owner's hogs. There they lived in the farmhouse and constructed various other buildings. Their hippie lifestyle included a diet of overripe fruit, vegetables, and brown rice and the use of psychedelics. They held Sunday afternoon "celebrations," which visitors frequently came to watch. In 1967, they purchased old buses and traveled around the country giving rock concerts. Because of the hostility of neighbors they relocated to another site near Llano, New Mexico. At the 1969 Woodstock festival in New York, they offered free food and medicine and gained national attention as the "Please Force" of the event. By then they had moved to New Mexico where communal members were soon overwhelmed feeding hundreds of visitors. Some Hog Farmers, led by Wavy Gravy, moved to a large house in Berkeley, California, that remains today as the headquarters of the community. In 1982, they purchased several hundred acres of land near Laytonville, California, to build Black Oak Ranch. Each Labor Day weekend they celebrate a "Pignic," or party, with a huge rock festival that brings in money to pay the mortgage on the ranch. Also, every summer Wavy Gravy runs a camp for children called Camp Winnarainbow, and another camp for adults. Hog Farmers devote themselves to charity work, mainly to treat blindness in Third-World countries. A flavor of Ben and Jerry's ice cream was created in Wavy's name and its sales provide royalties that go into a camp scholarship fund.

See Also Crashpads; Diggers; Drop City; Morning Star Ranch; Wheeler's Ranch

Sources:

Gravy, Wavy. 1974. *The Hog Farm and Friends*. New York: Links.
———. 1992. *Something Good for a Change: Random Notes on Peace through Living*. New York: St. Martin's Press.
Miller, Timothy. 1999. *The 60s Communes: Hippies and Beyond*. Syracuse, N.Y.: Syracuse University Press.

HOLY CITY. Holy City was the creation of William E. Riker (1873–1952), an Oakdale, California, native and mechanic who preached in the streets of San Francisco the message that whites alone should rule the world. In 1919, with land that he bought between Santa Cruz and San Jose, he founded a community dedicated to celibacy and white supremacy. Its sexually segregated members ran a rest stop for tourists, a soda pop factory, a zoo, a gas station, a grocery store, and a restaurant. They called their community the Headquarters for the World's Perfect Government. Riker completely dominated the colony and directed communal work in the various tourist-centered enterprises and in agriculture. No wages were given the members, who numbered 30, and they lived in crude cabins. But by the time Riker was arrested in 1942 for sedition because of his admiration for Adolph Hitler (he was acquitted of the charge), the colony was in serious decline. By 1952, there were just 12 residents at Holy City.

See Also Riker, William E.

Sources:

Fogarty, Robert S. 1980. *Dictionary of American Communal and Utopian History*. Westport, Conn.: Greenwood Press.
Hine, Robert V. 1983. *California's Utopian Colonies*. Berkeley: University of California Press.
Kagan, Paul. 1975. *New World Utopias: A Photographic History of the Search for Community*. New York: Penguin.
Lewis, Betty. 1992. *Holy City: Riker's Roadside Attraction in the Santa Cruz Mountains*. Santa Cruz: Otter B. Books.
Trahair, Richard C.S. 1999. *Utopias and Utopians: An Historical Dictionary*. Westport, Conn.: Greenwood Press.

HOME COLONY. Formally known as the Mutual Home Association, this Puget Sound community was one of the more notorious anarchist colonies founded in the state of Washington at the end of the nineteenth century. It was located on Joe's Bay, a remote enclave of the sound, and organized in 1896 by George H. Allen and B.F. Odell on 26 acres fronting the bay. It expanded eventually to 200 acres, purchased with a $20 down payment. The first two families moved in on February 10 and lived in frame houses, each placed on two acres. The purpose of the colony, as written in its charter adopted in January 1898, was to help "members in obtaining and building better social and moral conditions." The members together built a main communal building called Liberty Hall and ran cooperative stores, but the main emphasis was on individualism and personal liberty. The Home's newspaper, *Discontent: Mother of Progress,* began in May 1898 and almost immediately aroused the hostility of neighbors and the residents of Tacoma because of its radical articles on religion, politics, and sex. One Tacoma editor condemned the colony as a nest of anarchists, nude bathers, and free love practitioners. The threat of vigilante violence against them, plus a growing breach between the original anarchists, called radicals, and late-comers, called conservatives, led to constant quarrels and bickering. The colony dissolved in 1919.

See Also Burley Colony (Communal Brotherhood); Equality; Freeland

Sources:

Fogarty, Robert S. 1980. *Dictionary of American Communal and Utopian History.* Westport, Conn.: Greenwood Press.

LeWarne, Charles P. 1975. *Utopias on Puget Sound, 1885–1915.* Seattle: University of Washington Press.

Miller, Timothy. 1998. *The Quest for Utopia in Twentieth-Century America.* Syracuse, N.Y.: Syracuse University Press.

Trahair, Richard C.S. 1999. *Utopias and Utopians: An Historical Dictionary.* Westport, Conn.: Greenwood Press.

HORR, ALEXANDER. Alexander Horr (1871–1940) was a native of Hungary and an Orthodox Jew who immigrated to the United States in the 1880s. He lived in New York City, became involved with radical anarchists, and joined the newly formed Freeland Central Association. He wrote the introduction to the book by the Austrian economist Theodor Hertzka, *Freiland,* published in 1891. At the age of 34, he went to Equality with copies of *Freiland* and soon led a dissident group that tried to invigorate the colony. Instead of cooperative socialism, Horr urged a commitment to anarchism blended with the idealism and opportunism of Hertzka's book. At one point in the struggle for the leadership of Equality, Horr was physically beaten. Factionalism became so intense that in 1907 the community dissolved and Horr moved to San Francisco. By 1922, he had rejected his earlier anarchist ideas and ran for the governor of California as a Socialist. He died in poverty, living in a run-down shack south of San Francisco.

See Also Equality

Sources:

Fogarty, Robert S. 1980. *Dictionary of American Communal and Utopian History.* Westport, Conn.: Greenwood Press.

LeWarne, Charles P. 1975. *Utopias on Puget Sound, 1885–1915.* Seattle and London: University of Washington Press.

Miller, Timothy. 1998. *The Quest for Utopia in Twentieth-Century America.* Syracuse, N.Y.: Syracuse University Press.

Sutton, Robert P. 2004. *Communal Utopias and the American Experience: Secular Communities, 1824–2000.* Westport, Conn. and London: Praeger.

Trahair, Richard C. S. 1999. *Utopias and Utopians: An Historical Dictionary.* Westport, Conn.: Greenwood Press.

THE HOUSE OF DAVID. In 1903, Benjamin Franklin Purnell (1861–1927) founded the House of David when he gathered a group of followers at Benton Harbor, Michigan. Purnell proclaimed himself to be the seventh in a line of leaders of Joanna Southcott's nonmainstream Christian millennial sect. His announced mission was to pull together the scattered descendants of the tribes of Israel for the anticipated doomsday. By 1907, the population of the community had grown to 385, many of them from Australia where Purnell had gone on a mission in 1904. Purnell preached vegetarianism, rejection of alcohol, and the need for a man never to cut his hair or beard. He insisted on celibacy at The House of David, although he was married, and required that couples live as brother and sister. In the 1920s, the community prospered and, with a population of about 1,000, looked like a small Michigan town. It had an amusement park, zoo, theater, and ice cream parlor. Its baseball team, The House of David Nine, as well as its basketball team, gained a national reputation. Its marching band was immensely popular. The residents opened a lumber yard and saw mill on an island in Lake Michigan. The town had a power plant, streetcar operation, tailor shops, and extensive farm acreage. Legal difficulties plagued the community because of charges against Purnell of sexual misconduct that culminated in a 1926 arrest for statutory rape. At the 1927 trial, the judge evicted Purnell and his wife, Mary, from the community and placed The House of David into receivership. Purnell died, however, before the order was enforced. The House of David continued under outside legal control but a bitter internal dispute soon developed between Mary Purnell and Thomas Dewhirst. In 1930, the court awarded the Dewhirst group control of the communal property and gave Mary Purnell title to some buildings and $60,000. That same year, she founded a rival faction to The House of David called The Israelite House of David Community (shorthand called Mary's). The two groups, numbering totally about 50 members, still live at the sites in the year 2004.

See Also Purnell, Benjamin F.

Sources:

Adkin, Clare. 1990. *Brother Benjamin: A History of the Israelite House of David.* Berrien Springs, Mich.: Andrews University Press.

Fogarty, Robert S. 1981. *The Righteous Remnant: The House of David.* Kent, Ohio: Kent State University Press.

Miller, Timothy. 1998. *The Quest for Utopia in Twentieth-Century America.* Syracuse, N.Y.: Syracuse University Press.

Trahair, Richard C.S. 1999. *Utopias and Utopians: An Historical Dictionary.* Westport, Conn.: Greenwood Press.

HOWLAND, MARIE STEVENS. Marie Stevens Howland (1831–1921) was born in New Hampshire and as a young woman taught school in New York City. She received a degree from New York Normal College. In 1864, she married the publisher Edward Howland after she divorced her first husband, Lyman Case. The couple lived in Europe until the end of the Civil War when, in 1868, they settled in Hammonton, New Jersey. In 1874, Edward published the utopian romance, *Papa's Own Girl* (in subsequent editions changed to *Familisterie*), which many historians claim was the inspiration for Edward Bellamy's *Looking Backward.* In 1888, the Howlands joined the 500-resedent railroad community at Topolobampo Bay, Mexico, called Pacific City. Soon Edward became mortally ill from locomotor ataxia and died in 1890. When Pacific City failed in 1894, Marie moved to the Fairhope community, where she became the group's librarian and coeditor of its newspaper, the *Fairhope Courier,* until her death at the colony.

See Also Fairhope

Sources:

Fogarty, Robert S. 1980. *Dictionary of American Communal and Utopian History.* Westport, Conn.: Greenwood Press.
Sutton, Robert P. 2004. *Communal Utopias and the American Experience: Secular Communities, 1824–2000.* Westport, Conn. and London: Praeger.

HUBBARD, ELBERT GREEN. Hubbard (1856–1915) was born in Bloomington, Indiana, and became a journalist in Chicago in the 1870s. In 1895, he moved to East Aurora, New York, and opened the Roycroft Printing Shop and Press and shops for selling handicrafts. The name Roycroft referred to Thomas Roycroft, the king's printer under Charles II. The artisans who had their crafts sold in the shop organized a community called the "Roycrofters." Hubbard then started a magazine of social reform, *The Philistine,* that ran until he died in April 1915 as a passenger, along with his wife, on the *Lusitania.* His other publications include the *FRA,* the *Little Journeys to the Homes of Good Men and Great,* biographical sketches of famous individuals, and *Message to Garcia.*

See Also Roycroft

Sources:

Fogarty, Robert S. 1980. *Dictionary of American Communal and Utopian History.* Westport, Conn.: Greenwood Press.
Hoyle, John Thomas. 1915. *In Memoriam. Elbert and Alice Hubbard.* East Aurora, N.Y.: Roycrofters.
Miller, Timothy. 1998. *The Quest for Utopia in Twentieth-Century America.* Syracuse, N.Y.: Syracuse University Press.

Trahair, Richard C. S. 1999. *Utopias and Utopians: An Historical Dictionary*. Westport, Conn.: Greenwood Press.

HUNTSMAN, MASON T. (PAUL BLAUDIN MNASON). Huntsman (?–after 1910) was born in Stroudsburg, Pennsylvania, and, an orphan at the age of eight, was raised by a nearby farm family. He experienced an epiphany at the age of 31 and changed his name to Paul Blaudin Mnason in honor of Mnason of Cyrus. He let his hair grow long and grew a beard. In 1887, he was attacked by the residents of the village of Park Ridge, New Jersey, because of his vicious denouncement of what he called their immoral conduct. Two years later, he was arrested and sentenced to prison for abducting two female juveniles. When released later in 1889, he founded The Lord's Farm commune of 10 adults at Woodcliff, New Jersey. It soon became known as the place of the "Angel Dancers," who frolicked in the nude. Members were repeatedly arrested for breaking Sunday blue laws and for fraud. In 1903, Mnason was again arrested and sent to prison for a year. He stayed at the farm until 1910 when he went to New York City and opened a church for blacks called the Church of the Living God.

See Also The Lord's Farm

Sources:
Fogarty, Robert S. 1980. *Dictionary of American Communal and Utopian History*. Westport, Conn.: Greenwood Press.
Trahair, Richard C. S. 1999. *Utopias and Utopians: An Historical Dictionary*. Westport, Conn.: Greenwood Press.

HUTTERITE BRETHREN. The Hutterite Brethren originated as a radical faction of the Anabaptists in the Austrian province of Tyrol during the sixteenth century. They took their name after Jakob Hutter, an early leader who was burned at the stake for his beliefs. Fleeing persecution, they moved to Moravia where they organized communal farms called *Bruderhofs* (brothers farms) led by a *Vorsteher* (First Preacher). Many of the Hutterites during the eighteenth century relocated to Russia where they lived in areas settled by the Mennonites. After 1864, when the Czar introduced compulsory military service, some 800 Hutterites immigrated to the United States, where half of them abandoned communal living. The communal Hutterites built three designations of *Bruderhof*, each housing between 100 to 150 people and known by the name its founder: the *Schmiedeleut* (Blacksmith's People), *Dariusleut* (Darius's People), and *Lehrerleut* (Instructor's People). By 1917, there were 2,000 Hutterites living in 17 *Bruderhofs* in South Dakota and 2 in Montana. They were exclusively agricultural communes, except for the making of tools and household utensils. They raised grains, livestock, and waterfowl. During World War I, the federal government arrested and punished Hutterites who refused military service. This development, plus growing hostility from their American neighbors, caused most Hutterites to move to Manitoba, Canada. By the 1930s there were some 52 *Bruderhofs* there. But troubles developed with the Canadian government when it outlawed land sales to the Hutterites and restricted the location of any new *Bruderhofs*. Such harassment caused some Hutterites, mostly *Dariusleut* and *Lehrerleut,* to return to the United States. Between 1945 and 2000 they constructed *Bruderhofs* in Montana and Washington. By the end of the twentieth century, there were about 36,000 Hutterites living in 390 *Bruderhofs* in the United States and Canada. For a while there was some talk of merging with the the Bruderhof (Society of Brothers), a religious utopian community that was founded in Germany in the 1920s and which moved to Paraguay in 1941. But nothing came of the merger.

See Also Bruderhof; Arnold, Eberhard

Sources:

Hostetler, John A. 1983. *A Hutterite Life*. Scottdale, Pa.: Herald.

Janzen, Rod A. 1999. *The Prairie People: Forgotten Anabaptists*. Hanover, N.H.: University Press of New England.

Miller, Timothy. 1998. *The Quest for Utopia in Twentieth-Century America*. Syracuse, N.Y.: Syracuse University Press.

Oved, Yaacov. 1996. *The Witness of the Brothers: A History of the Bruderhof.* New Brunswick, N.J. and Oxford: Transaction.

Packhull, Werner O. 1995. *Hutterite Beginnings: Communitarian Experiments during the Reformation*. Baltimore: Johns Hopkins University Press.

Sutton, Robert P. 2003. *Communal Utopias and the American Experience: Religious Communities, 1732–2000*. Westport, Conn. and London: Praeger.

I

INTERNATIONAL SOCIETY FOR KRISHNA CONSCIOUSNESS (ISKCON). The International Society for Krishna Consciousness (ISKCON) was founded in the United States by Bhaktivedanta Swami Prabhupada, the leader of a Hindu sect that emphasized asceticism and devotion to the Hindu god Krishna. In 1965, he came to New York City and founded a mission dedicated to creating a "holy place of transcendental pastime." As the movement expanded, more missions were opened in other American cities. One of the most important communities was located in the Haight-Ashbury district of San Francisco. It housed more than 200 individuals drawn mainly from the youthful counterculture. The Swami required all of his "devotees," as they called themselves, to live communally and follow a strict daily routine of prayer, chanting, and study. They were vegetarians and renounced drugs, alcohol, coffee, tea, and tobacco. They engaged in *kirtan,* or street preaching, and *hare name,* or group chanting in public places. Marriage was allowed but sexual contact was only for procreation. By the time of Swami Prabhupada's death in 1977, he had published 70 volumes of commentaries on Hinduism and had organized a confederation of retreats, temples, schools, and rural communes. After his death, ISKCON went through a disturbing time reacting to sensational charges involving drug dealers, violent behavior, and crimes. A murder at one commune, New Vrindaban in West Virginia, resulted in the arrest and conviction of its leader, Keith Ham (Kirtanananda), for which ISKCON expelled both Ham and the New Vrindaban community. At the end of the twentieth century, there were several ISKCON temples that ran as religious communes and several rural communes.

See Also Morning Star Ranch

Sources:

Miller, Timothy. 1995. *America's Alternative Religions.* Albany: State University of New York Press.

———. 1999. *The 60s Communes: Hippies and Beyond.* Syracuse, N.Y.: Syracuse University Press.

Rochford, E. Burke, Jr. 1985. *Hare Krishna in America.* New Brunswick, N.J.: Rutgers University Press.

Shinn, Larry D. 1987. *The Dark Lord: Cult Images and the Hare Krishnas in America.* Philadelphia: Westminster.

J

JESUS PEOPLE USA. This commune was founded in Milwaukee in 1972 and two years later its members moved to Chicago and purchased a run-down hotel near Lake Michigan. There, over 450 communards ran a soup kitchen, homeless shelter, a jail chaplaincy, and a crisis pregnancy center. In addition to these social services, the Jesus People operated a construction business, a moving company, a t-shirt business, and a recording studio. All income was placed in a communal pool from which members could withdraw funds according to their needs, although the community lives under what should be called poverty conditions.

Source:
Miller, Timothy. 1999. *The 60s Communes: Hippies and Beyond*. Syracuse, N.Y.: Syracuse University Press

JONES, JAMES WARREN. James Warren Jones (1931–1978) was born in Lynn, Indiana, where his mother dominated the large family and saw "Jim" as destined for the ministry. He married in 1949 and the couple eventually had eight children. The following year, he entered Indiana University and then Butler University. While in school, he served as a pastor to the Indianapolis Christian Assembly of God Church. In 1960, he changed its name to the Peoples Temple Full Gospel Church. After graduating from Butler University in 1961 with a degree in secondary education, he worked as a missionary in Brazil to build orphanages. At that time, he visited Guyana. Back in the United States in 1964, he was ordained a minister of the Disciples of Christ Church and told the members of the Peoples Temple congregation that the end of the world was about to happen in a nuclear holocaust and that they must immediately relocate to California. In 1966, he led 70 families to Ukiah, California, about 100 miles north of San Francisco. Five years later, he moved the church again, this time to San Francisco, where he preached in black neighborhoods, organized social service programs for the poor, and established communal homes for the poor and elderly. He also became active in city politics and was chairman of the City Housing Authority. In 1977, he moved the church a third time to 27,000 leased acres in Guyana because he had become convinced that evil forces in the United States were combining to destroy his congregation and his social crusade for racial justice by charging him with brutalization of church members and sexual misconduct. In South America he built the 900-member Peoples Temple commune. In November 1978, after the murder in Guyana of Congressman Leo J. Ryan, who had gone there to investigate the community, Jones gathered his people together, told them of Ryan's murder, and led a "revolutionary suicide."

See Also Peoples Temple

Sources:
Fogarty, Robert S. 1980. *Dictionary of American Communal and Utopian History.* Westport, Conn.: Greenwood Press.
Hall, John R. 1987. *Gone from the Promised Land: Jonestown in American Cultural History.* New Brunswick, N.J.: Transaction.
King, Martin. 1993. *Preacher of Death.* Melbourne: Penguin.
Klineman, George, Sherman Butler, and David Conn. 1980. *The Cult That Died: The Tragedy of Jim Jones and the Peoples Temple.* New York: Putman.
Miller, Timothy. 1999. *The 60s Communes: Hippies and Beyond.* Syracuse, N.Y.: Syracuse University Press.
Reston, James, Jr. 1981. *Our Father Who Art in Hell: The Life and Death of Jim Jones.* New York: Times Books.

JORDAN, CLARENCE. Jordan (1912–1969), one of 10 children of a wealthy family, was born in Talbotton, Georgia, and graduated from the University of Georgia at Athens in 1933, and then from Southern Baptist Theological Seminary at Louisville, Kentucky. In 1939, he received a doctorate in divinity from the latter institution. He joined the faculty at Simmons University in Louisville and at the same time opened a mission in the black section of the city called the Sunshine Center. When he urged the officials of the Baptist Church to have his center integrated, they shut down the operation. He then laid plans to open a mission for poor whites in another part of the city and gathered together young men and women, mainly college students, to discuss racial equality, pacifism, and communalism. In 1940, they adopted the name "Koinonia" (Greek for "fellowship") for the group. The next year, after working with the philosopher Martin England, Jordan purchased 400 acres of arid land near the town of Americus, Georgia, and started an interracial colony called Koinonia Farm. By 1950, 60 people were living at Koinonia Farm and they had developed admissions standards and communal rules, which included a daily five o'clock afternoon worship. In 1954, after the Supreme Court handed down its decision on racial integration of the public schools in *Brown v. Board of Education,* local white residents, directed by the Ku Klux Klan, became increasingly hostile to the farm and the colony almost had to disband. They were able to endure by opening a mail-order business selling pecan products. In 1968, the colony started a low-cost house building operation that by the year 2004 has grown to worldwide proportions as the Habitat for Humanity.

See Also Koinonia Farm

Sources:

Fogarty, Robert S. 1980. *Dictionary of American Communal and Utopian History.* Westport, Conn.: Greenwood Press.

Fuller, Millard, and Diane Scott. 1986. *No More Shacks! The Daring Vision of Habitat for Humanity.* WAC, Texas: Word Books Publisher.

Inscoe, John C. ed. 1994. *Georgia in Black and White: Explorations in the Race Relations of a Southern State, 1865–1950.* Athens and London: The University of Georgia Press.

K'Meyer, Tracy Elaine. 1997. *Interracialism and Christian Community in Postwar South: The Story of Koinonia Farm.* Charlottesville and London: University Press of Virginia.

Lee, Dallas. 1971. *The Cotton Patch Evidence.* New York: Harper and Row.

Miller, Timothy. 1998. *The Quest for Utopia in Twentieth-Century America.* Syracuse, N.Y.: Syracuse University Press.

Sutton, Robert P. 2003. *Communal Utopias and the American Experience: Religious Communities, 1732–2000.* Westport, Conn. and London: Praeger.

K

KELLY, HARRY. Harry Kelly (1871–1953) was born in St. Charles, Missouri, and raised in that state. When his father died, Harry had to drop out of school and earn money for the family. He became a printer. The Panic of 1893 traumatized him and he became a hobo, wandering from city to city riding empty railroad cars. While in Boston in 1894, he converted to anarchism and wrote articles for Emma Goldman's magazine, *Mother Earth*. He later lived in New York City and along with Leonard Abbott and Joseph B. Cohen organized the Ferrer Colony at Stelton, New Jersey in 1916. He lived there until 1923 when he founded the Mohegan Colony at Lake Mohegan, New York, as a satellite of the Ferrer Colony. In 1925, he built Mt. Airy, at Harmon, New York. Next he purchased land 30 miles north of New York City to build a rural colony for Jewish immigrants. Kelly was coeditor along with Hippolyte Haves of an anarchist magazine, *The Road to Freedom*. He died in New Rochelle.

See Also Abbott, Leonard; Cohen, Joseph B.; Ferrer Colony

Sources:

Fogarty, Robert S. 1980. *Dictionary of American Communal History*. Westport, Conn.: Greenwood Press.
Trahair, Richard C.S. 1999. *Utopias and Utopians: An Historical Dictionary*. Westport, Conn.: Greenwood Press.
Veysey, Laurence. 1973. *The Communal Experience: Anarchist and Mystical Countercultures in America*. New York: Harper and Row.

KERISTA. In 1971, John Presmont, known as Brother Jud, and Eve Furchgott founded a group-marriage commune in San Francisco. The dozen or so members, mostly childless young adults, practiced "Polyfidelity," in which every person in a sub-family unit known as a B-FIC, or Best Friend Identity Cluster, had sexual intercourse with the opposite sex in a rotation system. The whole community practiced a group therapy called Gestalt-O-Rama to resolve conflicts and differences. The only children in the commune were those brought in by new members. Once a man became a member of Kerista, he had to have a vasectomy. When the AIDS epidemic began, they adopted a policy of sexual abstinence. In the 1970s and 1980s, the commune became wealthy in the computer business. In 1991, when Jud was ousted from his B-FIC and left the community, Kerista rapidly declined. About half of the members moved to Hawaii in 1994 and lived communally, making a living by doing gardening work and computer projects.

Sources:

Gruen, John. 1966. *The New Bohemia: The Combine Generation.* New York: Shorecrest.

Miller, Timothy. 1999. *The 60s Communes: Hippies and Beyond.* Syracuse, N.Y.: Syracuse University Press.

Polyfidelity: Sex in the Kerista Commune and Other Related Theories on How to Solve the World's Problems. 1984. San Francisco: Performing Arts Social Society.

KESEY, KEN. Ken Kesey (?–?) was one of the founders of the Merry Pranksters commune. In 1958, just after he was awarded a Woodrow Wilson Fellowship at Stanford University, he and his wife moved from Oregon to Perry Lane in Palo Alto, California, the bohemian area of the city. The following year, he became involved in controlled experiments with psychedelic drugs and soon other residents of the neighborhood were using LSD, mescaline, and psilocybin. For two years a hippie, drug-induced sharing prevailed until the summer of 1963 when the homes were purchased by a real estate developer. In the meantime, Kesey had written his best-selling first book, *One Flew over the Cuckoo's Nest,* and with money from its royalties he purchased a home outside La Honda. It became a refuge for many of the Perry Lane hippies and the site of a drug commune with sound speakers blaring music on the roof of the building and LSD in abundant supply. In the summer of 1964, Kesey and some of the communards boarded a gaudily painted 1939 bus and headed to New York City, calling themselves the Merry Pranksters. Enroute, at Millbrook, New York, Kesey stopped at the home of Timothy Leary, the Harvard professor involved with psychedelics, but did not meet the man. Back in California, the psychedelic drug–induced lifestyle of the Pranksters became more outrageous, especially after Kesey invited the Hell's Angels to the commune. Eventually the police arrested Kesey on marijuana charges and he was sentenced to five months on a work farm. After his release in the fall of 1967, he and his wife moved to Oregon and lived on a farm near Springfield owned by his brother. Soon afterwards, about 60 hippies from La Honda went there and began another version of the Merry

Pranksters commune. In August 1969, most of them traveled by bus to the Woodstock festival and never returned, leaving a rump colony largely made up of Kesey's extended family.

See Also Merry Pranksters

Sources:

Charters, Ann. 1983. *The Beats: Literary Bohemians in Postwar America*. Vol 1. Detroit: Gale.

Leary, Timothy. 1990. *Flashbacks: A Personal and Cultural History of an Era*. Los Angeles: Tarcher.

Lee, Martin A., and Bruce Shlain. 1987. *Acid Dreams: The CIA, LSD and the Sixties Rebellion*. New York: Grove.

Miller, Timothy. 1999. *The 60s Communes: Hippies and Beyond*. Syracuse, N.Y.: Syracuse University Press.

Perry, Paul. 1990. *On the Bus: The Complete Guide to the Legendary Trip of Ken Kesey and the Merry Pranksters and the Birth of the Counterculture*. New York: Thunder's Mouth.

Stevens, Jay. 1987. *Storming Heaven: LSD and the American Dream*. New York: Harper and Row.

KILGORE: ZION'S ORDER. In 1951, Marl V. Kilgore, a member of the Glendenning commune, formed his own Latter-Day Saints community on 1,175 acres near Mansfield, Missouri. He claimed to receive divine revelations and led his followers in an austere lifestyle near the poverty level. In the 1960s, they went on mission to the Navajo Indians, after which Kilgore resigned leadership of the commune and turned it over to his son. By that time, membership had reached its peak of 90, including children. In the 1995 *Communities Directory*, Kilgore called itself Zion's Order and described their "ranch" as consisting of timber, pastures, and hay fields, with a panoramic view of the countryside. They raised milk cows, rabbits for sale, and conducted a program of vaccinating chickens that were sold to commercial egg layers. They also operated a television repair service.

See Also Glendenning: The Levites/Order of Aaron

Sources:

Communities Directory: A Guide to Cooperative Living. 1995. Langley, Washington: Fellowship for Intentional Community.

Miller, Timothy. 1998. *The Quest for Utopia in Twentieth-Century America*. Syracuse, N.Y.: Syracuse University Press.

KOINONIA (MARYLAND). Glenn Harding founded this intentional community on January 1, 1952, on 45 acres north of Baltimore. Its purpose was to train "Christian Ambassadors" for social work in parts of the world that had been ravaged by World War II. For a while, community members conducted seminars dealing with the Christian commitment to world peace, hunger, literacy, race relations, and getting prepared to live overseas. But because the Peace Corps largely preempted its original mission, under David Poist, a new director in the 1960s, it changed its mission to one of dealing with the problems facing the young adults of the counterculture. Koinonia was run as a school that held seminars and retreats on cooperative living and spiritual growth. Its membership was about 50 full-time residents and a communal staff of 25 adults. The residents lived communally in terms of housing and meals. However, for financial reasons, Poist had to sell Koinonia to outside buyers in 1985, although some individuals still stayed on the property and those who left published a newsletter for a while.

Source:

Miller, Timothy. 1998. *The Quest for Utopia in Twentieth-Century America*. Syracuse, N.Y.: Syracuse University Press.

KOINONIA FARM. In 1941, Clarence Jordan (1912–1969), a Baptist minister with a doctorate in Greek New Testament, founded this interracial commune on 400 acres near Americus, Georgia. Within a few years, about 60 people, both blacks and whites, lived there communally. While white residents attended the nearby Rehobeth Baptist Church and some became Sunday School teachers. After a nine-month probation period, new members of the colony had to surrender all goods and personal possessions, after which families would receive living wages from a community fund. Koinonians had no formally elected leaders but met each morning and agreed on what work had to be done that day. All the meetings ended with prayer. Each evening they gathered for Bible study. A work coordinator kept track of all jobs and moved men from one assignment to another. The women performed household chores and watched the children who, at that age of six, attended the county school. Families lived in their own homes but everyone ate in a communal refectory. However, during the 1950s, as news spread throughout the area that the community was biracial, Koinonia was repeatedly attacked by white vandalism led by the Ku Klux Klan. With the help of a wealthy lawyer, Millard Fuller, who joined the community, Koinonia was able to survive economically. Revenues from Jordan's vernacular translation of the Bible, called the *Cotton Patch Version of the New Testament* (1968), and from a mail-order business selling pecan products sustained the colony. Under the leadership of Fuller in 1976 the Koinonians began a worldwide housing program called Habitat for Humanity, whose headquarters is in Americus. In 1995, Habitat had more than 11,000 projects in the United States and 164 abroad.

See Also Jordan, Clarence

Sources:

Fogarty, Robert S. 1980. *Dictionary of American Communal and Utopian History*. Westport, Conn.: Greenwood Press.

Fuller, Millard, and Diane Scott. 1986. *No More Shacks! The Daring Vision of Habitat for Humanity*. Waco, Tex.: Word Books Publisher.

Inscoe, John C., ed. 1994. *Georgia in Black and White: Explorations in the Race Relations of a Southern State, 1865–1950*. Athens and London: University of Georgia Press.

K'Meyer, Tracy Elaine. 1997. *Interracialism and Christian Community in the Postwar South: The Story of Koinonia Farm*. Charlottesville and London: University Press of Virginia.

Lee, Dallas. 1971. *The Cotton Patch Evidence*. New York: Harper and Row.

Miller, Timothy. 1998. *The Quest for Utopia in Twentieth-Century America*. Syracuse, N.Y.: Syracuse University Press.

Sutton, Robert P. 2003. *Communal Utopias and the American Experience: Religious Communities, 1732–2000*. Westport, Conn. and London: Praeger.

KORESH, DAVID (VERNON HOWELL). Vernon Howell, born in 1960, was a guitar player turned Adventist when he joined the Davidian movement founded by Victor Houteff in 1934 in Los Angeles as an offshoot of the Seventh-Day Adventists. The central belief of Houteff and his followers, calling themselves Branch Davidians, was that the Kingdom of David was soon to be recreated in Palestine and prior to that event they must live communally. By 1940, he had moved his sect of about 64 disciples to 189 acres west of Waco, Texas, and called the colony Mt. Carmel. Houteff died in 1978 and a woman, Lois Roden, became the head of the community. In 1981, Vernon Howell joined the colony and soon became its leader, taking the name David Koresh—David after the new kingdom in Palestine and Koresh after the Hebrew word for the messianic Persian king Cyrus. He preached that the Book of Revelation would be understood fully just before the upcoming millennium when the Seven Seals are opened and the four horses of the apocalypse appear. The sect believed that he was Jesus Christ. Koresh had at least seven wives and fathered numerous children at Mt. Carmel. Some members of the commune were licensed gun dealers and made money by retailing in guns and ammunition. On February 29, 1993, the Bureau of Alcohol, Tobacco and Firearms surrounded the building and after a 51-day siege the FBI, which by then had taken control of the situation, attacked the buildings, killing Koresh and other members of the community.

See Also Branch Davidians (Davidian Seventh-Day Adventists)

Sources:
King, Martin. 1993. *Preacher of Death: The Shocking Inside Story of David Koresh and the Waco Siege*. New York: Signet Books.

Miller, Timothy. 1999. *The 60s Communes: Hippies and Beyond*. Syracuse, N.Y.: Syracuse University Press.

Tabor, James D., and Eugene V. Gallagher. 1995. *Why Waco? Cults and the Battle for Religious Freedom in America*. Berkeley: University of California Press.

Trahair, Richard C.S. 1999. *Utopias and Utopians: An Historical Dictionary*. Westport, Conn.: Greenwood Press.

Valdemar, Richard. 1994. *Siege at Waco*. London: Constable.

Wright, Stuart A., ed. 1995. *Armageddon in Waco: Critical Perspectives in the Branch Davidian Conflict.* Chicago: University of Chicago Press.

KORESHAN UNITY. Cyrus Teed, known as Koresh (Hebrew for Cyrus) founded an exotic communal utopia at Estero, Florida, of followers who believed, as did Teed, that humans lived inside the shell of a hollow earth whose concave surface contained the universe. This knowledge came to him in an 1869 vision and he claimed that he could prove it scientifically. Teed had first organized his Koreshan Unity community in Chicago in 1888 but six years later he moved it to Estero at a 300-acre site south of Fort Myers. By 1897, he and his followers had built a three-story frame refectory with living quarters for women, a Master House for Teed, a school-dormitory, a sawmill, a post office, a bakery, and an Art Hall. A communal generator provided electrical power for all the buildings. Within seven years, they had acquired a total of 7,500 acres and incorporated the colony as Estero with a system of government. Eventually, more than 200 Koreshans lived there. They opened a "Pioneer University of Koreshan Universology" where Koreshans instructed children in Teed's ideas as well as a traditional academic curriculum and manual arts. At the "Bamboo Landing" next to the Estero River they enjoyed picnics and festivities. Their publishing house printed their periodical, *The Flaming Sword,* Teed's *The Cellular Cosmogony,* and pamphlets. Because the Koreshans voted as a bloc in local elections and threatened the area's Democratic machine, hostility developed against them. In 1906, Teed was physically assaulted in Fort Myers and two years later died of his injuries. Teed had told his followers that he was immortal and they sustained a three-day vigil expecting him to revive. The Lee County health officials discovered the vigil and interred the corpse. Koreshan Unity survived the death of its founder and continued to hold a variety of cultural activities for visitors. In 1961, they deeded their property to the state of Florida and it became the Koreshan State Historic Site. Since then an ambitious restoration program has been underway and visitors today can tour the Founder's House, General Store, Bakery, Planetary Court, Art Hall, the Machine Shops, and Generator Building. They can stand on the Bamboo Landing and walk a nature trail through pine flatwoods and scrub oaks. The state operates a 60-unit campground adjacent to the site. And east across Highway 41 is the Koreshan Unity Foundation, Inc., building, a round, wooden and glass structure that contains Teed's books, papers, and artifacts.

See Also Teed, Cyrus Read

Sources:

Carmer, Carl. 1949. *Dark Trees to the Wind: A Cycle of New York State Years.* New York: William Sloane Associates.

Miller, Timothy. 1999. *The Quest for Utopia in Twentieth-Century America.* Syracuse, N.Y.: Syracuse University Press.

Rea, Sara Weber. 1994. *The Koreshan Story.* Estero, Fla.: Guiding Star Publishing House.

Rainard, R. Lyn. 1981. "Conflict inside the Earth: The Koreshan Unity in Lee County." *Tampa Bay History* 3: 5–16.

Sutton, Robert P. 2003. *Communal Utopias and the American Experience: Religious Communities, 1732–2000.* Westport, Conn. and London: Praeger.

Trahair, Richard C.S. 1999. *Utopias and Utopians: An Historical Dictionary.* Westport, Conn.: Greenwood Press.

KRISHNA VENTA. Francis H. Pencovic, who was born in San Francisco in 1911, adopted the name of Krishna Venta and claimed that he was a savior who, like many before him, would lead mankind away from sin. In the early 1930s, he organized a community in Box Canyon near the San Fernando Valley in Southern California where members went barefoot and wore biblical robes. They embraced the goals of wisdom, faith, and love. The public knew of them as firefighters who helped to combat forest fires in the area. After building a second community at Homer, Alaska, in the mid-1950s, Krishna Venta had a few hundred followers. In December 1958, two members of the commune murdered him by setting off a bomb in the main community building because he had been having sex with their wives and with underage girls. The commune, however, continued under the leadership of his wife, Ruth, into the 1980s.

Sources:
Beam, Maurice. 1964. *Cults of America.* New York: Macfadden.

Mathison, Richard. 1960. *Faiths, Cults, and Sects of America.* Indianapolis: Bobbs-Merrill.

Melton, J. Gordon. 1994. *Encyclopedia of American Religions.* 4th ed. Detroit: Gale Research.

Miller, Timothy. 1998. *The Quest for Utopia in Twentieth-Century America.* Syracuse, N.Y.: Syracuse University Press.

KRISTENSTAET. John B. Christensen (1874–1930), a Dane, founded this colony 50 miles southwest of Fort Worth, Texas in January 1928 on 12,000 acres, 6,000 of which were used for pasture and the rest for farming and ranching. The residents, although not socialists, were committed to mutual assistance and cooperative work. The colony had a sawmill to cut the cottonwood, pecan, cedar, elm, and oak trees growing on the property. They used the lumber to construct houses and factories and to make charcoal for sale to outsiders. Residents used community scrip, from which each person was paid between $2.00 to $2.50 a day. Today nothing remains at Kristenstaet, half of the acreage of which is covered by the Brazos River Authority dam, but a few stone buildings.

See Also Christensen, John B.

Sources:
Fischer, Ernest G. 1980. *Marxists and Utopias in Texas.* Burnet, Tex.: Eakin Press.

Trahair, Richard C.S. 1999. *Utopias and Utopians: An Historical Dictionary.* Westport, Conn.: Greenwood Press.

KROTONA. Krotona was a Theosophical commune founded in 1911 by one of Helena Blavatsky's successors, Annie Besant, and a follower, Albert P. Warrington, on 23 acres in "Old Hollywood," about halfway between Santa Barbara and Point Loma. Its 45 residents ran the Krotona School of Theosophy and offered classes on Blavatsky's ideas. The colony had a number of buildings including a vegetarian cafeteria, print shop, library, and temple. Financial problems appeared almost immediately and, despite donations of land and money by new members, most of the property was sold in 1924 to pay off the debts. Krotona lingered as a marginal commune until the 1960s when it was revitalized by offering regular classes and workshops in its School of Theosophy from September through May.

See Also Point Loma (Universal Brotherhood and Theosophical Society); Temple of the People; Tingley, Katherine Augusta Westcott

Sources:

Hine, Robert V. 1983. *California's Utopian Colonies.* Berkeley: University of California Press.

Miller, Timothy. 1998. *The Quest for Utopia in Twentieth-Century America.* Syracuse, N.Y.: Syracuse University Press.

Sutton, Robert P. 2003. *Communal Utopias and the American Experience: Religious Communities, 1732–2000.* Westport, Conn. and London: Praeger.

KWAN UM ZEN SCHOOL. This commune was one of several Zen communities founded during the 1960s and 1970s. Unlike most of the other colonies, which were based on the Japanese Soto school of Zen, this one was in the Korean Chogye Zen tradition.

In 1972, Seung Sahn immigrated to America and organized a temple at Providence, Rhode Island. From there he branched out to create centers in other American cities and in university towns. Sahn moved the communal headquarters to the nearby town of Cumberland where members lived a meditative, celibate life. But when it was discovered that the master had sexual relations with female students, some of his followers left the movement.

See Also San Francisco Zen Center; Zen Center of Los Angeles

Sources:

Boucher, Sandy. 1993. *Turning the Wheel: American Women Creating the New Buddhism.* Boston: Beacon.

Miller, Timothy. 1999. *The 60s Communes: Hippies and Beyond.* Syracuse, N.Y.: Syracuse University Press.

Mitchell, Stephen, ed. 1976. *Dropping Ashes on the Buddha: The Teaching of Zen Master Seung Sahn.* New York: Grove.

L

LAMA FOUNDATION. Steve Durkee and some friends founded the Lama Foundation in 1967 as a combination intentional community and religious retreat on top of an 8,000-foot mountain in New Mexico about 20 miles north of Taos. Its emphasis was on spiritual and emotional health. The residents, many of whom lived there part time, put up a central communal domed complex and two kitchens. Individual houses and retreat huts were placed outside the central areas. The daily routine involved communal meals, work, meditation, and regular conferences. The colony's spiritual leader was Ram Dass (Richard Alpert), who received nationwide attention for the book he published in 1971, *Be Here Now,* which sold 500,000 copies. One historian called the book the "countercultural Bible." After a forest fire ravaged the site and razed 24 of its buildings (but not the central complex), some members left the colony. A few stayed on and rebuilt.

Sources:

Dass, Ram. 1971. *Be Here Now.* San Cristobal, N.M.: Lama.

Miller, Timothy. 1999. *The 60s Communes: Hippies and Beyond.* Syracuse, N.Y.: Syracuse University Press.

Sutton, Robert P. 2004. *Communal Utopias and the American Experience: Secular Communities, 1732–2000.* Westport, Conn. and London: Praeger.

Trahair, Richard C. S. 1999. *Utopias and Utopians: An Historical Dictionary.* Westport, Conn.: Greenwood Press.

THE LAND OF SHALAM. This community was one of the spiritualist experiments funded by physician and dentist John B. Newbrough. He based the colony on a reinterpretation of scripture called *Oahspe* that he published in

1882. Claiming that he was responding to spiritual communications, he stated that his messages located a place for a community on 1,490 acres near Doña Ana, New Mexico. His followers, calling themselves the "Faithists," moved there in 1884 and opened an orphanage. The following year, they incorporated with the state of New Mexico as the "First Church of Tae." They constructed a 42-room main building known as the "Fraternum" and a "Temple of Tae." A wealthy businessman, Andrew M. Howland, subsidized the community. Residents included the children at the colony orphanage and a dozen adult Faithists. Internal dissension and an epidemic of influenza, during which Newbrough died, were serious setbacks. But after Howland married Newbrough's widow, Frances, and gave more money to the colony, it lasted until 1907. Selling milk to nearby El Paso helped Shalam to carry on even when Howland ran out of cash in 1900.

See Also Lily Dale and Cassadaga; Preston; The Societas Fraternia

Sources:

Miller, Timothy. 1998. *The Quest for Utopia in Twentieth-Century America.* Syracuse, N.Y.: Syracuse University Press.

Oahspe: A New Bible in the Word of Jehovah and His Angel Ambassadors. 1967. Los Angeles: Kosmon Press, 1942; originally published in 1882.

LEBARON. In the 1920s, Alma Dayer LeBaron and his six sons moved from Utah to Colonia Juárez, Mexico, in order to continue practicing polygamy and live communally. The eldest of his sons, Joel, founded his intentional community in 1955 called Joel's Church of the First Born and of the Fullness of Times. He soon was involved with a dispute with another son, Ervil, and in 1971 excommunicated his younger brother. Ervil then founded his Church of the Lamb of God. In 1972, he directed some of his followers to murder Joel. After Joel's murder, Ervil's men committed at least 20 homicides, including that of a local physician, Dr. Rulon C. Allred. The authorities arrested Ervil for Allred's death and he was sent to prison in 1980, where he died. There is evidence that Ervil's followers continued their killings and that the church still survives in Mexico along with two other small LeBaronite churches.

Sources:

LeBaron, Verlan M. 1981. *The LeBaron Story.* Lubbock, Tex.: Keels and Co.

Miller, Timothy. 1998. *The Quest for Utopia in Twentieth-Century America.* Syracuse, N.Y.: Syracuse University Press.

Shields, Steven L. 1982. *Divergent Paths of the Restoration: A History of the Latter Day Saint Movement.* Bountiful, Utah: Restoration Research.

LEMURIAN FELLOWSHIP. In 1936, Robert D. Stelle founded the Lemurian Fellowship in Chicago to lay plans for a communal utopia for individuals who believed in the tale of Lemuria. This was the name given to a mythical lost continent in the Pacific that was about to rise again and bring about devastation on North America. The Lemurians felt that they had special knowledge passed down through the ages that would enable them to survive the disaster. In 1941, Stelle purchased 260 acres near Ramona, California, where his followers built a school, library, chapel, and living quarters. The colony also started a craft manufacturing industry, the Lemurian Crafts, that brought in profits. Their main focus was on developing a correspondence school with a national audience for which they charged fees for those enrolled. An offshoot Lemurian colony was created south of Chicago in 1973 by Richard Kieninger called the Stelle Community. He started another satellite colony, the Adelphi Group, shortly after he was expelled from Stelle in 1976.

See Also Stelle Community

Sources:

Miller, Timothy. 1998. *The Quest for Utopia in Twentieth-Century America*. Syracuse, N.Y.: Syracuse University Press.

Sutton, Robert P. 2004. *Communal Utopias and the American Experience: Secular Communities, 1824–2000*. Westport, Conn. and London: Praeger.

LERMOND, NORMAN WALLACE. Lermond (1862–1944) was born in Warren, Maine, and was one of the founders of the Populist Party in that state. In his early adulthood, he was a bookstore employee, accountant, newspaper reporter, and then a farmer. He was also the founder, along with two Warren neighbors, of the Brotherhood of the Co-operative Commonwealth (BCC) and formed the first local chapter of that labor union in Maine in October 1895. The next year, he was a delegate to the Populist convention in St. Louis. That year he was also elected national secretary of the BCC and pushed for the creation of a chain of cooperative colonies as a means of spreading socialism. In 1895, he wrote an article for the *New York Commonwealth* magazine urging full commitment to colonize in the state of Washington. Notable Socialists such as Eugene V. Debs supported the idea. Lermond purchased land near Edison, Washington, in November 1897 and established the first BCC utopian community called Equality, after Edward Bellamy's novel. He moved his family to the colony in March 1898, but stayed only five months. He returned to Maine, became editor of the magazine *Harmony,* and ran for governor in 1900. Later in life he focused on natural science and made his home into a park and arboretum where he held meetings of likeminded individuals.

See Also Equality

Sources:

Fogarty, Robert S. 1980. *Dictionary of American Communal and Utopian History*. Westport, Conn.: Greenwood Press.

LeWarne, Charles P. 1975. *Utopias on Puget Sound, 1885–1915*. Seattle: University of Washington Press.

LIBRE. In 1967, Dean Fleming, a successful New York City artist, and his wife, Linda, moved to Colorado and bought a home near the Drop City commune at Trinidad. They quickly became friends with some of the Droppers and with them they decided to start a similar, less chaotic, community for creative artists. In 1968, they purchased 360 acres a few miles north of the New Mexico border at Gardner. The 20 or so members of Libre (meaning "free" in Spanish) built a domed structure modeled on the geodesic structures at Drop City and other unconventional buildings, but no central communal hall. They wanted members to construct their own houses and to have responsibility for their own finances, food, and clothing. Working in separate shops they developed their skills at painting, sculpture, making jewelry, and writing. They got along well with neighbors, except for a 1979 police raid to confiscate marijuana.

See Also Drop City

Source:
Miller, Timothy. 1999. *The 60s Communes: Hippies and Beyond.* Syracuse, N.Y.: Syracuse University Press.

LILA. In 1969, a wealthy Taos and Questa, New Mexico, community patron, Charles Lonsdale, purchased 600 acres of land north of the latter city where he hoped to found Lorien, an intentional community based on open land principles. During Lonsdale's absence in the first year, quarreling factions soon degenerated into gunfights that resulted in arrests. Discouraged, Lonsdale went to Lila, a small yoga community located on his land a mile away at El Rito. Lila members lived in small, temporary cabins, practiced communal labor and religious activities, and proscribed both drugs and alcohol. When Lonsdale demanded that they pay him $500 annual rent the colony dissolved. In 1972, Lonsdale sold off his land as individual plots.

See Also Lama Foundation

Sources:
Gardner, Hugh. 1978. *The Children of Prosperity: Thirteen Modern American Communes.* New York: St. Martin's Press.
Miller, Timothy. 1999. *The 60s Communes: Hippies and Beyond.* Syracuse, N.Y.: Syracuse University Press.

LILY DALE AND CASSADAGA. Lily Dale, a spiritualist colony founded in southwestern New York in 1897, began as a summer camp but soon had year-round residents. Because of the severe winters in that state, they started the community of Cassadaga, Florida. Residents of both colonies included practicing mediums. At Cassadaga, a prominent medium, George Colby, communicated messages from a Seneca Indian. During the first half of the twentieth century, wealthy northern spiritualists opened the Cassadaga Hotel to attract visiting spiritualists during the winter. It survived into the twenty-first century as a popular center for visitors.

See Also The Land of Shalam; Preston; The Societas Fraternia

Sources:

Harrold, Robert. 1979. *Cassadaga: An Inside Look at the South's Oldest Psychic Community with True Experiences of People Who Have Been There.* Miami: Banyan Books.

Miller, Timothy. 1998. *The Quest for Utopia in Twentieth-Century America.* Syracuse, N.Y.: Syracuse University Press.

THE LITTLE LANDERS. Along with Fellowship Farm (Westwood, MA) and Fellowship Farm (Puente, CA), The Little Landers was an example of a new type of communal living that appeared at the beginning of the twentieth century: communities of modest size dedicated to self-sufficient living through subsistence agriculture and small craft shops. William E. Smythe, a San Diego historian who was inspired by Boston Hall's book, *A Little Land and a Living,* became convinced that a family could live by self-sufficient farming on a one-acre plot. With this idea in mind, in 1909 he founded The Little Landers colony on 550 acres south of San Diego in the Tijuana River Valley. He charged an admission fee of between $330 and $550 to each individual for a one-acre farm. He planned streets, waterlines, and sewage disposal. He designed a community flag. By 1912, 116 families raised crops and animals and had opened a cooperative store in San Diego where they sold their produce. A number of the settlers were professionals and encouraged a vigorous intellectual life. Largely due to the favorable publicity given the colony in San Diego and Los Angeles newspapers, by 1915 there were 500 residents living in 200 frame homes. However, the community was plagued almost from the start by fiscal mismanagement and by the fact that many colonists had no agricultural skills. The irrigation system was woefully inadequate and, at the other extreme, in 1916 the Tijuana River flooded the community and devastated 100 family plots. The colony thereafter slowly disintegrated.

See Also Fellowship Farm (Puente CA); Fellowship Farm (Westwood, MA); Smythe, William Ellsworth

Sources:

Fogarty, Robert S. 1980. *Dictionary of American Communal and Utopian History.* Westport, Conn.: Greenwood Press.

Hine, Robert V. 1983. *California's Utopian Colonies.* Berkeley: University of California Press.

Miller, Timothy. 1998. *The Quest for Utopia in Twentieth-Century America.* Syracuse, N.Y.: Syracuse University Press.

Pourade, Richard F. 1965. *Gold in the Sun: The History of San Diego.* San Diego: Union-Tribune Publishing Co.

Trahair, Richard C.S. 1999. *Utopias and Utopians: An Historical Dictionary.* Westport, Conn.: Greenwood Press.

LITTLEFIELD, GEORGE ELMER. George Elmer Littlefield (1862–1930) was a Boston printer who, in 1888, joined Edward Bellamy's Nationalist Club and enrolled the same year at Harvard University. In 1892, after graduation, he became a Unitarian minister. In 1910, he organized the Fellowship Farm at Westwood, Massachusetts, and began running the Ariel Press. Two years later, he helped Kate D. Buck organize a similar cooperative colony near Santa Barbara at Puente. The last year of his life he published a magazine called *Joy.*

See Also Fellowship Farm (Puente, CA); Fellowship Farm (Westwood, MA)

Sources:

Bedford, Henry. 1966. *Socialism and the Workers of Massachusetts.* Amherst: University of Massachusetts Press.

Fogarty, Robert S. 1990. *All Things New: American Communes and Utopian Movements 1860–1914.* Chicago: University of Chicago Press.

Hine, Robert V. 1983. *California's Utopian Colonies.* Berkeley: University of California Press.

Littlefield, George Elmer. 1911. *The Fellowship Farm Plan: How One Fellow Makes an Honest Living on the Land and Is a Free Man.* Westwood, Mass.: Ariel Press on Fellowship Farm.

_____. 1928. *Illumination and Love.* Santa Barbara, Calif.: Red Rose Press.

LLANO DEL RIO/NEWLLANO. In 1914, Job Harriman (1861–1925) began construction of Llana del Rio on 1,000 acres of desert land near Palmdale, California. Initially, the 100 colonists lived in tents and adobe huts and named the colony after a creek on the property. Then they constructed small family houses and a stone dormitory for bachelors and visitors. Soon they had a hotel, barns, and workshops. They cleared the land of joshua trees and creosote and planted alfalfa, corn, and grain. They added cattle, an apiary, a community laundry, a cannery, and a print shop where they published their newspapers, *Western Comrade* and *Llano Colonist.* The *Western Comrade* described a lavish, but as it turned out imaginary, circular "Socialist City" with six sections of houses and workshops located around a hub called the Civic Center. This building was to include administration offices, an assembly hall, library, post office, a theater, and a bank. Close to the Center, colonists planned a restaurant, market, church, schools, and a department store. The colony lasted for four years and charged residents between $500 and $1,500 for shares of stock. The amount of shares purchased determined the individual's housing and work assignment. Residents were a diverse group in terms of occupations. Wages were the same for everyone, four dollars a day. Men outnumbered women two-to-one. Both sexes, though, had an equal voice in a general assembly. But they faced a serious problem in not having enough water and they built irrigation ditches to pull water from a nearby creek, but this venture failed. Consequently, in 1918, they moved to Stables, in Vernon Parish, Louisiana, and named the new colony "Newllano" and had hopes of making money from oil drilling. However, all the wells were dry. Even so, the community held together until the Great Depression forced it to dissolve in 1938.

See Also Harriman, Job

Sources:

Fogarty, Robert S. 1980. *Dictionary of American Communal and Utopian History.* Westport, Conn.: Greenwood Press.

Hayden, Dolores. 1976. *Seven American Utopias: The Architecture of Communitarian Socialism, 1790–1975.* Cambridge, Mass. and London: MIT Press.

Hine, Robert V. 1983. *California's Utopian Colonies.* Berkeley: University of California Press.

Miller, Timothy. 1998. *The Quest for Utopia in Twentieth-Century America.* Syracuse, N.Y.: Syracuse University Press.

Oved, Yaacov. 1988. *Two Hundred Years of American Communes.* New Brunswick, N.J. and Oxford: Transaction.

Sutton, Robert P. 2004. *Communal Utopias and the American Experience: Secular Communities, 1824–2000.* Westport, Conn. and London: Praeger.

LONGLEY, ALCANDER. Longley (1832–1918), an active promoter of secular communal utopias, was born in Oxford, Ohio. He sponsored a number of nineteenth-century communities such as the Moores Hill, Indiana (1857), Black Lake, Michigan (1858), and Foster's Crossing, Ohio (1865). His most successful communal experiment was begun near Carthage, Missouri, and was called the Reunion Colony. Between 1867 and 1897, he tried to establish three other communal groups in Missouri, all of them short-lived. In 1907, at Sulphur Springs, located 22 miles south of St. Louis, he organized the Altruist Community. There he published a magazine, the *Altruist,* and pamphlets on communal living.

See Also The Altruist Community

Sources:

Fogarty, Robert S. 1980. *Dictionary of American Communal and Utopian History.* Westport, Conn.: Greenwood Press.

Miller, Timothy. 1998. *The Quest for Utopia in Twentieth-Century America.* Syracuse, N.Y.: Syracuse University Press.

Trahair, Richard C.S. 1999. *Utopias and Utopians: An Historical Dictionary.* Westport, Conn.: Greenwood Press.

LOPEZ ISLAND. The Reverend Thomas Gourley was running a Pentecostal mission in Seattle, Washington, preaching that the Bible required humans to renounce the temptations of society and gather with the elect to commune with God. In 1912, he and 175 followers built a religious utopia on Lopez Island in a remote part of Puget Sound. They had to live in tents until they were able to construct houses, a refectory, a school, and other buildings. They had their own power plant and tools and a boat they navigated on the Sound. They were a vegetarian ascetic community and prohibited smoking, dancing, and alcohol. Marriages were encouraged and all ceremonies were performed by Gourley. Most of the money needed to support the colony came from selling lumber to a mill on another nearby island. Unfortunately, Lopez Island was hit with epidemics of typhoid and tuberculosis. Only a few new members came to the colony. Daily life involved Bible study and prayer and two religious services on Sunday. Because Gourley preached pacifism, he told his male followers not to serve in the military during World War I. As a consequence, he was arrested for violating the Espionage Act of 1917. The charges were dismissed, however. Gourley was criticized by some of his followers for having mishandled the colony's finances and, after an emotional confrontation with them, he left the colony in 1920. Shortly after his departure the remaining residents decided to disband. They sold their communal holdings and divided the proceeds, which came to about $175 a family.

Sources:
LeWarne, Charles P. 1975. *Utopias on Puget Sound, 1885–1915.* Seattle: University of Washington Press.

Miller, Timothy. 1998. *The Quest for Utopia in Twentieth Century-America.* Syracuse, N.Y.: Syracuse University Press.

THE LORD'S FARM. Mason T. Huntsman, who called himself Paul Blaudin Mnason following a conversion to Christianity, was a revivalist preacher who impersonated Jesus Christ. In 1889, he organized a religious communal farm near Woodcliff, New Jersey, that eventually had 40 members. Mnason's religious beliefs focused exclusively on the Sermon on the Mount. He allowed anyone to join The Lord's Farm and soon neighbors called members the "Angel Dancers" because of the nude dances at the community. The farm grew and sold fruit for income. Due to the open admissions policy, the colony soon had a number of eccentric members, some with criminal records. As a result of persistent complaints of scandals—nude dancing and sexual promiscuity—county authorities closed the farm down in 1910. Mnason spent the rest of his life in New York City; the date of his death is unknown.

See Also Huntsman, Mason T.

Sources:
Fogarty, Robert S. 1980. *Dictionary of American Communal and Utopian History.* Westport, Conn.: Greenwood Press.

Miller, Timothy. 1998. *The Quest for Utopia in Twentieth-Century America.* Syracuse, N.Y.: Syracuse University Press.

Schroeder, Theodore. 1987. *Anarchism and the Lord's Farm* (Microform). Alexandria: Chadwyck-Healey.

Trahair, Richard C. S. 1999. *Utopias and Utopians: An Historical Dictionary.* West-
    port, Conn.: Greenwood Press.
Wooster, Ernest S. 1924. *Communities of the Past and Present.* Newllano, La.: Llano
    Colonist.

LOVE ISRAEL FAMILY. In 1980, Love Israel (Paul Erdman) founded
this primitive escapist communal utopia in Seattle, Washington. He was a
television salesman who underwent a mystical epiphany after he moved to
Haight-Ashbury, San Francisco, in the mid-1960s. The experience convinced
him that humanity had to realize that they were all one person and that they
had to "come together." Under the name of Love Israel, he preached that
people should live in a community modeled on biblical Israel. He rented a
house in Seattle and several individuals moved in to live with him. Soon the
number grew to 400 members and Love Israel had to rent more homes.
Dressed in robes and sandals, they took as their surnames "Israel," and Erdman gave them moralistic first names such as "Understanding," "Devotion,"
and "Honesty." Their main activity was operating an inn that provided free
food and lodging and landscaping public parks in the Queen Anne Hill area
of the city. In 1985, internal squabbles led to the departure of large number
of members, including Love Israel, who temporarily left with his female com-
panion to live in Los Angeles for two years before returning to the community. When they were sued by a former member to recover donations that he
had made to the group, Love Israel Family was forced into bankruptcy. By
the late 1980s, there were only 50 members living on a 280-acre ranch 50
miles north of Seattle. They were hardworking and persistent in their commitment to religious communal life, however, and by the mid-1990s the
colony had grown to 100 members living in a dozen family units. They
opened businesses that marketed flower salads and garlic and began farming
operations. Minor problems arose when local officials discovered that some
of the Family homes were built without building permits, but these difficulties were resolved. Love Israel and the other members of the Family believed
that they were immortal and will never die. The group stated in the 2000 edition of *Communities Directory* that "we are not here to perpetuate religion
but to discover who we really are when we create together in service and
love."

Sources:

Communities Directory: A Guide to Intentional Communities and Cooperative Living.
    2000. Rutledge, Mo.: Fellowship for Intentional Community.
Miller, Timothy. 1999. *The 60s Communes: Hippies and Beyond.* Syracuse, N.Y.: Syra-
    cuse University Press.

M

MacDOWELL COLONY. Edward MacDowell (?–1908), a professor of music at Columbia University, had long planned to establish an art colony at Peterborough, New Hampshire, but before he could implement the plan he was stricken with mental illness. His wife, Marian, moved him to Peterborough and built a log cabin. By the time of Edward's death in 1908 several other artists had formed the nucleus of a community. Marian converted farm buildings into dormitories and added several hundred acres to the colony. In 1911, a visitor reported that 50 artists were living there. By the 1920s, there were 25 widely scattered homes and private studio buildings at the 600-acre colony, where residents lived and worked year round. Although they were separated during the day working in their studio-homes, each evening they gathered for a communal dinner and socializing. When the MacDowell Colony celebrated its fiftieth anniversary in 1957, it had 95 studio buildings and an application list of more than 1,000. By this time, many famous artists had lived there, including 18 winners of the Pulitzer Prize. The colony continues to thrive at the beginning of the twentieth-first century

Source:
Miller, Timothy. 1998. *The Quest for Utopia in Twentieth-Century America*. Syracuse, N.Y.: Syracuse University Press.

MACEDONIA COOPERATIVE COMMUNITY. In 1937, a teacher, Morris Mitchell, bought land near Clarkesville, Georgia, to found a communal cooperative of families committed to pacifism, communal education, and the preservation of natural resources. There was community ownership of the property, an economically profitable dairy, and a children's toy business called "Community Playthings." In 1953–54, seven families of the Bruder-hof lived at Macedonia for a while and some members of the Macedonia Cooperative joined the Bruderhof. In 1958, after 15 more members joined the Bruderhof, the Macedonia Cooperative property was sold.

Sources:

Miller, Timothy. 1998. *The Quest for Utopia in Twentieth-Century America.* Syracuse, N.Y.: Syracuse University Press.

Orser, W. Edward. 1981. *Searching for a Viable Alternative: The Macedonia Cooperative Community, 1937–1958.* New York: Burt Franklin and Co.

Zablocki, Benjamin. 1971. *The Joyful Community.* Chicago: University of Chicago Press.

THE MA-NA-HAR COOPERATIVE FELLOWSHIP AND THE BHOODAN CENTER OF INQUIRY. The name of this fellowship means "harmony of man and nature" and "bhoodan" was a land-sharing plan invented by Mohandas Gandhi where surplus land was given to the landless. The Bhoodan Center was a Quaker-like intentional community organized in 1953 on 80 acres near Oakhurst, California. The members of the ashram, or community, conducted seminars on low-cost construction and sought spiritual perfection through meditation, study, and mutual sharing. The actual communal organization of the center was called the Ma-Na-Har Cooperative Fellowship, in which members lived in private homes but engaged in work where the tools and equipment were communally owned. By the 1990s, the experiment had been abandoned.

Sources:

Manahar Cooperative Fellowship Handbook. 1970. Oakhurst, Calif.: Bhoodhan Center.

Miller, Timothy. 1998. *The Quest for Utopia in Twentieth-Century America.* Syracuse, N.Y.: Syracuse University Press.

MANKIND UNITED. This religious community promised, as did Heaven City, salvation from a looming earthly disaster. In 1934, Arthur L. Bell, call-ing himself the "Voice of the Right Idea," said he knew of a plot to destroy and enslave mankind based on secret plans of "Hidden Rulers" who for decades had been engaged in a conspiracy to commit the dastardly deed. He organized his followers into the "pioneers of the Mankind United" to save the world and then usher in a new Golden Age. This new age would see everyone having a guaranteed four-hour-day employment in a four-day work week. Over just eight months everyone would earn a minimum salary of $3,000. They would retire at the age of 40. All these utopian advantages would be brought about by a new technology that would produce food and clothing. One historian claims that thousands of individuals in California were attracted to the program. But the FBI, in 1942, arrested some of the leaders and they were convicted of interfering with the war effort. Thereupon

Bell, in January 1944, organized the communal Christ's Church of the Golden Rule. Over 850 members donated all personal and real property to the community and lived in spartan conditions until 1951 when the church went into bankruptcy and Bell disappeared. A handful of people continued on as a community near Willits, California, and ran cottage industries and raised livestock. By the mid-1990s, about 100 residents were living there communally in a colony with a school, library, dining hall, and print shop all dedicated to making the world free from want.

See Also Heaven City

Sources:

Dohrman, H.T. 1958. *California Cult: The Story of "Mankind United."* Boston: Beacon.

Miller, Timothy. 1998. *The Quest for Utopia in Twentieth-Century America.* Syracuse, N.Y.: Syracuse University Press.

THE MAVERICK. Internal dissension at Byrdcliffe was the reason for the creation of another art colony on a nearby 102-acre farm near Woodstock, New York. Hervey White, one of Byrdcliffe's officers, purchased the farm in 1904 and erected a small cabin. Within months residents put up other cabins and those who could paid White rent to live in the colony. All poor members, however, were given free lodging and food. Like Byrdcliffe, Maverick was a utopia of prominent artists and intellectuals, including Thorstein Veblen. White started the Maverick Press in 1910 and the next year published a literary magazine called *The Wild Hawk* and then *The Plowshare*. In 1915, they began the "Maverick Festival," an outdoor music festival held in an abandoned stone quarry. The community published a literary magazine edited by James P. Cooney, *The Phoenix,* that promoted the socialist ideas of D.H. Lawrence and announced the community's rejection of mechanization and its condemnation of all industrial labor. It pleaded for a return to living a more simple life of small cooperative communities devoted to subsistence agriculture and handicrafts.

See Also Byrdcliffe

Sources:

Evers, Alf. 1987. *Woodstock: History of an American Town.* Woodstock: Overlook Press.

"The Maverick." 1933. *Publications of the Woodstock Historical Society* 11 (Aug.–Sept.): 3–11.

Miller, Timothy. 1998. *The Quest for Utopia in Twentieth-Century America.* Syracuse, N.Y.: Syracuse University Press.

MAVERICK, MAURY. Maverick (?–?) was the tax collector of Bexar County, Texas, in which the city of San Antonio is located. During the Great Depression, he persuaded executives of the Humble Oil Company to let him use its land to build a communal cooperative utopia called Diga. He then put abandoned railroad cars on the 35 acres as living quarters. Remodeled boxcars were converted into a hospital, a service station, and a school. At its peak in the winter of 1933, it had 171 members. As relief became available from President Franklin D. Roosevelt's New Deal programs, Diga steadily declined. Maverick later was elected mayor of San Antonio.

See Also Diga

Sources:

Miller, Timothy. 1998. *The Quest for Utopia in Twentieth-Century America*. Syracuse, N.Y.: Syracuse University Press.

Sutton, Robert P. 2004. *Communal Utopias and the American Experience: Secular Communities, 1824–2000*. Westport, Conn. and London: Praeger.

McCOWEN, HENRY. McCowen (1890–1970) was born in Las Cruces, New Mexico, and became a wealthy, college-educated dairy farmer and newspaper editor in the town of Elida. He wanted to create cooperative villages organized around the principles of planning and efficiency. In his book, *Moneyless Government or Why and Why Not,* published in 1933, he advocated the building of 100,000 cooperative communes in the United States, each with 2,000 residents. The following year, he organized his first communal experiment in a rented building in Elida and advertised it in the newspaper the *Roosevelt County Record,* inviting members to join his cooperative colony. Just one family responded and only a handful of local ranchers backed the utopia. McCowen himself did not move to the building. When town residents resented the appearance of a "communist" experiment, he abandoned the "Old Moneyless" plan. McCowen died in Elida after publishing another book, *Old Moneyless and Prescription* in 1966.

Sources:

Fogarty, Robert S. 1980. *Dictionary of American Communal and Utopian History*. Westport, Conn.: Greenwood Press.

Sutton, Robert P. 2004. *Communal Utopias and the American Experience: Secular Communities, 1824–2000*. Westport, Conn. and London: Praeger.

McCOY, DON. In the 1960s, Don McCoy (1940–?) came into a substantial family inheritance and, which, added to the money that he and his brother made owning and renting houseboats in Sausalito, California, made McCoy a wealthy man. In 1967, after living with some friends, he decided to use his money to start a hippie community. He rented 690 acres and a large house at Novato, California, and soon 26 residents were living at the commune. McCoy paid all of the operating expenses. Calling themselves the Chosen Family, they lived a comfortable life using the property's swimming pool and smoking marijuana. They organized a commercial baking factory and sold loves of bread in San Francisco. In 1969, when some members of

Morning Star Ranch came to Olompali, McCoy welcomed them. But the two groups of hippies found each other's lifestyle incompatible and disagreements soon arose. Trouble really began when McCoy's family took him to court and stopped all further expenditures on the colony. Police twice came to the place because of the pervasive use of marijuana. In 1969, a fire gutted the mansion and residents began to leave the colony. A few remained and tried to continue communal living by running an alternative school for children. When two small girls drowned in the swimming pool and newspapers reported on the antisocial activities (marijuana and nudism), the remaining hippies were evicted and that summer Olompali closed down. In the mid-1990s, McCoy told Timothy Miller that living at Olompali Ranch was "the most colorful time in my life."

See Also Morning Star Ranch; Olompali Ranch

Source:
Miller, Timothy. 1999. *The 60s Communes: Hippies and Beyond.* Syracuse, N.Y.: Syracuse University Press.

MELBOURNE VILLAGE. In 1947, Ralph Borsodi (1886–1977), author of the utopian tract *Flight from the City* and founder of the subsistence homestead cooperative community called the School of Living near Dayton, Ohio, promoted the establishment of Melbourne Village at Melbourne, Florida. He and others planned a subsistence homestead on 80 acres where 50 family homes were to be built on plots ranging from one-half to one acre. Forty acres were set aside as communal land. They built a community store and a recreation hall. Within a year, Melbourne Village was a prosperous commune of 21 homes, craft shops, and small businesses. A second School of Living was opened to provide education for the residents. In 1950, six years after Borsodi himself had moved to Melbourne Village, he started Melbourne University, a graduate school emphasizing human thought and action in "praxiological philosophy." However, only a few seminars and courses were ever offered. Internal disputes arose in the late 1950s and local real estate developers started subdivisions around the community and the village never realized Borsodi's grandiose communal ideas.

See Also Borsodi, Ralph; School of Living

Sources:
Crepeau, Richard C. 1988. *Melbourne Village: The First Twenty-five Years (1947–1971).* Orlando: University of Central Florida Press.
Loomis, Mildred J. 1982. *Alternative Americas.* New York: Universe Books.
Miller, Timothy. 1998. *The Quest for Utopia in Twentieth-Century America.* Syracuse, N.Y.: Syracuse University Press.

MERRY PRANKSTERS. Ken Kesey and his wife created this hippie colony, one of the first. In 1963, a congenial group of young men and women who had been living a bohemian life at Perry Lane in Palo Alto, California, were forced to move when a real estate developer purchased the properties they had been renting. With the royalties from his first best-selling novel, *One Flew over the Cuckoo's Nest*, Kesey purchased a mountain home near La Honda and it became a raucous colony of drug-using hippies. In 1974, some of them, led by Kesey, traveled to New York City in an outlandishly painted bus converted into a recreational vehicle. Following the trip, Kesey asked the Hell's Angels to visit the colony and the subsequent noisy LSD parties had four police cars stand guard at the entrance. In 1967, Kesey was arrested on drug charges and spent five months on a work farm. When released, he left the mountain top commune to go with his family to a brother's farm near Springfield, Oregon, where about 60 of the Merry Pranksters came to live. But by that time, Kesey had tired of communal life and when most of the Pranksters left to attend the Woodstock festival in August 1969, he told them not to come back to the farm. Some returned, though, but they did not live with Kesey and stayed with other friends in the Springfield area.

See Also Kesey, Ken; Millbrook

Sources:

Charters, Ann. 1983. *The Beats: Literary Bohemians in Postwar America*. Vol. 1. Detroit: Gale.

Leary, Timothy. 1990. *Flashbacks: A Personal and Cultural History of an Era*. Los Angeles: Tarcher.

Lee, Martin A., and Bruce Shlain. 1985. *Acid Dreams: The CIA, LSD and the Sixties Rebellion*. New York: Grove.

Miller, Timothy. 1999. *The 60s Communes: Hippies and Beyond*. Syracuse, N.Y.: Syracuse University Press.

Perry, Paul. 1990. *On the Bus: The Complete Guide to the Legendary Trip of Ken Kesey and the Merry Pranksters and the Birth of the Counterculture*. New York: Thunder's Mouth.

THE MESSIANIC COMMUNITIES (TWELVE TRIBES). These Jesus movement communes were founded by Elbert and Marsha Spriggs in 1972 as an outgrowth of the large number of young people who came to their Christian coffeehouse in Chattanooga, Tennessee. The couple eventually had a total of five communal houses and a health-food business. Because of local opposition to their racially integrated commune they moved to Island Pond, Vermont, in 1978. From that headquarters they built more than 15 communes in five countries. All the communes stressed an imminent millennium and remained largely isolated from outsiders. They educated and strictly disciplined their children, dressed them the same, and used a unique religious language that calls Jesus "Yahshua." They were patriarchal and insisted upon only male leadership and husbands dominating their wives. They have adopted some Jewish practices such as celebrating a Saturday Sabbath and calling each other by Hebrew names. Some communes operated restaurants. The Messianic Communities grew rapidly in the 1990s to claim a membership of between 1,000 to 1,500.

Sources:

Miller, Timothy. 1999. *The 60s Communes: Hippies and Beyond*. Syracuse, N.Y.: Syracuse University Press.

Swantko, Jean, and Ed Wiseman. 1995. "Messianic Communities, Sociologists, and the Law." *Communities: Journal of Cooperative Living* 88 (fall): 34–35.

MILLBROOK. This psychedelic commune, much resembling the Merry Pranksters, existed from 1963 to 1967 in Millbrook, New York, about a two-hour drive from New York City. Earlier, Harvard University adjunct professor Timothy Leary, another professor, Richard Alpert, a graduate student, Ralph Metzner, and others had formed a commune in two houses in Newton, Massachusetts. But when their bizarre antics and loud music offended their neighbors, Leary and Alpert accepted the offer of one of their wealthy members, Peggy Hitchcock, to relocate to an estate her family had purchased in Millbrook. The property they moved to in August 1963 included several buildings, a large mansion, and several thousand acres. About 25 individuals lived at the Castalia Foundation, the name they gave to the community, and included academics, graduate students, and spiritualists. Psychologist Art Kleps ran a psychedelic New-American Church in the gatehouse. Members donated their personal libraries to the commune and they published a scholarly journal called the *Psychedelic Review*. Although they used LSD, as did the Merry Pranksters, they were much more serious. Instead of having wild parties, they developed psychedelic light shows and painted images of mandalas and Asian deities on the inside and outside of the mansion. Also, unlike the Merry Pranksters, they tried to maintain some discipline in assigning communal duties. Wealthy individuals in the colony took care of paying the bills. After LSD was made illegal, things began to deteriorate. In December 1965, Leary was arrested on drug charges and sentenced to 30 years in prison. The following April, a county prosecutor, G. Gordon Liddy, later involved in the Watergate burglary, ordered a raid on the property. Internal squabbles began to arise in the face of these frustrations and Peggy's brother, Billy Hitchcock, closed down the commune in the spring of 1967.

See Also Merry Pranksters

Sources:

Hollingshead, Michael. 1973. *The Man Who Turned on the World*. New York: Abelard-Schuman.

Kleps, Art. 1977. *Millbrook: The True Story of the Early Years of the Psychedelic Revolution*. Oakland, Calif.: Bench Press.

Miller, Timothy. 1999. *The 60s Communes: Hippies and Beyond*. Syracuse, N.Y.: Syracuse University Press.

Stevens, Jay. 1987. *Storming Heaven: LSD and the American Dream*. New York: Harper and Row.

THE MOLOKAN COMMUNITIES. This ethnic community of Russian immigrants represents the tendency of some ethnic groups arriving in the United States to band together communally for cultural integrity against American influences. The Molokans, or Russian Spiritual Christians, formed in that country in the eighteenth century and de-emphasized the importance of the leader's teachings as the final interpretation of God's will. Instead, they relied on the Bible. In 1904, they left Russia in order to avoid military conscription and settled in Canada, but soon moved to East Los Angeles because of its more hospitable climate. Several families lived in various city houses but ran a communal grocery store. In 1906, a second and third Molokan commune was started at Potrero Hill, San Francisco, and in the Guadalupe Valley of Baja California. At the latter site, 50 families purchased 13,000 acres and built a village from which they farmed the land communally. This venture lasted until the 1950s when troubles with Mexican squatters in the area caused most families to move back to the United States. Between 1906 and 1910, about 20 families formed a communal utopia near Ukiah, California, but these families went back to the San Francisco commune in 1918. Still another colony was established in 1915 near Kerman, California, although the land was held by individuals. In 1911, some families from the Los Angeles community started a commune near Glendale, Arizona, that soon had more than 100 families. With such a high number of communards living there, they organized four separate villages, not unlike the Amana Society in Iowa, and developed a profitable cotton farm. When cotton prices fell drastically after the end of World War I, most families returned to the Los Angeles community. By the 1990s, only the urban Molokan colonies remained and the rural ones had vanished.

Sources:

Berokoff, John K. 1969. *Molokans in America*. Los Angeles: Stockton-Doty.
Conybeare, Frederick. 1962. *Russian Dissenters*. New York: Russell and Russell.
Miller, Timothy. 1998. *The Quest for Utopia in Twentieth-Century America*. Syracuse, N.Y.: Syracuse University Press.

MONTAGUE FARM. In 1968, this literary commune was started at Montague, Massachusetts, not far from the Packer Corner colony by members of the Liberation News Service. Its most notable member was Stephen Diamond, author of *What the Trees Said*. He and other residents preached a message of abandoning the city to live in the friendlier rural environment. Like Packer Corner residents, the writers at Montague Farm worked at outside jobs.

See Also Packer Corner

Sources:
Diamond, Stephen. 1971. *What the Trees Said: Life on a New Age Farm*. New York: Dell.
Miller, Timothy. 1998. *The Quest for Utopia in Twentieth-Century America*. Syracuse, N.Y.: Syracuse University Press.

MOON, SUN MYUNG. In 1920, the Reverend Sun Myung Moon was born in northwest Korea and received a traditional Chinese education until, at the age of 10, his family converted to Presbyterianism. He attended a western-style elementary school and a high school in Seoul and later took courses at the Pentecostal Church. He claimed that on Easter morning, 1936, Jesus appeared to him and told him to lead a world mission to establish the Kingdom of Heaven on Earth. He had other visions—of Moses, Buddha, and God the Father. In 1938, he studied electrical engineering in Tokyo. In 1943, when the Japanese occupied Korea, the police arrested him for involvement in a resistance underground. After the war, he organized his church in North Korea; but the police arrested him on the charge that he was a spy for South Korea and sent him to a labor camp. He was liberated when the American armed forces invaded the country in the summer of 1950. He then went to a refugee colony in Pusan and the next year moved to Seoul and worked as a day laborer in the docks. He organized the Holy Spirit Association for the Unification of World Christianity and in 1956 relocated the church's headquarters to Chungpadong. The next year he published the *Divine Principle*, a book that explained his new religion as a combination of Christianity, Korean shamanism, Taoism, and Confucianism. In 1959, he established his headquarters in the United States as the Freedom Leadership Foundation, which brought his message of a "Day of Hope" to American audiences. In 1971, he relocated to Tarrytown, New York. His estimated 40,000 followers lived communally as local congregations that rented houses and pooled property and finances. The living accommodations were separated by sex because Sun Myung Moon condemned premarital sex as an abomination. In 1982, he was convicted of tax evasion, sentenced to 18 months in federal prison, and fined $25,000. After serving the sentence, he presided at mass weddings of his disciples in South Korea. In 1990, in Moscow, he delivered the "True Unification and One World" speech that claimed there were congregations of the Unification Church in 35 countries that earned money selling soft drinks, computers, and fish.

See Also Moonies (Unification Church)

Sources:
Miller, Timothy. 1999. *The 60s Communes: Hippies and Beyond*. Syracuse, N.Y.: Syracuse University Press.
Owen, Roger J. 1982. *The Moonies: A Critical Look at a Controversial Group*. London: Ward Lock Educational.

Trahair, Richard C. S. 1999. *Utopias and Utopians: An Historical Dictionary.* Westport, Conn.: Greenwood Press.

MOONIES (UNIFICATION CHURCH). In the mid-1950s, Young Oon Kim (later called Miss Kim), then a professor at Ewha University in Seoul, joined Sun Myung Moon's Holy Spirit Association for the Unification of World Christianity at its Korean headquarters at Chungpadong. In 1960, she opened the first Unification Church missions in America, called "Family Centers," in Oregon, Washington, D.C., and San Francisco. In the Bay Area, Miss Kim targeted discontented youth by stressing the hope and excitement involved in creating the "International Ideal City," as she called it. Within 10 years, she had established 55 United Family Centers in Berkeley and other cities. Each year church membership doubled and by 1971 it had an operating budget of $250,000. All the while Moon remained in Korea and paid little attention to what was happening in America. In 1965, when he visited the United States as part of a worldwide tour, he did some work with the Unification Church. But when he came to New York City in 1971 to begin a third world tour he took control. He moved to Tarrytown, New York, to live. He gave television interviews and delivered impassioned sermons to large crowds. He preached that Americans must abandon traditional Protestant denominations and find a new relationship with God. He predicted that in 1981 the entire world would accept him as Lord of the Second Advent and inaugurate this Kingdom of Heaven. In the meantime, he started three United Family Centers to train Unification Church missionaries. The centers made candles and retailed them by the thousands in teams of 15 members called the MFTs or Mobile Fund-raising Teams. By the mid-1970s, candle sales averaged over $1,000 weekly. In 1981, Moon claimed more than 500,000 followers in the United States, although the actual numbers were somewhere between 3,000 and 5,000. They lived communally in small colonies of about a half-dozen to a dozen members who combined finances and practiced celibacy with a strict separation of the sexes. In the 1980s, though, Moon allowed many followers who had served the church as brothers and sisters to enter into a church-blessed marriage. Afterward, many couples abandoned communalism and lived as private families. By 1981, Moon had constructed the Unification Theology Seminary in New York, had purchased the New Yorker Hotel in Manhattan for $5 million, and had paid $2.5 million for Tiffany's. He opened a fishing industry in Gloucester, Massachusetts. He published two daily newspapers, the *News World* and the *Washington Times*. But on July 16, 1982, Moon was found guilty of tax evasion, sentenced to 18 months in federal prison, and fined $25,000. By the beginning of the twenty-first century the movement had largely abandoned its communal life. It clams to have more than 1,000 worldwide disciples, two million associate members, and United Family Centers in 120 countries.

See Also Moon, Sun Myung

Sources:

Bromley, David G., and Anson D. Shupe, Jr. 1979. *"Moonies" in America: Cult, Church, and Crusade.* Beverly Hills, Calif.: Sage.

Miller, Timothy. 1999. *The 60s Communes: Hippies and Beyond.* Syracuse, N.Y.: Syracuse University Press.

Owen, Roger J. 1982. *The Moonies: A Critical Look at a Controversial Group.* London: Ward Lock Educational.

Trahair, Richard C. S. 1999. *Utopias and Utopians: An Historical Dictionary.* Westport, Conn.: Greenwood Press.

THE MOREHOUSES. The Morehouse communities, like Synanon, were established to improve health and personal growth. In 1967, a former professional football player, Victor Baranco, established the first Morehouse (or More House) in San Francisco. He stressed fun and entertainment. Its Institute of Human Abilities offered seminars on "Basic Sensuality," "Basic Communication," and "Jealousy, Money and Possession." It also provided living quarters in one of the houses that was purchased in the Bay Area. In the 1970s, these Morehouses flourished because of income from the seminar and the labor donated by the residents. But information on its later development is scanty.

See Also Synanon

Source:

Miller, Timothy. 1999. *The 60s Communes: Hippies and Beyond.* Syracuse, N.Y.: Syracuse University Press.

MORGAN, ARTHUR. Morgan (1878–1975) was the founder of the Celo community in North Carolina's Great Smoky Mountains in 1936. Before becoming involved in utopian communities during the Great Depression, he had a distinguished career as an engineer and served as president of Antioch College. At Antioch, he developed a curriculum that combined class lectures with jobs in the city of Yellow Springs, Ohio. In 1940, President Franklin D. Roosevelt appointed him chairman of the Tennessee Valley Authority, in which capacity he not only constructed the dam system but built cooperative villages for project's workers. That same year he organized Community Service, Inc., to encourage living in small towns modeled on the English "garden city" movement. Such communities, he believed, would serve as an ideal alternative to the overcrowded urban environment and would encourage cooperation, mutual respect, and interaction with one's neighbors. He held regular meetings in Yellow Springs to promote his small-town utopias. After World War II, he created the InterCommunity Exchange. Then, under Art Wiser, it was called the FIC. This organization expanded his utopia building to the international setting, promoted pacifist communitarianism, and protested against Cold War militarism. This movement, however, declined in the 1960s because of the Peace Corps and its call for selfless service on the world scene. Morgan's Celo Community survives today on 1,100 acres with 34 independent households.

See Also Celo; Fellowship for Intentional Communities

Sources:

Communities Directory: A Guide to Intentional Communities and Cooperative Living. 2000. Rutledge, Mo.: Fellowship for Intentional Community.

Fogarty, Robert S. 1980. *Dictionary of American Communal and Utopian History.* Westport, Conn.: Greenwood Press.

Intentional Communities: 1959 Yearbook of the Fellowship of Intentional Communities. 1959. Yellow Springs, Ohio: Fellowship of Intentional Communities.

Miller, Timothy. 1998. *The Quest for Utopia in Twentieth-Century America.* Syracuse, N.Y.: Syracuse University Press.

Morgan, Arthur. 1984. *The Community of the Future and the Future of Community.* Yellow Springs, Ohio: Community Service (Ohio), 1957.

———. 1945. *Philosophy of Edward Bellamy.* New York: King's Crown Press.

———. 1946. *Nowhere Was Somewhere: How History Makes Utopias and How Utopias Make History.* Chapel Hill: University of North Carolina Press.

MORNING STAR EAST. In 1969, some residents from Morning Star Ranch moved to New Mexico and established an open-land community next to the Reality Construction Company commune in Taos County. They built crude adobe huts for living quarters without running water or electricity. For a brief time residents shared communal corn farming with their Reality neighbors. Morning Star East had a communal kitchen where women prepared meals. In the summer, its 100 or so members hand-plowed, seeded, irrigated, and weeded the fields in temperatures that ran into the nineties. In the winter, temperatures dropped below zero and the closest firewood was 30 miles from the colony. The community gradually deteriorated and it dissolved in 1972.

See Also Morning Star Ranch; Reality Construction Company

Sources:

Houriet, Robert. 1971. *Getting Back Together.* New York: Avon.

Miller, Timothy. 1999. *The 60s Communes: Hippies and Beyond.* Syracuse, N.Y.: Syracuse University Press.

MORNING STAR RANCH. In March 1966, the talented musician and music critic for the *San Francisco Chronicle* Lou Gottlieb began inviting friends to spend time with him in one of two houses that stood on property he had purchased, with financial help from Bill Wheeler, in Sonoma County. By the summer, a number of others had moved into Gottlieb's houses and they called the place "Morning Star Ranch," a name given to it by the former owner. For a year the number of residents remained small. In the summer of

1967, young people from San Francisco's Haight-Ashbury district began to arrive. The large number of teenagers at the ranch soon attracted the attention of local police because of open drug use, nudity, and promiscuous sex. Many of the residents practiced yoga and studied Asian spiritualism. In April, Swami A. C. Bhaktivedanta, or Prabhupada, of the International Society for Krishna Consciousness (ISKCON) spoke at the community. In the fall of 1968, Gottlieb met Don McCoy of the Olompali Ranch. Unfortunately, as Morning Star Ranch's population increased both its neighbors and the police became hostile. And as tales of rape and violence spread, the hostility intensified. Gottlieb was arrested in July 1967 on the charge of violating state sanitation laws. In September, Sonoma County officials obtained a court order to close down the ranch. In January 1968, officials arrested and fined the 20 people still living there. In May 1969, Gottlieb announced that he had deeded the property to God, but a judge vacated the transfer. Soon afterwards the county bulldozed the colony's houses and shacks, and three other leveling efforts followed. Each time the residents rebuilt crude shelters and defied the officials. A few stayed on until 1973 but by then most had left.

See Also Diggers; Gottlieb, Lou; International Society for Krishna Consciousness (ISKCON); McCoy, Don; Morning Star East; Olompali Ranch; Wheeler's Ranch

Sources:

Gardner, Hugh. 1978. *The Children of Prosperity: Thirteen Modern American Communes.* New York: St. Martin's Press.

Fogarty, Robert S. 1980. *Dictionary of American Communal and Utopian History.* Westport, Conn.: Greenwood Press.

Miller, Timothy. 1999. *The 60s Communes: Hippies and Beyond.* Syracuse, N.Y.: Syracuse University Press.

MORTON, JAMES FERDINAND. Morton (1870–1941) was born in Littleton, Massachusetts, the son of a Baptist minister. In 1892, he received an M.A. degree from Harvard and while a student there became an enthusiastic socialist. After graduation, he signed on as a writer for the left-wing publication *Free Society,* located in San Francisco. He joined the Home Colony in 1900 and for five years was the editor of its newspaper, *Discontent: Mother of Progress,* and other publications. In 1906, he left home to become a writer for the anarchist journal *Truth Seeker.* That same year his book, *The Curse of Race Prejudice,* appeared. He also was a field secretary for the New York Single-Tax League. In 1925, he moved to Patterson, New Jersey, and served as curator of that city's museum until his death.

See Also Home Colony

Sources:

Fogarty, Robert S. 1980. *Dictionary of American Communal and Utopian History.* Westport, Conn.: Greenwood Press.

LeWarne, Charles. 1975. *Utopias on Puget Sound, 1885–1915.* Seattle: University of Washington Press.
Sutton, Robert P. 2004. *Communal Utopias and the American Experience: Secular Communities, 1824–2000.* Westport, Conn. and London: Praeger.

MOVE. In 1974, Vincent Leaphart founded this back-to-nature commune on the west side of Philadelphia, in a house on North Thirty-Third Street. From that time on, Leaphart took a new name, John Africa, as did the other members of the colony, most of them African Americans. Their goal was to show how the corrupt "cancerous system" was the cause of America's social and economic problems. These vegetarian communards all wore blue denim clothes and never bathed or cut their hair. A large number of cats and dogs roamed the premises and the place was inundated with rats, termites, and other insects. High-volume rock music blared from loudspeakers day and night. A number of its members were arrested before the police raided the house in August 1978. At that time a shot from inside killed an officer. The members were charged with murder and city authorities razed the building. They tried to recreate MOVE in another house but in May 1985 the police dropped a bomb on the roof of the premises and the resulting fire destroyed a city block of 60 homes. John Africa and 11 MOVE members were killed in the attack.

Sources:

Anderson, John, and Hilary Hevenor. 1987. *Burning Down the House: MOVE and the Tragedy of Philadelphia.* New York: Norton.
Miller, Timothy. 1999. *The 60s Communes: Hippies and Beyond.* Syracuse, N.Y.: Syracuse University Press.

MOVEMENT FOR A NEW SOCIETY (MNS). Movement for a New Society (MNS), like MOVE, was located in Philadelphia but it was a much more respectable commune that was dedicated to social reform. MNS was a network of intentional communities that was started in 1970 from a reform organization known as A Quaker Action Group. By 1980, there were 20 MNS houses in West Philadelphia, each with its own social reform focus. Most residents took part-time jobs in the city. From Philadelphia MNS established social action communal homes in seven other cities as schools for sharing and working toward world peace and justice.

Sources:

Best, James S. 1978. *Another Way to Live: Experiencing Intentional Community.* Wallingford, Pa.: Pendle Hill.
Miller, Timothy. 1999. *The 60s Communes: Hippies and Beyond.* Syracuse, N.Y.: Syracuse University Press.

N

NELSON, NELSON O. Nelson (1844–1922) was born in Lillisand, Norway, and immigrated with his parents to Missouri. He served in the Union Army and after the war opened a plumbing business in St. Louis and became wealthy. Following the economic depression of 1886, he sponsored cooperative settlements and communal utopias as a remedy for America's economic and social problems. He established a cooperative factory on 250 acres near Edwardsville, Illinois, and at the same time subsidized Edward Bellamy's magazine, *The New Nation*. He also supported the Ruskin colony in Tennessee and wrote articles for its newspaper. In the first decade of the twentieth century, he turned to financing garden cities and rural cooperatives in the South. In 1922, he opened cooperative grocery stores in New Orleans. After this venture went bankrupt, he had a nervous breakdown and died in Los Angeles.

See Also Ruskin

Source:
Fogarty, Robert S. 1980. *Dictionary of American Communal and Utopian History*. Westport, Conn.: Greenwood Press.

NEVADA COLONY. The Nevada Colony was founded by C. V. Eggleston, the fiscal agent of Llano del Rio who, in August 1915, left that colony to start a cooperative community at Nevada City, in Churchill County, Nevada. He established two corporations, the Nevada Colony Corporation and the Union Security Company, to run the colony. The state wanted to encourage such colonies in order to rebuild Nevada's economy, which had gone into a slump with the closing of the mines. So, it built irrigation projects to encourage settlement in that area. Between 1916 and 1918, 200 individuals moved to the colony to live on its 1,540 scattered acres. Nevada Colony activities included a furniture store, mill, print shop, and farming. Almost from the start, however, disagreements emerged among the members, especially local ranchers who had joined the colony and traded land for stock in the two corporations. Within a month of the first annual meeting in November 1916, three of the five members of the board of directors were expelled. The following June, Eggleston resigned and then difficulties steadily multiplied, including lawsuits. In May 1919, the colony went into receivership and Nevada Colony became a ghost town.

See Also Llano del Rio/Newllano; Eggleston, C.V.

Sources:
Fogarty, Robert S. 1980. *Dictionary of American Communal and Utopian History.* Westport, Conn.: Greenwood Press.
Miller, Timothy. 1998. *The Quest for Utopia in Twentieth-Century America.* Syracuse, N.Y.: Syracuse University Press.
Shepperson, Wilbur S. 1966. *Retreat to Nevada: A Socialist Colony of World War I.* Reno: University of Nevada Press.

NEW BUFFALO. In 1967, Rick Klein financed the purchase of 100 acres north of Taos, New Mexico, at Arroyo Hondo for 25 residents who moved there in June and built adobe communal buildings. They also lived in tepees. But conditions were crowded because the population doubled within months and the buildings and tents were adequate for only the original communards. Turnover during the first year was high, with only five of the original settlers still there by 1968. New Buffalo grew corn and made adobe bricks, but life was difficult because in the summer the community was overpopulated and in the winter there were only a few residents. By the 1980s, only Rick Klein and his wife remained, and they opened a bed and breakfast on the property. But within a decade this operation closed and Klein sold the property.

See Also Morning Star East; Reality Construction Company

Sources:
Fairfield, Richard [Dick]. 1972. *Communes USA: A Personal Tour.* Baltimore: Penguin.
Hedgepeth, William, and Dennis Stock. 1970. *The Alternative: Communal Life in New America.* New York: Macmillan.
Miller, Timothy. 1999. *The 60s Communes: Hippies and Beyond.* Syracuse, N.Y.: Syracuse University Press.

NEW CLAIRVAUX. In 1900, Edward Pearson Pressey, a Unitarian minister, and his wife moved to Montague, Massachusetts, where he preached reform through rural self-sufficiency and salvation through arts and crafts. In

1902, he started a magazine, *Country Time and Tide,* to promote back-to-the-land artist cooperatives. That year he founded New Clairvaux, a commune named after the monastery St. Bernard built in France in the twelfth century. Its 21 residents grew produce on a farm and opened a school named the New Clairvaux that offered courses in crafts and academics. They also made craft items for sale. But these items never brought in enough income to support the colony and it dissolved in 1909.

Sources:

Boris, Eileen. 1986. *Art and Labor: Ruskin, Morris, and the Craftsman Ideal in America.* Philadelphia: Temple University Press.

Miller, Timothy. 1998. *The Quest for Utopia in Twentieth-Century America.* Syracuse, N.Y.: Syracuse University Press.

NEW DEAL COOPERATIVES. In the New Deal (1932–1941), the federal government for the first time became involved in building utopian communities as a refuge for those unemployed because of the Great Depression. These federal communities were just one of two types of utopian experiments that appeared during the New Deal. The other communities were started and financed by individuals. These included Ralph Borsodi's School of the Living at Suffern, New York; Henry McCowen's Communist colony at Elida, New Mexico; Maury Maverick's Diga community at San Antonio; and the anarchist colony at Alicia, Michigan. But by far the most ambitious communal programs were under the authority of President Franklin D. Roosevelt's New Deal. Between 1933 and 1937 alone, these federal agencies with a budget of over $100 million planned more than 100 utopias, all conceived as permanent settlements because of the government's assumption that full employment might never again be possible in America. One kind of New Deal commune was the rural resettlement colonies, essentially rural subsistence homesteads, the most notable being at Arthurdale, West Virginia, near Reedsville. Eleanor Roosevelt personally took charge of the construction of this model community, even to the point of supervising the type of furniture to be used in the prefabricated cottages. At Highstown, New Jersey, Milburn L. Wilson, who worked under Harold Ickes as head of a new Division of Subsistence Homesteads (DSH), started an unsuccessful homestead for the urban unemployed. Wilson advanced Benjamin Brown, a Ukraine labor organizer, $500,000 as a loan to purchase 2,300 acres of land that he advertised as the Jersey Homestead. It was open to garment workers who would pay a $500 admissions fee. More than 100 individuals applied to work in its communal garment factory and to farm. But the factory was mismanaged and none of the residents was interested in agriculture. In 1942, it was bought out by a hat manufacturer. Harry Hopkins's Federal Emergency Relief Administration (FERA) had a special division called the Division of Rural Rehabilitation and Stranded Populations (DRRSP) that erected large farm homesteads at Woodlake (Texas), Dyess Colony (Arkansas), Pine Mountain Valley (Georgia), and

Cherry Lake Farm (Florida). But all four projects filed for bankruptcy. Frustrated by the failure of the FERA homesteads, Roosevelt formed the Resettlement Administration (RA) and named Rexford G. Tugwell, then Undersecretary of Agriculture, as its director. Tugwell built two types of communities, collective farms and the greenbelt towns. He developed large, staple-crop collective farms at Lake Dick (Arkansas), Casa Grande Farms (Arizona), and Terrebonne Parish (Louisiana). They disbanded after the outbreak of World War II. Tugwell's experiments were called "garden cities" and were the showcase communities of the New Deal that aimed to provide the advantages of rural and city life for low-income families. Three of these towns were built: at Greenbelt, Maryland, close to Washington D.C.; Greenhills, Ohio, 11 miles north of Cincinnati; and Greendale, just west of Milwaukee. Labeled "Tugwell Towns," they had both enthusiastic supporters and vocal critics, and as the latter group increased, Tugwell, frustrated, resigned in November 1936. The next month, Roosevelt transferred the RA to the Department of Agriculture where, renamed as the Farm Security Administration (FSA) in September 1937, it assumed responsibility for the towns. In 1942, it placed them under the Public Housing Authority which, after the war, sold the buildings in Greenhills and Greendale to private individuals, mostly veterans, or to the cities of Cincinnati and Milwaukee. In 1950, veterans bought 1,580 Greenbelt properties and over the next four years the rest were sold at public auctions. Tugwell purchased a Greenbelt home in 1957 and went there to live.

See Also FERA (Federal Emergency Relief Administration) Homesteads

Sources:

Arnold, Joseph L. 1971. *The New Deal in the Suburbs: A History of the Greenbelt Town Program 1935–1945.* Columbus: Ohio State University Press,

Conkin, Paul K. 1959. *Tomorrow a New World: The New Deal Community Program* Ithaca, N.Y.: Cornell University Press.

Cutler, Phoebe. 1985. *The Public Landscape of the New Deal.* New Haven, Conn.: Yale University Press.

Miller, Timothy. 1998. *The Quest for Utopia in Twentieth-Century America.* Syracuse, N.Y.: Syracuse University Press.

Sternsher, Bernard. 1964. *Rexford Tugwell and the New Deal.* Brunswick, N.J.: Rutgers University Press.

Sutton, Robert P. 2004. *Communal Utopias and the American Experience: Secular Utopias, 1824–2000.* Westport, Conn. and London: Praeger.

NEW HOUSE OF ISRAEL. This evangelical Protestant community was established in 1895 on 144 acres between the towns of Livingston and Leggett in Polk County, Texas. The 75 families living there in 1900, calling themselves Israelites, had formerly belonged to an Adventist movement in England that was begun in the late-eighteenth century by Joanna Southcott. They were vegetarians, followed the Mosaic Law, and did not cut their hair.

The men wore beards. Information about the community is sparse, but they led a communal life until leadership problems beset them after the death of their "high priest," and by the early 1920s, the community was abandoned.

See Also The Olive Branch Mission; Shiloh: Church of the Living God; The Woman's Commonwealth

Sources:

Fogarty, Robert S. 1980. *Dictionary of American Communal and Utopian History.* Westport, Conn.: Greenwood Press.

Miller, Timothy. 1998. *The Quest for Utopia in Twentieth-Century America.* Syracuse, N.Y.: Syracuse University Press.

O

THE OLIVE BRANCH MISSION. Rachel Bradley, a Free Methodist, organized this evangelical Protestant community in Chicago in 1876 as an outreach program to help the poor. Made up of adults and children living communally as an extended family, the inner-city mission helped the down-and-out people of West Madison Avenue. In 1984, there were 14 adults and 3 children living there. Families had private rooms for sleeping but meals and worship were communal. Today it is run as a communal rescue mission with housing, food, and clothing for the homeless. It offers Bible studies and a summer day camp for children.

Source:
Miller, Timothy. 1999. *The Quest for Utopia in Twentieth-Century America*. Syracuse, N.Y.: Syracuse University Press.

OLOMPALI RANCH. In 1967, Don McCoy, a wealthy businessman from Sausalito, California, and some friends rented 690 acres near Novato that had a large mansion with a swimming pool. McCoy personally paid all of the expenses for the 26 hippies who lived there enjoying a happy life as the "Chosen Family" that included nude parties by the pool and ever-present marijuana. But business enterprises occupied the colony, such as running a commercial baking operation that shipped hundreds of loaves of bread to San Francisco hippie communes. In 1966, the place became a retreat for the Grateful Dead rock band. In 1969, some residents of Morning Star Ranch, which had run into difficulties with the law in Sonoma County, came to the Olompali Ranch. Not all of the residents approved of McCoy's welcoming this radical group that camped on their land and refused to take proper sanitation measures. When McCoy's family stopped sending him money, the communards were forced to take up collections for food. The rent went into arrears. Twice the police raided the property because of the ubiquitous use of marijuana. In February 1969, the mansion caught fire. That spring commune members began to leave, although some remained and attempted to start an alternative school to bring in money. But after newspapers recounted the death of two little girls by drowning in the swimming pool, the owners of the property evicted the remaining Olompalians.

See Also Black Bear Ranch; McCoy, Don; Morning Star Ranch

Source:

Miller, Timothy. 1999. *The 60s Communes: Hippies and Beyond*. Syracuse, N.Y.: Syracuse University Press.

P

PACKER CORNER (TOTAL LOSS FARM). In 1969, a fatal division developed among the staffers on the New Left organization called the Liberation News Service (LNS) between the radical "Vulgar Marxists" and the more idealistic "Virtuous Caucus." Many of the second group, led by Raymond Mungo, Marty Jezer, and Marshall Bloom, moved to southern Vermont and purchased a $26,000 property in Guilford. The colony was self-sufficient and raised its own livestock, cultivated a garden, and cut firewood. Royalties from Mungo's books, *Famous Long Ago* and *Total Loss Farm,* and from Alicia Bay Laurel's *Living on the Earth,* helped finance the communal treasury, against which any member could write checks without accountability. Most members voluntarily contributed their own money to the fund. The commune published a periodical called the *Green Mountain Post.* Troubles began to appear when the community was inundated with uninvited young hippies and the original residents forced them to leave. After this upheaval only about 13 communards remained. By 1996, this number had shrunk to eight who lived by taking outside jobs.

See Also Montague Farm

Sources:

Miller, Timothy. 1999. *The 60s Communes: Hippies and Beyond.* Syracuse, N.Y.: Syracuse University press.

Mungo, Raymond. 1971. *Total Loss Farm: A Year in the Life.* New York: Bantam.

PADANARAM SETTLEMENT. In 1966, an independent minister, Daniel Wright, led a dozen followers to an 80-acre farm in the rolling hill country of Martin County, Indiana, near the town of Williams. He called the utopian community Padanaram, from the Book of Genesis, and founded a colony based on teamwork and love. The property had only a run-down house without toilet facilities, but soon the hard-working residents constructed a multistory log village that comfortably housed the community's 200 residents. It had a large dining room where men and women ate at separate times. They opened a preschool, kindergarten, and grade school. They grew their own vegetables in an organic farm and raised cattle and hogs. By the late 1970s, Padanaram had developed a profitable logging and sawmill business. All work was gender based. Men logged, ran the mill, drove the trucks, operated the equipment, butchered the livestock, and kept business records. Women cooked, washed, canned, and cleaned the buildings. The sexes worked together at harvest time, however. Seven men governed the village as a board of trustees. Wright described the community in its 1994 publication, *Padanaram Settlement*, as a "twentieth-century communitarian settlement" that concentrated on five principles: the Golden Rule, hold all things in common, distribution according to need, one who has much from him much is required, and those who do not work do not eat. Wright's ideology, "Kingdomism," predicted a future age in which the corrupt present political system will disappear. Meanwhile, Padanaram residents must prepare for this new kingdom. Wright welcomes visitors who might want to attend the community's spring and fall conventions or its annual open house in October.

Sources:

Communities Directory: A Guide to Intentional Communities and Cooperative Living. 2000. Rutledge, Missouri: Fellowship for Intentional Community.

Miller, Timothy. 1999. *The 60s Communes: Hippies and Beyond.* Syracuse, N.Y.: Syracuse University Press.

Padanaram Settlement. 1994. Williams, Ind.: Padanaram Press.

Sutton, Robert P. 2003. *Communal Utopias and the American Experience: Religious Communities, 1732–2000.* Westport, Conn. and London: Praeger.

Wagner, Jon, ed. 1982. *Sex Roles in Contemporary American Communes.* Bloomington: Indiana University Press.

PARAMAHANSA YOGANANDA. Paramahansa Yogananda (1893–1952) was born in India and when his mother died when he was 11 years old, he became a disciple of Sri Yuktesnari Giri. In 1920, Giri ordered him to go to the United States as a missionary. In 1946, he published *Autobiography of a Yogi*, a book that became a best-seller and was issued as a second edition in 1971. The book was a rare example of one written by a yogi that discussed Hindu saints and religions. It gained the guru a large national following and he was able to acquire a number of properties, such as a desert retreat at Twentynine Palms, California, and two churches, one in Long Beach, California, and the other in Phoenix, Arizona. By the time of his death in 1952, he claimed thousands of followers.

See Also Ananda World Brotherhood Village; Walters, James Donald (Swami Kriyananda)

Sources:

Trahair, Richard C.S. 1999. *Utopias and Utopians: An Historical Dictionary.* Westport, Conn.: Greenwood Press.

Walters, Donald. 1977. *The Path: Autobiography of a Western Yogi (Swami Kriyananda).* Nevada City, Calif.: Ananda.

PARAMANANDA, SWAMI. Swami Paramananda (1833–1940) was born in East Bengal, the youngest of 11 children of a wealthy and westernized family. He was trained at a Ramakrishna monastery at Behu and at the age of 21 immigrated to New York City. He gathered together an ashrama, or a religious community, and was its guru, or spiritual teacher. In 1912, he moved to Boston, purchased a house at 1 Queensberry Street, and established another ashrama that included two Harvard professors. In 1923, he founded Ananda Ashrama, a 135-acre estate at La Crescenta, California, just north of Los Angeles. Within five years, the colony had a Cloister, a Community House, and a Temple where eight nuns, one monk, and twenty-five "residents," most of them women. They had a herd of goats and cows, a vegetable garden, and an orchard. Paramananda commuted between the California and Massachusetts ashrams and promoted the Vedanta Society in lectures throughout the United States. He also was the editor of a periodical called *Message of the East.* In the summer of 1933, a fire destroyed part of the California ashrama and afterwards the community declined.

See Also Ananda Ashrama

Sources:

Fogarty, Robert S. 1980. *Dictionary of American Communal and Utopian History.* Westport, Conn.: Greenwood Press.

Miller, Timothy. 1998. *The Quest for Utopia in Twentieth-Century America.* Syracuse, N.Y.: Syracuse University Press.

Vesey, Laurence. 1973. *The Communal Experience: Anarchist and Mystical Countercultures in America.* New York: Harper and Row.

PEACE MISSION. The founder of Peace Mission, a charismatic leader known as Father Divine (George Baker), was born in 1879 into a poor laborer's family in Rockville, Maryland. Before coming to Harlem in 1915, he was an itinerant preacher in Baltimore and Valdosta, Georgia, and claimed that he was God's spokesman. In 1919, he moved to Sayville, Long Island, where he gave lavish dinners at his home that attracted large crowds from both Harlem and Newark, New Jersey. His sermons stressed a Christian duty to aid the poor and the outcast. After whites joined the crowds he changed his name to Father Divine. In 1933, he opened his first Peace Mission in Harlem and his followers lived communally in Divine Peace Mission Cooperatives. Eventually, the Peace Mission included 25 restaurants, 10 barber shops, 2 groceries, and other businesses. By the mid 1930s, he had purchased properties in other cities where he opened Houses of Prayer. He claimed a half-million followers of both races. His message was simple and focused on a few basic points: all members should live communally, promote racial integration, and condemn alcohol, tobacco, and cosmetics. In 1942, he moved the headquarters of the mission from New York to Philadelphia. After World War II, the Peace Mission changed as Father Divine reduced his direct participation and his assistants took over. They erected a complicated administrative hierarchy with special names and functions. With this bloated bureaucracy and lack of charismatic leadership, the membership declined rapidly and by 1950 only the missions in Harlem, Newark, and Philadelphia remained open. Father Divine died in New York City on September 10, 1965.

See Also Divine, Father

Sources:

Brunham, Kenneth. 1979. *God Comes to America: Father Divine and the Peace Mission Movement.* Boston: Lambeth Press.

Fogarty, Robert S. 1980. *Dictionary of American Communal and Utopian History.* Westport, Conn.: Greenwood Press.

Harris, Sara, with the assistance of Harriet Crittendon. 1953. *Father Divine.* New York: Doubleday.

Watts, Jill. 1992. *God, Harlem U.S.A.: The Father Divine Story.* Berkeley: University of California Press.

Weisbrot, Robert. 1983. *Father Divine and the Struggle for Racial Equality.* Urbana: University of Illinois Press.

PENN-CRAFT. This was a nongovernmental resettlement community for unemployed coal miners founded by the Quakers near Uniontown, Pennsylvania, during the Great Depression. It was located on the 200-acre Craft farm and was named for the state and for the family. Penn-Craft was funded with money from the American Friends Service Committee. Two directors of the New Deal Division of Subsistence Homesteads colony at nearby Norvelt came to direct the Quaker project. Resident families were carefully interviewed to be sure they were willing to undergo job training and eventually own their own homes. Initially, the residents built 50 homes using nearby materials. They also put up a cooperative store, as well as a knitting mill, and other cooperative industries. The community provided activities through a number of social clubs and organizations. The experiment worked so well that in 1946, the Quakers constructed 15 more homes on land connected to Penn-Craft.

Sources:

Hoagland, Alison K., and Margaret M. Mulrooney. 1991. *Norvelt and Penn-Craft, Pennsylvania: Subsistence-Homestead Communities of the 1930s.* Washington,

D.C.: Historic American Buildings Survey/Historic American Engineering Record, America's Industrial Heritage Project, National Park Service.

Miller, Timothy. 1998. *The Quest for Utopia in Twentieth-Century America.* Syracuse, N.Y.: Syracuse University Press.

PEOPLES TEMPLE. The Peoples Temple was a tragic experiment in Christian communalism that became horrifyingly perverted and ended with the suicide/murder of more than 900 individuals in Jonestown, Guyana, in November 1978. James Warren Jones, its charismatic leader, was born in 1931 in Lynn, Indiana, and even as a child preached to his playmates. In the late 1950s, he organized the Peoples Temple and promoted Christian brotherhood and helping the poor. He moved the the group to Ukiah, California, in 1965. The commune soon became noticed for its social service programs for the poor and for its racial integration. By the late 1960s, Jones had opened 19 communal homes for the elderly and poor in San Francisco. In 1974, he started a commune in Jonestown, and three years later he and his followers moved there to escape criticism that they were misusing the donations that many elderly members had given to the Temple. In November 1978, Congressman Leo J. Ryan went to Jonestown to investigate charges of misconduct. On November 18, after Ryan was murdered, Jones led his followers in a prerehearsed "revolutionary suicide."

See Also Jones, James Warren

Sources:

Fogarty, Robert S. 1980. *Dictionary of American Communal and Utopian History.* Westport, Conn.: Greenwood Press.

King, Martin. 1993. *Preacher of Death.* Melbourne: Penguin.

Klineman, George, Sherman Butler, and David Conn. 1980. *The Cult That Died: The Tragedy of Jim Jones and the Peoples Temple.* New York: Putnam.

McCormick, Maaga, and Catherine Wessinger. 1988. *Hearing the Voices of Jonestown.* Syracuse, N.Y.: Syracuse University Press.

Miller, Timothy. 1998. *The Quest for Utopia in Twentieth-Century America.* Syracuse, N.Y.: Syracuse University Press.

Reston, James, Jr. 1981. *Our Father Who Art in Hell: The Life and Death of Jim Jones.* New York: Times Books.

Trahair, Richard C.S. 1999. *Utopias and Utopians: An Historical Dictionary.* Westport, Conn.: Greenwood Press.

PISGAH GRANDE. In 1894, Finis E. Yoakum, a Los Angeles physician, opened a Pentecostal mission for the poor called Pisgah Home. It had a store that dispensed free food and clothing and gained a reputation as a place for the homeless and for faith healing. In 1914, he purchased a 3,200-acre ranch near Santa Susana, on the Ventura-Los Angeles county line and called it Pisgah Grande. Its 300 or so residents included people from the Los Angeles mission as well as farmers, professionals, and artists. They lived mostly in shacks but survived until Yoakum's death in 1920, when his successor, James Cheek, relocated the colony to Pikesville, Tennessee. Although the buildings at Pisgah Grande gradually disappeared, the Pisgah Home in Los Angeles survived until the late 1990s.

Sources:

Fogarty, Robert S. 1980. *Dictionary of American Communal and Utopian History.* Westport, Conn.: Greenwood Press.

Kagan, Paul. 1975. *New World Utopias: A Photographic History of the Search for Community.* New York: Penguin.

Miller, Timothy. 1998. *The Quest for Utopia in Twentieth-Century America.* Syracuse, N.Y.: Syracuse University Press.

POINT LOMA (UNIVERSAL BROTHERHOOD AND THEOSOPHICAL SOCIETY). In 1897, Katherine Tingley (1847–1929) founded the most famous Theosophical community at this 330-acre site on a peninsula close to San Diego. It became the headquarters of the Universal Brotherhood and Theosophical Society. By 1910, 200 adults and 300 children resided in the community, valued at over $300,000 and consisting of three main buildings, bungalows, an amphitheater that seated 2,500, gardens, and orchards. Tingley required a $500 admissions fee and charged a monthly rent. Members were allowed to keep private investments and own property outside the colony. All land and buildings, however, were in Tingley's name as trustee and she was Point Loma's "Leader and Official Head" for life. Women did domestic chores and made the simple uniforms worn by every resident. The men raised avocados, oranges, and honey, all of which they sold in San Diego. Communal meals were taken in a refectory where adults and children sat in separate rooms. Tingley ran a community school called Raja Yoga or Kingly Union, and children were taught spiritual development, culture, and academics. Most students were not members of the colony and paid a tuition that sometimes ran as high as $4,000. In 1901, Tingley purchased the San Diego opera house and renamed it the Isis Theater and in it members of Point Loma performed Greek tragedies and dramas. Despite generous financial donations by famous Americans such as sporting goods magnate Albert Spalding and Florida citrus tycoon William Chase Temple, the community's expenses by the 1920s vastly exceeded its income. At the time of Tingley's death in an automobile accident in July 1929, it owed creditors over $400,000. The stock market crash of the same year and the ensuing Great Depression made Point Loma's financial situation so critical that it was forced by creditors in 1940 to sell all the real estate except the central compound. During World War II, the army took over that facility as a barracks. Tingley's successor, Gottfried de Purucker, liquidated all assets and moved with a few followers to Covina, California. In 1950, the national headquarters for the Universal Brotherhood and Theosophical Society moved to Pasadena.

See Also Tingley, Katherine Augusta Westcott

Sources:

Fogarty, Robert S. 1980. *Dictionary of American Communal and Utopian History.* Westport, Conn.: Greenwood Press.

Greenwalt, Emmett A. 1978. *The Point Loma Community in California: 1897–1942—A Theosophical Experiment.* Berkeley: University of California Press, 1955. Rev. ed. Published as *California Utopia: Point Loma: 1897–1942.* San Diego: Point Loma Publications.

Hine, Robert V. 1983. *California's Utopian Colonies.* Berkeley: University of California Press.

Miller, Timothy. 1998. *The Quest for Utopia in Twentieth-Century America.* Syracuse, N.Y.: Syracuse University Press.

Sutton, Robert P. 2003. *Communal Utopias and the American Experience: Religious Communities, 1732–2000.* Westport, Conn. and London: Praeger.

PRESTON. Preston was one of four spiritualist colonies that appeared in the last half of the nineteenth century (the others being Lily Dale/Cassadaga, The Societas Fraternia, and The Land of Shalam) and lasted into the twentieth century. It was a small community founded by Emily Preston two miles north of Cloverdale, California, the site of the last Icarian community called Icaria Speranza (1882–1885). She moved there from San Francisco with her husband, H. L. Preston, in 1869 and purchased 1,500 acres. Soon more than 100 individuals arrived and lived in small shacks with the community operating a school and water supply. Mrs. Preston preached the ideal of a "Religion of Inspiration" in the communal church called the "Free Pilgrims Covenant." In the 1940s, a handful of spiritualists were still using the church for meditation, and an artists' colony flourished there until a fire destroyed most of the buildings in 1988.

See Also The Land of Shalam; Lily Dale and Cassadaga; The Societas Fraternia

Source:

Miller, Timothy. 1998. *The Quest for Utopia in Twentieth-Century America.* Syracuse, N.Y.: Syracuse University Press.

PROJECTS ONE, TWO, AND ARTAUD. These three artist communities were founded in large San Francisco warehouses. Project One and Project Artaud were started in 1971 and provided living quarters, studios, food co-ops, and computer centers for the members. Project Two, begun the following year, had the same facilities but added some light industries such as a print shop. Project One's large building had public toilet facilities and showers. The resident artists paid a small rent. All three communities were informally governed by monthly meetings and by boards of directors. It was estimated that 650 artists lived in Project One. Project Artaud housed 125 residents. They all had a variety of artistic pursuits plus open sexual experimentation. There was a high turnover of membership in all the colonies. Project One lasted the longest, into the late 1980s.

Source:

Miller, Timothy. 1999. *The 60s Communes: Hippies and Beyond*. Syracuse, N.Y.: Syracuse University Press.

PURNELL, BENJAMIN F. Benjamin F. Purnell (1861–1927), a member of the House of David colony at Benton Harbor, Michigan, was born in Greenup City, Kentucky. Possessing a rudimentary education, he became an itinerate minister in Ohio and Indiana. Having married a Kentucky girl in 1877, in 1880 he married another woman without obtaining a divorce. In 1892, he joined the New House of Israel and three years later became its guiding personality as the "seventh messenger" who would supervise the gathering of Israel. The following year, the community purchased land east of Benton Harbor and started to erect communal buildings such as the Ark and Bethlehem, residences, a school and a print shop. Purnell called the community The House of David and its celibate members awaited the 1905 millennium predicted by him. In 1904, he went to Australia and recruited 85 new converts. Even though the millennium failed to happen, some 385 colonists continued to live there and by 1907 the community purchased more land and put up more buildings. That year, Purnell opened the Eden Springs Amusement Park with carnival rides, games, stage shows, and a zoo. In the 1920s, the colony had a baseball team well known for wearing long beards. But in 1926, the state of Michigan arrested him and charged him with fraud and seducing women who were under age. In 1926, during a protracted trial, Purnell died.

See Also The House of David

Sources:

Fogarty, Robert S. 1980. *Dictionary of American Communal and Utopian History*. Westport, Conn.: Greenwood Press.

Miller, Timothy. 1998. *The Quest for Utopia in Twentieth-Century America*. Syracuse, N.Y.: Syracuse University Press.

Trahair, Richard C. S. 1999. *Utopias and Utopians: An Historical Dictionary*. Westport, Conn.: Greenwood Press.

Q

QUARRY HILL. This community was an artists' colony founded in 1946 by Irving Fiske and his wife, Barbara, on an old farm near Rochester, Vermont, and it was still a vital community as of 2004. Irving, a playwright, and Barbara, a painter, encouraged friends to join them, erect houses, and develop a community. The main focus of the colony was opposition to the current methods of child rearing and to all corporal punishment of children. They formed an advocacy group called "Free the Kids!" By the late 1970, when young hippies moved into its community center, the number of residents reached about 100. Although communal, families had private meals. They built a small dormitory to accommodate visitors. In 2000, it advertised itself in the *Communities Directory* as being "Vermont's oldest and largest alternative community...."

Sources:

Communities Directory: A Guide to Intentional Communities and Cooperative Living. 2000. Langley, Washington: Fellowship for Intentional Community.

Miller, Timothy. 1998. *The Quest for Utopia in Twentieth-Century America*. Syracuse, N.Y.: Syracuse University Press.

R

RANCHO RAJNEESH. In 1981, the "rich man's guru," Bhagwan Shree Rajneesh, founded a communal utopia on 64,229 acres close to Antelope, Oregon. He was born in 1931 in Kuchwada, India, and raised by his grandparents. He took an active part in the resistance to British control of India. At the age of 29, he was appointed a professor of philosophy at Hitkarini College in Jabalpur, a post he resigned in 1966 to open a meditation camp south of Bombay at the outskirts of Poona. The community attracted over 2,000 educated, middle-class disciples as permanent residents. Seeking medical treatment, he came to the United States in 1981 and established Rancho Rajneesh. It had a network of paved roads, prefabricated homes, warehouses, a sewage system, electricity, and water. The following year, he laid out an administrative center and constructed a two-acre greenhouse. In July, the community sponsored an inaugural commemoration of its founding and put up 2,000 tents for visitors. By 1985, the 4,000 residents of Rancho Rajneesh had an airplane, a satellite television station, and a gambling operation. But in October 1985, everything turned negative. The guru was arrested in North Carolina for violating immigration laws, given a 10-year suspended sentenced, and fined $400,000. He put the Oregon community up for sale for $40 million. Bhagwan Shree Rajneesh then left the country and his followers scattered to other places.

Sources:

Carter, Lewis F. 1990. *Charisma and Control in Rajneeshpuram: The Role of Shared Values in the Creation of a Community.* Cambridge: Cambridge University Press.

Mullan, Bob. 1983. *Life as Laughter: Following Bhagwan Shree Rajneesh.* London: Routledge and Kegan Paul.

Trahair, Richard C. S. 1999. *Utopias and Utopians: An Historical Dictionary.* Westport, Conn.: Greenwood Press.

REALITY CONSTRUCTION COMPANY. This community was the hippie colony constructed in 1969 a few hundred yards from Morning Star East by Max Finstein, cofounder of New Buffalo, on land owned by Michael Duncan near Taos, New Mexico. Led by two black adult males, the 25 residents, mostly radicals from New York City and San Francisco, built adobe structures like those in Morning Star East. The primitive colony had no running water or electricity. The communards were suspicious of unwanted visitors and an armed person met them at the gate of the community and refused them entrance. Their goal was to prepare a camp for anticipated armed conflict with outsiders. Michael Duncan, upset with what was going on at Reality, closed it down in 1972.

See Also Morning Star East; New Buffalo

Sources:

Gardner, Hugh. 1978. *The Children of Prosperity: Thirteen Modern American Communes.* New York: St. Martin's.

Houriet, Robert. 1971. *Getting Back Together.* New York: Avon.

Miller, Timothy. 1999. *The 60s Communes: Hippies and Beyond.* Syracuse, N.Y.: Syracuse University Press.

REBA PLACE FELLOWSHIP. In 1957, John Miller, a Mennonite biblical scholar at Goshen College, Indiana, founded the Reba Place Fellowship modeled on the Hutterites *Bruderhof* communities, but placed in an urban setting. He hoped to create a close-knit group of families and friends that would enable the residents to overcome the isolation of the "lonely crowd." He and his "pioneers" bought a house located in Evanston, Illinois, at 727 Reba Place. By 1987, the community had expanded to own 21 homes with a membership of 120 communards. In 2000, it had "forty-some members and children" living in in "large multifamily homes and apartment buildings," according to the *Communities Directory.* Most adults were vegetarians. Members had outside jobs but deposited their earnings in a communal fund. All members of the colony were committed to extensive social service programs. Reba Place Fellowship has been in contact with Koinonia Farm, the Bruderhof, the Sojourners Community, and the Forest River Hutterite community. A rural imitation of Reba Place was founded in 1971 called the Plow Creek Fellowship in Tiskilwa, Illinois. Internal disagreements appeared over the role of women, because the highest office in the community was always held by a man. After they started to admit noncommunal members, some original residents left the colony and by the 1990s only half of the Reba Place residents were living communally. In 2000, they advertised their ministries as including a shelter for the homeless, care of refugees from Cambodia and

Central America, low-income housing, personal counseling, and a peace witness program.

See Also Bruderhof; Hutterite Brethren; Koinonia Farm; Sojourners Community.

Sources:

Communities Directory: A Guide to Intentional Communities and Cooperative Living. 2000. Rutledge, Missouri: Fellowship for Intentional Community.

Jackson, David, and Neta Jackson. 1987. *Glimpses of Glory: Thirty Years of Community: The Story of Reba Place Fellowship.* Elgin, Ill.: Brethren Press.

Miller, Timothy. 1998. *The Quest for Utopia in Twentieth-Century America.* Syracuse, N.Y.: Syracuse University Press.

RED ROCKERS. In the spring of 1969, some classmates at Beverly Hills High School started a hippie commune at Farisita, Colorado, near the Libre community. They constructed only one structure, a 60-foot geodesic dome, in which the 30 members of the commune lived and worked. There was no privacy. The main activity was to put on musical and theatrical events. It dissolved in early 1970.

See Also Libre

Source:

Miller, Timothy. 1999. *The 60s Communes: Hippies and Beyond.* Syracuse, N.Y.: Syracuse University Press.

RENAISSANCE COMMUNITY/BROTHERHOOD OF THE SPIRIT.
In 1968, when 17-year-old Daniel Metelica, later known as Michael Rapunzel, returned to his hometown of Leyden, Massachusetts, after participating in the "Summer of Love" at Haight-Ashbury, he organized a small group of hippies to build a treehouse, which the neighbors burned down. Then he and about a half-dozen young people rented a small bunkhouse in a summer camp near the town of Heath. A dozen individuals were soon crammed into the structure and lived without out heat, toilets, and cooking facilities. By the 1970s, they called themselves the Brotherhood of the Spirit, but in 1974 decided to name the colony the Renaissance Community. By then they had relocated to land in Warwick and about 350 members lived in a large dormitory and worked at jobs in the town or on nearby farms. Their economic expansion was remarkable. They formed a rock band called the "Spirit Flesh" and gave concerts throughout New England. They had the Renaissance Recording Studio, a business called the Rockets that converted old school buses into recreational vehicles, a Renaissance Builders, a Renaissance Excavating Company, and a Top-notch Cleaning Service. In the town of Turners Falls, they opened a plumbing and refrigeration business, a grocery store, a natural foods restaurant, a pizza parlor, and a youth center. Near the town of Gill was the 2001 Center, a self-sufficient community home with a school

heated by solar panels. They had a solar greenhouse and a fenced garden where they grew organic food. They opened a Renaissance Greeting Card Company that distributed cards wholesale to other stores. Most members were in their twenties and, although they approved of a nuclear family, only five couples were legally married. All members took a vow of poverty and donated their assets to the community. They allowed beer and wine but banned drugs. A variety of communal structures appeared, from large hotel-like barracks to small cabins and tepees. Some Renaissance members actively participated in outside activities. One individual was the town clerk of Gill, and Metelica ran for Selectman in Turners Falls. They invited visitors to come to their dances at the 2001 Center. In 1995, the group described itself as located on a 90-acre tract near Turners Falls "on a hill with beautiful views of the rolling farm country of the Connecticut Rover Valley." Shortly afterwards, however, troubles beset the community. The proscription against drugs lapsed and it gained a reputation for drug dealing. Metelica's leadership was challenged by some members and they began leaving the community disillusioned. It was not listed in the 2000 edition of *Communities Directory.*

Sources:

Communes Directory: A Guide to Cooperative Living. 1995. Langley, Washington: Fellowship for Intentional Communities.

McLaughlin, Corinne, and Gordon Davidson. 1985. *Builders of the Dawn: Community Lifestyles in a Changing World.* Walpole, N.H.: Stillpoint Publishing.

Miller, Timothy. 1999. *The 60s Communes: Hippies and Beyond.* Syracuse, N.Y.: Syracuse University Press.

Popenoe, Cris, and Oliver Popenoe. 1984. *Seeds of Tomorrow: New Age Communities That Work.* San Francisco: Harper and Row.

Sutton, Robert P. 2004. *Communal Utopias and the American Experience: Secular Communities, 1824–2000.* Westport, Conn. and London: Praeger.

RIKER, WILLIAM E. Riker (1873–1952) was born in Oakdale, California, and worked as a mechanic in San Francisco after receiving only a fourth-grade education. In 1918, he claimed to have received divine messages and became a self-proclaimed street revivalist and the sole authority for what he called the Perfect Christian Divine Way. He was a racist who believed in white supremacy. In 1919, he founded the Holy City in the Santa Cruz Mountains, where 30 disciples lived in crude cabins. He published a monthly newspaper, the *Enlightener,* and books entitled *The Philosophy of the Nerves Revealed* and *World Peace and How to Have It.* He ran unsuccessfully for governor in 1937. At various times, he was charged with criminal acts such as murder, tax evasion, and fraud. He became a Roman Catholic before his death.

See Also Holy City

Sources:

Fogarty, Robert S. 1980. *Dictionary of American Communal and Utopian History.* Westport, Conn.: Greenwood Press.

Hine, Robert. 1983. *California's Utopian Colonies.* Berkeley: University of California Press.

Trahair, Richard C. S. 1999. *Utopias and Utopians: An Historical Dictionary.* Westport, Conn.: Greenwood Press.

THE ROCHESTER FOLK ART GUILD (EAST HILL FARM). In 1967, Louise March, a student of G. I. Gurdjieff, organized an arts community at Naples, New York, on a 318-acre farm. A dozen residents created art works in wood, iron, glass, and fabrics. By 1945, 45 adults had joined as resident members along with 12 children. They made little money but supplemented their income from the sale of their craft items by selling grapes raised on the farm. Some members worked outside the community for extra money.

Sources:

Miller, Timothy. 1999. *The 60s Communes: Hippies and Beyond.* Syracuse, N.Y.: Syracuse University Press.

Popenoe, Cris, and Oliver Popenoe. 1984. *Seeds of Tomorrow: New Age Communes That Work.* San Francisco: Harper and Row.

ROSENTHAL, HERMAN. Herman Rosenthal (1843–1917) was born in Friedrichsstadt, Russia, and was a founder of the Sicily Island colony and a resident of the Woodbine colony. Working as a printer in the Ukraine, he learned German, Russian, and Hebrew and translated Russian poems into German. At the age of 27, his own poems appeared under the title of *Gedichte,* meaning "poems." In Kiev, he published a daily newspaper, the *Zarya.* When the pogroms began in 1881, he immigrated to the United States and joined the Sicily Island community. In the late 1880s, he published *Der Yidisher Farmer,* or the Yiddish farmer. In 1891, he joined the industrial-agricultural community at Woodbine, New Jersey. James Hill, the railroad tycoon, sent him to Japan, China, and Korea to explore the possibilities of railroad building. In 1894, he moved to New York City and worked in the Immigration Bureau at Ellis Island. After 1898, he was head of the Slavonic Department of the New York Public Library and served as the editor of the *Jewish Encyclopedia*'s Department of Russian Jewry.

See Also Woodbine

Sources:

Brandes, Joseph. 1971. *Immigrants to Freedom Jewish Communities in Rural New Jersey since 1882.* Philadelphia: University of Pennsylvania Press.

Eisenberg, Ellen. 1995. *Jewish Agricultural Colonies in New Jersey 1882–1920.* Syracuse, N.Y.: Syracuse University Press.

Herscher, Uri D. 1981. *Jewish Agricultural Utopias in America, 1880–1910.* Detroit: Wayne State University Press.

Fogarty, Robert S. 1980. *Dictionary of American Communal and Utopian History.* Westport, Conn.: Greenwood Press.
Sutton, Robert P. 2003. *Communal Utopias and the American Experience: Religious Communities, 1732–2000.* Westport, Conn. and London: Praeger.

ROSE VALLEY. This art colony was founded in 1901 on 100 acres outside Philadelphia by William Lightfoot Price, a famous architect, and Horace Traubel, a bohemian disciple of both Walt Whitman and Henry George's single-tax theory. Price had started a single-tax community at Arden, Delaware, the previous year and because of its success, he and his business partner, Hawley McLanahan, purchased a number of vacant mill buildings and homes at the Pennsylvania site. In April, he incorporated the community as the Rose Valley Association and sold stock to begin craft industries there. Members would rent housing and some could purchase tracts of land at the edge of the colony. Traubel was one of the early members of the community and in the fall of 1903, he ran the Rose Valley Print Shop in Philadelphia to put out their magazine, *The Artsman.* Rose Valley attracted students and faculty from Swarthmore College. They opened a furniture shop, a ceramics shop, and a book bindery, all powered by old water mills on the property. One of the mills was refurbished to serve as a theater they called Artsman's Hall. The community was democratic, run by monthly meetings called Folk Mores. They enjoyed a lively social life of concerts, plays, and lectures. But economic problems appeared. There were not enough jobs for all the resident artisans. The furniture was too expensive to market. By 1907, members started to leave, the shops closed down, and the following year, the association dissolved. In 1910, McLanahan's father-in-law, Charles T. Schoen, purchased all the land and buildings, except one known as the Guild Hall, which survived as a place for social and cultural life, but not communal living. Traubel continued to run the Rose Valley press until he died in 1921.

Sources:

Ayres, William, ed. 1983. *A Poor Sort of Heaven, a Good Sort of Earth: The Rose Valley Arts and Crafts Experiment.* Chadds Ford, Pa.: Brandywine Rover Museum.
Cumming, Elizabeth, and Wendy Kaplan. 1991. *The Arts and Crafts Movement.* New York: Thames and Hudson.
Karsner, David. 1919. *Horace Traubel: His Life and Work.* New York: Egmont Arens.
Miller, Timothy. 1998. *The Quest for Utopia in Twentieth-Century America.* Syracuse, N.Y.: Syracuse University Press.
Shi, David. 1985. *The Simple Life: Plain Living and High Thinking in American Culture.* New York: Oxford University Press.

ROYCROFT. This semicommunal corporation of artisans who shared its profits was established by Elbert Green Hubbbard, a wealthy salesman for the Larkin Soap Company. In 1895, he founded Roycroft in East Aurora, New

York, and soon had between 300 and 500 members. At least as many non-members were hired to work its farm, bank, printing plant, book bindery, blacksmiths shop, and furniture factory. The colony had a hotel for visitors. The variety of craft products included copperware, stained glass, wrought iron, food specialties, and handmade paper works. Although Hubbard owned all the property, and so the economic aspect of Roycroft was not communal, its commitment to communal living was seen in its phalanstery, the Roycroft Inn, communal meals, meetings, and recreation. Most members were committed to socialism and progressive reforms. After Hubbard and his wife died aboard the *Lusitania,* sunk by Germany in April 1915, the Roycrofters became exclusively a commercial organization, selling handicrafts and publishing the magazine *The Roycrofter* until the demise of the business in 1939.

See Also Hubbard, Elbert Green

Sources:

Champney, Freeman. 1968. *Art and Glory: The Story of Elbert Hubbard.* New York: Crown.

Fogarty, Robert S. 1980. *Dictionary of American Communal and Utopian History.* Westport, Conn.: Greenwood Press.

Ludwig, Coy L. 1983. *The Arts and Crafts Movement in New York State, 1890s–1920s.* Hamilton, N.Y.: Gallery Association of New York State.

Miller, Timothy. 1998. *The Quest for Utopia in Twentieth-Century America.* Syracuse, N.Y.: Syracuse University Press.

Shay, Felix. 1926. *Elbert Hubbard of East Aurora.* New York: William H. Wise.

RUSKIN. Julius A. Wayland (1854–1912), the principle influence on the founding and shaping of Ruskin, was a newspaper editor and publisher of the nationally circulated socialist weekly *The Coming Nation.* In 1894, he announced in that publication that he was opening a socialist cooperative 50 miles west of Nashville, Tennessee. By August, Wayland, his family, and 40 people had arrived. A year later, 120 residents were there, and by 1896 the community numbered 250 residents. Wayland admitted only white Americans. There were no Jews or Catholics at Ruskin. Most members were professionals or skilled artisans with only about 15 percent being day workers. In order to join the colony a person had to pass an examination on socialism and show how socialist views had impacted their lives. Even so, admissions were lenient and almost anyone could become a member. The colonists chose Wayland as the first president and voted him the authority to own and run a print shop to publish *The Coming Nation.* All work at Ruskin was communal, as were meals, housing, and medical treatment. Members purchased clothing in the communal store with work vouchers. When the water supply at the original site of the colony proved unsafe, some members moved to another location five miles away called Cave Mills. It lasted about a year. Because of disputes with some Ruskinites, Wayland left in the summer of 1895 and stared a new publication called the *Appeal to Reason,* which eventually exceeded the circulation of *The Coming Nation.* Although Ruskin prospered economically, fierce internal fights erupted over marriage, religion, and education. After a number of court battles, the colony was dissolved in 1899 and its assets were sold at auction. Some colonists combined their resources and purchased these assets. Then they joined a group of socialist called the American Settlers Association who had founded the Duke Colony near Waycross, Georgia. They renamed the Georgia colony Ruskin and the two groups briefly merged. But internal factionalism, disease, and economic difficulties forced the colony to sell the printing press, land, and buildings and close down in 1902. At that point, Wayland merged *The Coming Nation* with his *Appeal to Reason* and operated the weekly until his death by suicide in 1912. Ruskin was the inspiration for colonies at Niksur and Kinderlou, a Ruskin Commongood Society that financed community improvements. Some former members of Ruskin founded Ruskin, Florida, in 1906. Some Ruskinites joined the single-tax colony at Fairhope. Still others went to the socialist cooperative at Burley in the Puget Sound.

See Also Burley Colony (Cooperative Brotherhood); Fairhope; Wayland, Julius A.

Sources:

Brundage, W. Fitzhugh. 1996. *A Socialist Utopia in the New South: The Ruskin Colonies in Tennessee and Georgia 1894–1901.* Urbana and Chicago: University of Illinois Press.

Fogarty, Robert S. 1980. *Dictionary of American Communal and Utopian History.* Westport, Conn.: Greenwood Press.

Miller, Timothy. 1998. *The Quest for Utopia in Twentieth-Century America.* Syracuse, N.Y.: Syracuse University Press.

Oved, Yaacov. 1987. *Two Hundred Years of American Communes.* New Brunswick, N.J. and Oxford: Transaction.

Sutton, Robert P. 2004. *Communal Utopias and the American Experience: Secular Communities, 1824–2000.* Westport, Conn. and London: Praeger.

RUSSELL, CHARLES TAZE. Charles Taze Russell (1852–1916) was one of the founders, in 1904, of the Bethel Home community, better known as the Jehovah's Witnesses, along with Joseph Franklin Rutherford (1869–1942). It was Russell who kept alive the ideas of the Adventist Millerites, some of whom were disillusioned when the predicted date of the Second Coming of October 22, 1844, failed to happen. By the 1870s, Russell was one of the most prominent preachers of an Adventist eschatology that specified 1914 as the date for the end of the world. He rejected the Trinity and the divinity of Christ and condemned military service and blood transfusions. Russell eventually established the headquarters of the Jehovah's Witnesses in Brooklyn, New York, where its officers lived communally.

See Also Bethel Home

Sources:

Harrison, Barbara Gruzzuti. 1978. *Visions of Glory: A History and a Memory of Jehovah's Witnesses.* New York: Simon and Schuster.

Miller, Timothy. *The Quest for Utopia in Twentieth-Century America.* Syracuse, N.Y.: Syracuse University Press.

Penton, M. James. 1985. *Apocalypse Delayed: The Story of Jehovah's Witnesses.* Toronto: University of Toronto Press.

Trahair, Richard C.S. 1999. *Utopias and Utopians: An Historical Dictionary.* Westport, Conn.: Greenwood Press.

S

SAN FRANCISCO ZEN CENTER. In 1959, Zen master Shunryu Suzuki came to San Francisco and founded a Zen temple that attracted a large white American following. These American Zennists then opened the San Francisco Zen Center inside the Suzuki temple and in 1969 they moved to a separate headquarters in the city. The master moved to the new center and stayed there as its teacher until his death in 1971. His successor, Richard Baker, guided the community until he resigned in 1983 and relocated to Santa Fe to start a new Zen community called Dharma Sangha. Baker then went to Colorado and opened the Creston Mountain Zen Center.

See Also Kwan Um Zen School; Zen Center of Los Angeles

Sources:

Miller, Timothy. 1999. *The 60s Communes: Hippies and Beyond.* Syracuse, N.Y.: Syracuse University Press.

Rawlinson, Andrew. 1997. *The Book of Enlightened Masters: Western Teachers in Eastern Traditions.* Chicago: Open Court.

Tworkov, Helen. 1994. *Zen in America.* New York: Kodansha International.

SANDFORD, FRANK. Frank Sandford (1862–1948) was born in Bowdoinham, Maine, and attended Bates College, graduating in 1888. He then enrolled in Cobb Divinity School and was a pastor in Free Baptist churches at Topsham, Maine, and Great Falls, New Hampshire. After receiving a revelation in 1893, he announced that he was another Elijah and would build a temple called Shiloh: Church of the Living God, at a site between Lewiston and Brunswick, Maine. Daily prayer meetings were held at a communal center and the colony's 300 members occupied a prayer tower. By 1900, Sandford had overseen the completion of an imposing temple. That year he was charged with manslaughter when a child died at the community but this charge was withdrawn. In 1905, he was convicted of manslaughter in leading a pilgrimage of members to missionary sites in Africa in which some of them died. He served just over six years in prison. He then returned to Shiloh and led the colony until it was dissolved in 1920. He died in Hobart, New York.

See Also Shiloh: Church of the Living God

Sources:

Fogarty, Robert S. 1980. *Dictionary of American Communal and Utopian History.* Westport, Conn.: Greenwood Press.

Miller, Timothy. 1998. *The Quest for Utopia in Twentieth-Century America.* Syracuse, N.Y.: Syracuse University Press.

SANDHILL FARM. Sandhill Farm is one of a number of communities that appeared in the 1970s founded on principles similar to the Twin Oaks community. The farm's main tenets were nonviolence, opposition to sexism, and environmental protection. In 2000, it was located on 135 acres near Rutlegde, Missouri, close to the Amana colony and was dedicated to back-to-the-land living in producing sorghum, molasses, and honey. Its membership was deliberately small, numbering just six adults and two children in 2000. They practiced self-sufficiency in growing their own food, running the farm, home healing, and home schooling. They lived communally in sharing daily meetings, and in sharing income and vehicles. They are active in recycling, community theater, and hospice assistance.

Sources:

Communities Directory: A Guide to Intentional Communities and Cooperative Living. 2000. Rutledge, Missouri: Fellowship for Intentional Community.

Miller, Timothy. 1999. *The 60s Communes: Hippies and Beyond.* Syracuse, N.Y.: Syracuse University Press.

SCHOOL OF LIVING. In 1936, Ralph Borsodi founded the School of Living at his home on seven acres near Suffern, New York, where he had moved from Manhattan with his family in 1919. After the failure of his federally funded community homestead project at Dayton, Ohio, in 1936, he became determined to build a self-sufficient community without federal assistance or control. He organized two-acre homesteads and a common land area called Bayard Lane near his Suffern home and called it the School of Living. Residents were paid low wages while working on their homesteads in return for guaranteed, year-round jobs. They were taught practical skills that enabled them to operate their homesteads. In 1940, Borsodi resigned as director when some residents complained about his dictatorial administrative style. He eventually abandoned interest in communal homesteads and instead turned to research and writing about monetary theories until his death in 1977. In 1945, Borsodi sold the School of Living to one of the residents.

See Also Borsodi, Ralph; Melbourne Village

Sources:
Fogarty, Robert S. 1980. *Dictionary of American Communal and Utopian History.* Westport, Conn.: Greenwood Press.
Miller, Timothy. 1998. *The Quest for Utopia in Twentieth-Century America.* Syracuse, N.Y.: Syracuse University Press.
Shi, David. 1985. *The Simple Life: Plain Living and High Thinking in America Culture.* New York: Oxford University Press.

SENDER BARAYON, RAMÓN. In the late 1980s, Sender (?–?) was the founder and editor of a newsletter of critics of the Bruderhof. It was called *KIT,* or "Keep In Touch," and consisted mostly of letters to the editor. He was born in Spain where his father was a noted writer and affiliated with the anarchist communes of Catalonia. He came with his parents to the United States at the age of four and at the age of sixteen, he met the great-granddaughter of John Humphrey Noyes at the Oneida Community. After his marriage to her, Sender and his wife joined the Bruderhof in 1957 but he did not remain there. His wife and their daughter, however, did become permanent members. Afterwards, he only saw his daughter once before she died of cancer at the age of 33. Sender joined the Morning Star Ranch as one of its first residents and later moved to live at Wheeler's Ranch and other communities.

See Also Bruderhof; Morning Star Ranch; Wheeler's Ranch

Sources:
Miller, Timothy. 1998. *The Quest for Utopia in Twentieth-Century America.* Syracuse, N.Y.: Syracuse University Press.
_____. 1999. *The 60s Communes: Hippies and Beyond.* Syracuse, N.Y.: Syracuse University Press.

SHAKER COMMUNITIES. The Shakers were founded in England by Ann Lee (1736–1784) after she had become a member of a radical group of evangelicals led by James Wardley. They were known as the Shaking Quakers because of their violent physical gyrations and speaking in loud voices. After her marriage and four miscarriages, she had visions of Adam and Eve and adopted celibacy. She also preached that God was both masculine and feminine, with Christ being the masculine expression and herself the feminine expression. One of her visions led her and a small band of followers to immigrate to America in 1774; she established her first community at Watervliet (Niskeyuna), New York (near Albany), the following year. After a missionary tour of New England, she died in 1784 and her successor, James Whittaker, moved the community to New Lebanon. Under his leadership, and then that of Joseph Meacham, 10 Shaker villages were established in New York and New England by 1796, each with a "family" of between 30 and 100 adults. A strict celibacy and separation of the sexes was practiced in each community. Under Meacham, a detailed listing of the rules of daily Shaker life developed in the *Gospel Order* and other publications. Upon Meacham's death in 1796, Lucy Wright (Mother Lucy) led the Shakers as "the elder or first born" for 25 years. Mother Lucy sent a second mission in the trans-Appalachian frontier under the direction of Benjamin Seth Youngs and Issachar Bates. In the first stage of development (1787–1796), the Shakers founded 12 villages in the northeast. In the second stage (1796–1836), they built seven villages in the Ohio Valley and three more in the northeast. In the last phase (1894–1898), they opened villages in Narcoosee, Florida, and White Oak, Georgia. Atrophy of membership because of celibacy eventually led to the closing of all but one village at Sabbathday Lake, Maine, by the end of the twentieth century.

Sources:

Berry, Brian J. L. 1992. *America's Utopian Experiments: Communal Havens from Long-Wave Crises.* Hanover, N.H. and London: University Press of New England.

Brewer, Priscilla J. 1986. *Shaker Communities, Shaker Lives.* Hanover, N.H. and London: University Press of New England.

Fogarty, Robert S. 1990. *All Things New: American Communes and Utopian Movements 1860–1914.* Chicago: University of Chicago Press.

Oved, Yaacov. 1987. *Two Hundred Years of American Communes.* New Brunswick, N.J. and Oxford: Transaction.

Stein, Stephen J. 1992. *The Shaker Experience in America: A History of the United Society of Believers.* New Haven, Conn.: Yale University Press.

Sutton, Robert P. 2003. *Communal Utopias and the American Experience: Religious Communities, 1732–2000.* Westport, Conn. and London: Praeger.

Trahair, Richard C. S. 1999. *Utopias and Utopians: An Historical Dictionary.* Westport, Conn.: Greenwood Press.

SHILOH: CHURCH OF THE LIVING GOD. In 1893, Frank Sandford (1862–1948) founded this Christian commune in Maine at a site between Lewiston and Brunswick. Soon individuals and families moved to the place and turned over to Sandford all of their property. They constructed a number of elaborate Victorian buildings, including a school, and lived daily lives according to the Acts of the Apostles. When six members of the community died of smallpox in the winter of 1902–1903, Sandford was charged and convicted of cruelty for his refusal to treat the individuals with modern medicine. In a tragic ocean voyage in 1910–1911 aboard their ship the *Coronet,* which left Portland in December, Sandford and 66 followers traveled to Africa and Trinidad, then headed north for Greenland; but finally they were forced to land in Maine. By that time nine passengers had died and others were gravely ill. Sandford was convicted of manslaughter and served just over six years in an Atlanta penitentiary. After his release in 1918, he joined 100 or so disciples who had remained at Shiloh, who by then were living on outside charity donations. But within two years, the community dissolved.

See Also Sandford, Frank

Sources:

Fogarty, Robert S. 1980. *Dictionary of American Communal and Utopian History*. Westport, Conn.: Greenwood Press.

Miller, Timothy. 1998. *The Quest for Utopia in Twentieth-Century America*. Syracuse, N.Y.: Syracuse University Press.

Nelson, Shirley. 1989. *Fair Clear and Terrible: The Story of Shiloh, Maine*. Latham, N.Y.: British American Publishing.

SHILOH FARMS. Shiloh Farms was an independent Christian community founded in Chautauqua County, New York, in 1941 by Eugene Crosby Monroe. Monroe preached a Christian perfectionism that stressed spiritual development rather than social reform and the importance of divine revelation from the Holy Spirit. Monroe died at the colony in 1961. After receiving one such revelation in 1968, more than half of the 100-member community moved to Sulphur Springs, Arkansas. In 1968, they purchased a hotel in the Arkansas Ozarks that served as their main building with offices, a bakery, a health food store, a cafeteria, and a retirement center. They opened a nursery and preschool and the Shiloh Christian Retreat Center. More than 50 new converts joined the community in the 1970s. They developed a profitable business of selling health foods under the label of Shiloh Farms and baked goods under the label of Sun Rise Acres Bakery. By the end of the twentieth century, a number of associate members lived on nearby properties and worked inside the community.

Sources:

Communities Directory: A Guide to Intentional Communities and Cooperative Living. 2000. Rutledge, Mo.: Fellowship for Intentional Community.

Miller, Timothy. 1998. *The Quest for Utopia in Twentieth-Century America*. Syracuse, N.Y.: Syracuse University Press.

SHILOH YOUTH REVIVAL CENTERS. In 1969, John Higgins founded one of the largest Jesus movement communities that grew from a small gathering in a house in Costa Mesa, California, to include more than 1,000 members living in 170 communal houses across the country by the mid-1970s. The first house was called the House of Miracles and its lifestyle of poverty, "loving Jesus," and long hours of hard work set the pattern for the other Revival Centers. In a few years, they purchased a 90-acre site near Eugene, Oregon, that became Shiloh's main colony of more than 100 members. In the other Shiloh Houses, members earned a living by farming, fishing, canning, automobile repair, and other such businesses. Leadership was patriarchal, with women restricted to traditional roles. However, membership rapidly declined and by 1989, the Internal Revenue Service took their property for unpaid taxes.

Source:

Miller, Timothy. 1999. *The 60s Communes: Hippies and Beyond.* Syracuse, N.Y.: Syracuse University Press.

SHORT CREEK (COLORADO CITY). This community was one of the most popular polygamist colonies founded by Latter-Day Saints communitarians. It was started in 1928 by Lorin C. Woolley under the auspices of his organization, the United Effort Plan, as a haven for the outlawed polygamists. Located on the Utah border just north of the Grand Canyon, he hoped that it would offer a safe retreat from law enforcement. Although isolated, the public soon knew of their presence and in August 1935, the Mohave County Attorney, E. Elmo Bollinger, arrested its leaders, an action taken with the approval of the Mormon Church officials in Salt Lake City. Two men were given prison terms. In March 1944, U.S. Attorney John S. Boyden conducted raids on all polygamist communities in Utah, Arizona, and Idaho, including Short Creek. Its leaders were arrested and charged with mailing obscene literature, kidnapping, and violating the White Slave Trade Act. In 1953, the governor of Arizona, Howard Pyle, sent police officers across the border to Short Creek in a pre-dawn raid. They arrested 36 men and 8 women. They then took the mothers and children to Phoenix and placed the children in foster homes. After this raid, Short Creek was renamed Colorado City and public officials have left the 5,000 residents alone. Satellite polygamist communities were then started at Lister, British Columbia, and other places, and by the end of the twentieth century there were an estimated 7,600 communal polygamists in the United Effort Plan.

Sources:

Bradley, Martha Sonntag. 1993. *Kidnapped from That Land: The Government Raids on the Short Creek Polygamists.* Salt Lake City: University of Utah Press.
Miller, Timothy. 1998. *The Quest for Utopia in Twentieth-Century America.* Syracuse, N.Y.: Syracuse University Press.

SINCLAIR, UPTON. Upton Sinclair (1878–1968) was a novelist and the founder of the Helicon Hall colony (1906–1907), a group of young couples who gathered to live cooperatively in a former boys' school in Englewood, near the New Jersey Palisades. Financed with royalties from *The Jungle* (1904), it attracted 46 adults, many of them well-known authors, and 15 children. They led a comfortable bohemian lifestyle that abruptly ended when a fire destroyed the school building in March 1907. In the summer of 1908, the property was sold to private residential developers. Sinclair was born in Baltimore and moved with his family to New York City at the age of

10. He graduated from New York City College in 1897 and briefly attended Columbia University Law School. He then wrote short stories for *Wilshires Weekly* and *The Appeal to Reason*. After the Helicon fire, Sinclair tried to promote another such community but abandoned the idea to become active in socialist politics. In 1920, he ran unsuccessfully for the House of Representatives in California as a socialist, then for the U.S. Senate in 1922, and for governor in 1926 and 1930. In 1934, he was the Democratic Party candidate for governor with the slogan "End Poverty in California" but lost to incumbent Frank Merriam. In addition to socialism, he championed the American Civil Liberties Union and the temperance reform movement. His 1935 novel, *Co-op,* dealt with the pros and cons of cooperative organizations. He died in Los Angeles.

See Also Helicon Hall Colony

Sources:
Fogarty, Robert S. 1980. *Dictionary of American Communal and Utopian History.* Westport, Conn.: Greenwood Press.

Harris, Leon. 1975. *Upton Sinclair: American Rebel.* New York: Thomas Y. Crowell.

Sutton, Robert P. 2004. *Communal Utopias and the American Experience: Secular Communities, 1824–2000.* Westport, Conn. and London: Praeger.

Trahair, Richard C. S. 1999. *Utopias and Utopians: An Historical Dictionary.* Westport, Conn.: Greenwood Press.

Yoder, John A. 1975. *Upton Sinclair.* New York: Ungar.

SKINNER, B. F. Burrhus Frederic Skinner (1904–1990) was born in Susquehanna, Pennsylvania. He was on the faculty of Harvard University from 1931 to 1936, then at University of Minnesota from 1936 to 1945. When he returned to Harvard in 1946 he developed new ideas in behavior psychology. Although he was a prolific writer, his most important contribution to utopian communalism was *Walden Two,* published in 1948. Some historians consider the impact of the book on 1960s-era communalism as profound. The novel depicts a visitor to an ideal community who describes what is found there as a paradise. Members perform satisfying work that each individual chooses to do, enjoy leisure activities, and live in small homes that they built themselves. Community planners and managers organize Walden's routine and work assignments. Skinner's ideas became the inspiration for three utopian communities. The first was Walden House in Washington, D.C., which opened in 1956. The second was Waldenwoods near Ann Arbor Michigan, which opened in 1966. In 1967, the most significant communal experiment modeled on *Walden Two* was founded at Twin Oaks at Louisa, Virginia.

See Also Twin Oaks

Sources:
Miller, Timothy. 1999. *The 60s Communes: Hippies and Beyond.* Syracuse, N.Y.: Syracuse University Press.

Kinkade, Kat. 1973. *A Walden Two Experiment: The First Five Years of the Twin Oaks Community.* Louisa, Va.: Twin Oaks Publishing.

Skinner, B. F. 1948. *Walden Two.* New York: Macmillan.

Trahair, Richard C. S. 1999. *Utopias and Utopians: An Historical Dictionary.* Westport, Conn.: Greenwood Press.

SMYTHE, WILLIAM ELLSWORTH. Smythe (1861–1922) was born in Worcester, Massachusetts, and lived as an adult in San Diego. He was the editor of *Irrigation Age,* promoted irrigation projects in the American West, and organized conferences on the topic in Nebraska. He was active in the Californian Constructive League and pushed for irrigation and water conservation. He supervised the building of The Little Landers community near the Mexican border in Southern California. But the irrigation system failed to provide enough water to grow crops and most of the colonists had no experience in agriculture. After a 1916 flood all but destroyed the colony, the experiment was abandoned. Smythe also founded Little Landers of Los Angeles in 1913. Just before his death in 1922, he published *City Homes on Country Lanes* and *Homelanders of America.*

See Also The Little Landers

Sources:

Fogarty, Robert S. 1980. *Dictionary of American Communal and Utopian History.* Westport, Conn.: Greenwood Press.

Hine, Robert V. 1983. *California's Utopian Colonies.* Berkeley: University of California Press.

Miller, Timothy. 1998. *The Quest for Utopia in Twentieth-Century America.* Syracuse, N.Y.: Syracuse University Press.

Trahair, Richard C.S. 1999. *Utopias and Utopians: An Historical Dictionary.* Westport, Conn.: Greenwood Press.

SOCIETAS FRATERNIA. In 1876, an English immigrant and businessman, George Hinde, started this spiritualist colony on 24 acres near Fullerton, California. Residents lived in a 14-room house with an octagonal tower. They followed the messages of Dr. Louis Schlesinger, which demanded communal living, vegetarianism, and sharing of sexual partners. Pressure by neighbors forced Schlesinger to leave and he was replaced by Walter Lockwood, a former Methodist minister, who led the small colony until he died in 1921. The Societas Fraternia then dissolved.

See Also The Land of Shalam; Lily Dale and Cassadaga; Preston

Sources:

Colman, Fern. 1967. "Vegetarian Health Seekers of Orange County." In *Rawhide and Orange Blossoms,* Quill Pen Club, ed., 227–31. Santa Ana, Calif.: Pioneer Press.

Miller, Timothy. 1998. *The Quest for Utopia in Twentieth-Century America.* Syracuse, N.Y.: Syracuse University Press.

SOJOURNERS COMMUNITY. The 1995 edition of *Communities Directory* described Sojourners Community as "an ecumenical, Christian community in inner-city Washington D.C." that was "rooted in the teachings of the bible and the call of daily application of faith in our lives." It had its origins in the Jesus movement of the 1970s, during which some students at Trinity Evangelical Divinity School organized an intentional community in a suburb of Chicago and published a newspaper called the *Post American*. Focusing on urban problems, they relocated in 1974 to Washington, D.C., and dedicated themselves to living among the poor and feeding the hungry. They opened a learning center for children and a food distribution program for more than 200 families and published a new magazine called *Sojourners*. Members of the Sojourners Community took on service-related jobs in the Columbia Heights neighborhood and pooled their incomes and assets. They remained committed to traditional marriage, condemned abortion, corporate greed, and imperial exploitation of third-world countries. Their Sunday afternoon worship service at five o'clock was open to the public.

Sources:

Communities Directory: A Guide to Cooperative Living. 1995. Langley, Washington: Fellowship for Intentional Community.

Miller, Timothy. 1999. *The 60s Communes: Hippies and Beyond.* Syracuse, N.Y.: Syracuse University Press.

Wallis, Jim. 1996. *Who Speaks for God? An Alternative to the Religious Right—A New Politics of Compassion, Community, and Civility.* New York: Delacorte.

SOUTHERN CO-OPERATIVE ASSOCIATION OF APALACHI-COLA. This community was a descendant of the Christian Commonwealth Colony founded by Ralph Albertson near Columbus, Georgia, in 1896. In 1900, after surviving members of that colony liquidated their assets to satisfy their debts, some members moved to Apalachicola, in Franklin County, Florida. Led by Harry C. Vrooman, they purchased 1,700 acres and continued to be dedicated to the Commonwealth's goals of social Christianity, the remaking of society, and unselfish fellowship. After Vrooman died in 1904 the community dissolved.

See Also Albertson, Ralph

Sources:

Fogarty, Robert S. 1980. *Dictionary of American Communal and Utopian History.* Westport, Conn.: Greenwood Press.

Miller, Timothy. 1998. *The Quest for Utopia in Twentieth-Century America.* Syracuse, N.Y.: Syracuse University Press.

SPIRIT FRUIT SOCIETY. In 1901, Jacob Beilhart (1867–1908), third son of an immigrant German father, founded the Spirit Fruit Society at his home in Lisbon, Ohio, when he gathered together 13 spiritualists and theosophists. They called the commune "The Home" and believed in a universal spirit and the need to work unselfishly and to do good works to attain the "full fruit" of mankind, or the Spirit of Christ. They practiced sexual freedom and renounced traditional monogamy. In 1905, Beilhart moved the community away from its critical Lisbon neighbors to a 90-acre site northwest of Chicago. Here they constructed a large communal living quarters and a barn. Beilhart died from peritonitis after an appendix operation in 1908 and the colony relocated to a rural spot near Santa Cruz, California, called Hilltop Ranch. But without a leader, the community atrophied and finally dissolved in 1930.

See Also Beilhart, Jacob

Sources:

Fogarty, Robert S. 1980. *Dictionary of American Communal and Utopian History.* Westport, Conn.: Greenwood Press.

Grant, H. Roger. 1988. *Spirit Fruit: A Gentle Utopia.* DeKalb: Northern Illinois University Press.

Miller, Timothy. 1999. *The 60s Communes: Hippies and Beyond.* Syracuse, N.Y.: Syracuse University Press.

Murphy, James L. 1989. *The Reluctant Radicals: Jacob Beilhart and the Spirit Fruit Society.* Lanham, Md.: University Press of America.

Trahair, Richard C.S. 1999. *Utopias and Utopians: An Historical Dictionary.* Westport, Conn.: Greenwood Press.

STELLE COMMUNITY. In 1963, Richard Kieninger, a Chicago businessman, published *The Ultimate Frontier* under the pen name of Eklal Kueshana, in which he purported to transmit messages from ancient brotherhoods about the impending millennium in the year 2000 where only those chosen for modern-day brotherhoods would survive. In 1973, he and his followers pooled their money and resources to buy land at Stelle, in rural northern Illinois. They had a woodworking business, the Stellewood Company, that made cabinets, wood bumpers for pool tables, and rulers. They also ran a plastics company and a print shop. The community had 30 homes, an office building, and a school. After Kieninger left the community in 1964 following a sex scandal, the remaining 216 members concentrated on improving the physical environment, conservative living, and family values that prohibited smoking, alcohol, and drugs. They developed an elaborate educational program at their Learning Center with a 12-month curriculum without grading that allowed each child to progress at his or her own pace. They experimented with new methods of house construction and alternative fuel sources such as solar heat. They ran a holistic health center and published a community newspaper, the *Stelle Letter.* In 1982, they opened the community to nonbelievers and all community matters were then decided by a Stelle Community Association made up of property owners.

See Also Lemurian Fellowship

Sources:

Miller, Timothy. 1998. *The Quest for Utopia in Twentieth-Century America*. Syracuse, N.Y.: Syracuse University Press.

Popenoe, Cris, and Oliver Popenoe. 1984. *Seeds of Tomorrow: New Age Communities That Work*. San Francisco: Harper and Row.

Sutton, Robert P. 2003. *Communal Utopias and the American Experience: Religious Communities, 1732–2000*. Westport, Conn. and London: Praeger.

Trahair, Richard C.S. 1999. *Utopias and Utopians: An Historical Dictionary*. Westport, Conn.: Greenwood Press.

STRAIGHT EDGE INDUSTRIAL SETTLEMENT.   This colony, a social gospel community modeled on the Christian Commonwealth Colony in New York City, was founded in New York City in 1899 by Wilbur F. Copeland and his wife as a way to provide jobs for those who had worked in cooperative industries. There were two locations of the settlement. One was in lower Manhattan where workers joined and worked in a "co-operative enterprise founded upon the Golden Rule." During the first seven years, a total of more than 200 individuals became members, although the usual annual resident membership was about 18 persons. Copeland published a periodical called *The Straight Edge*. The second part of the community was located at Alpine, New Jersey, and was a residence for workers. Financial difficulties brought about the closing of both communities in 1918.

See Also Copeland, Wilbur F.

Source:

Miller, Timothy. 1998. *The Quest for Utopia in Twentieth-Century America*. Syracuse, N.Y.: Syracuse University Press.

SUNRISE. In July 1933, Joseph B. Cohen, a Russian-born Jewish immigrant who lived in New York City, founded a utopian community in Michigan named after J. William Lloyd's 1904 novel *Dwellers in the Vale Sunrise*. He planned a self-sufficient community made up of physicians, teachers, farmers, and skilled artisans. All means of production would be held in common and members would be provided the necessities of life. Personal items, however, such as clothes, furniture, and books were allowed. There was an admission fee of $500 and members had to be under the age of 45 and without large numbers of children. More than half of the 80 families who resided there were Jewish. They lived in individual homes while single members lodged in a dormitory. Everyone ate in a communal dining hall. Morale was high during the first year when they were inspired by the dream of building a new social order. But as early as the winter of 1934, troubles surfaced. Quarrels arose over the constitution and election of officers. Some members, including Cohen, were anarchists and wanted no elections of any kind. Cohen tried to run Sunrise by himself and for a while the community stabilized. However, when the fall harvest of 1934 fell way below expectations because of a severe drought, Cohen had to borrow $55,000 from New Deal agencies to keep Sunrise going. When he reorganized the work system to replace individual choice of jobs with arbitrary assignments, members began to leave. By the spring of 1935, 50 families remained. Cohen became discouraged and the following spring he sold Sunrise to the federal government. He and 19 families relocated to Virginia to live on a 640-acre farm. But soon families were quarreling and open fights broke out among some younger men. Roads from the farm to the main highway were impassible in the spring mud. By November 1938, the 12 families that remained voted to sell the property and dissolve Sunrise.

See Also Cohen, Joseph B.

Sources:

Cohen, Joseph J. 1957. *In Quest of Heaven: The Story of the Sunrise Co-operative Farm Community.* New York: Sunrise History Publishing Committee.

Conkin, Paul K. 1959. *Tomorrow a New World: The New Deal Community Program.* Ithaca, N.Y.: Cornell University Press.

Fogarty, Robert S. 1980. *Dictionary of American Communal and Utopian History.* Westport, Conn.: Greenwood Press.

Miller, Timothy. 1998. *The Quest for Utopia in Twentieth-Century America.* Syracuse, N.Y.: Syracuse University Press.

Oved, Yaacov. 1988. *Two Hundred Years of American Communes.* New Brunswick, N.J. and Oxford: Transaction.

Sutton, Robert P. 2003. *Communal Utopias and the American Experience: Religious Communities, 1824–2000.* Westport Conn. and London: Praeger.

SUNRISE COOPERATIVE FARMS. This Jewish cooperative, funded by Jewish philanthropists, was organized near Hightstown, New Jersey, in 1933 on 1,000 acres. It, like the Michigan Sunrise, wanted to resettle poor, urban Jews in a rural farm community. Most of the 100 settlers came from the garment district of New York City and held radical socialist ideas. Each family had a one-acre tract for farming and a private home. The founders planned to start a clothing factory but no records show that it ever was opened. Settlers did not remain long in the colony and it closed in 1936.

See Also Sunrise

Source:

Miller, Timothy. 1998. *The Quest for Utopia in Twentieth-Century America.* Syracuse, N.Y.: Syracuse University Press.

SUNRISE HILL. In the summer of 1966, Gordon Yaswen and 20 communards moved to a 40-acre farm near Conway, Massachusetts, owned by one member of the group to create a communal "nest" where bodies, minds, and possessions would be shared. They worked in the open and lived in the single house on the property. There was no formal communal organization and members had the choice of donating possessions to Sunrise Hill or keeping them. They held meetings where decisions were reached by consensus. While the weather was warm everything was idyllic. But as autumn apporached, they recognized that the single house was inadequate for winter and discussed building a second structure. Nothing came of the planning, however. They ran out of money. Work on the farm led to dissension and conflicts. In February 1967, the few remaining residents left the colony, four of them moving to join another commune at Hobart, New York, called Cold Mountain Farm.

See Also Cold Mountain Farm

Sources:

Fogarty, Robert S. 1980. *Dictionary of American Communal and Utopian History.* Westport, Conn.: Greenwood Press.
Heinlein, Robert. 1961. *Stranger in a Strange Land.* New York: Putnam's.
Houriet, Robert. 1971. *Getting Back Together.* New York: Avon.
Miller, Timothy. 1999. *The 60s Communes: Hippies and Beyond.* Syracuse, N.Y: Syracuse University Press.
Richard, Jerry, ed. 1973. *The Good Life.* New York: New American Library.

SUNRISE RANCH. This New Age religious utopia was started in 1945 at the foot of the Rocky Mountains near Loveland, Colorado, by Lloyd Meeker, founder of the Emissaries of Divine Light, and a British aristocrat, Lord Martin Cecil. The dozen residents built living quarters, a domed auditorium, a hydroponic greenhouse, and conference buildings and practiced organic farming. They emphasized "attunement," or the body's mental energy for healing diseases. They had an Attunement Center to practice the synchronization of this physical and mental energy. Its population increased to the hundreds by the late twentieth century.

See Also The Emissary Communities

Sources:

Communities Directory: A Guide to Intentional and Cooperative Living. 2000. Rutledge, Missouri: Fellowship for Intentional Community.
Miller, Timothy. 1998. *The Quest for Utopia in Twentieth-Century America.* Syracuse, N.Y.: Syracuse University Press.

SYNANON. This commune was the largest of the communal utopias founded during the 1960s to improve health and personal growth. The others included the Gesundheit Institute in Arlington, Virginia, and the Morehouses in California and Hawaii. Charles Dederich founded Synanon in 1958 in Santa Monica, California, as a drug and alcohol rehabilitation center, and for the first decade all residents were addicts. In the late 1960s, however, nonaddicts were admitted with a nonrefundable admissions fee and Synanon became an intentional community rather than a treatment center. It organized encounter groups of mutual criticism called the "game," somewhat reminiscent of the sessions at the Oneida Community in the mid-nineteenth century. These "games," held several times a week, were supplemented by other exercises designed to promote well-being. The colony had communal kitchens, dormitories, and schools. Other Synanon communities opened throughout California. A severe economic setback occurred in the early 1990s, however, when the community had to forfeit its tax-exempt status and pay back taxes. That event resulted in bankruptcy and the closing of the residences.

See Also Gesundheit Institute; The Morehouses

Sources:

Janzen, Rod. 2001. *The Rise and Fall of Synanon.* Baltimore, Md.: Johns Hopkins University Press.

Kanter, Rosabeth Moss. 1972. *Commitment and Community: Communes and Utopias in Sociological Perspective.* Cambridge, Mass.: Harvard University Press.

Miller, Timothy. 1999. *The 60s Communes: Hippies and Beyond.* Syracuse, N.Y.: Syracuse University Press.

Yablonsky, Lewis. 1967. *Synanon: The Tunnel Back.* Baltimore: Penguin.

T

TABLE MOUNTAIN RANCH. Table Mountain Ranch was founded at Albion, in the Redwood country of Mendocino County, California, in 1968 when two wealthy men from Haight-Ashbury purchased 120 acres as a retreat from the hectic environment of San Francisco's hippie enclave. They converted the farmhouse into a communal meetinghouse with a living room/library, a rope swing hanging from the ceiling, and a few dilapidated chairs. Residents lived in 12 small cabins. They had no electricity and no telephone. Kerosene and wood were used for fuel and for light at night. A Quonset hut served as a workshop for blacksmithing, upholstering car seats, and repairing vehicles. They opened a school for the children in a small building near the hut. Its curriculum included academics, mechanical arts, and crafts. Adults stressed peace, love, spontaneity, and spirituality. Drugs were openly used. Although Table Mountain Ranch experienced a decline of membership in the 1980s, by the beginning of the twenty-first century it had revived considerably.

See Also Black Bear Ranch

Sources:

Berger, Bennett M. 1981. *The Survival of a Counterculture: Ideological Work and Everyday Life among Rural Communards.* Berkeley: University of California Press.

Miller, Timothy. 1999. *The 60s Communes: Hippies and Beyond.* Syracuse, N.Y.: Syracuse University Press.

Sutton, Robert P. 2004. *Communal Utopias and the American Experience: Secular Communities, 1824–2000.* Westport, Conn. and London: Praeger.

TARTHANG TULKU. In 1959, Tibetan abbot Tarthang Tulku, along with Chogyam Trungpa, fled his country when the Chinese took over. He went to India and in 1968 came to Berkeley, California. There he founded the Nyingma Institute and lived communally with his students in a refurbished fraternity house called Padma Ling. It served as a meditation center for the members. He kept the institute's headquarters in another part of the city and used it as a communal living center. Tarthang Tulku kept strictly to Tibetan traditions and stressed its ritual, chants, prostrations, and meditations. In 1975, he purchased 900 acres near Jenner, California, and created the Nyingma Country Center as a self-sufficient farming community. By 1996, it had expanded to become a Buddhist monastery on 1,100 acres with six temples along with stupas, meditation sites, 1,242 electric prayer wheels, 800 prayer flags, and more than 108,000 statues of Padmasambhava, the person who converted Tibetans to Buddhism.

See Also Trungpa, Chogyam

Sources:
Fields, Rick. 1981. *How the Swans Came to the Lake: A Narrative History of Buddhism in America*. Boulder, Colo.: Shambhala.
Miller, Timothy. 1999. *The 60s Communes Hippies and Beyond*. Syracuse, N.Y.: Syracuse University Press.
Prebish, Charles. 1979. *American Buddhism*. North Scituate, Mass.: Duxbury Press.

TEED, CYRUS READ. Cyrus Read Teed (1839–1908), the founder of the Koreshan Unity community, was born in Teedsville, New York. He served in the Medical Corps of the Union Army during the Civil War. He entered the New York Eclectic School of Medicine in 1865 and received his degree three years later. He then opened a practice in Syracuse. In 1880, after experiencing a vision of a male and female god, he organized a small community in Moravia, New York, dedicated to "cellular cosmology," which purported that humans lived inside a hollow earth with seven shells, the outer one being made of precious metals. The sun was at the center of the hollow earth and planets rotated around the sun as "Mercurial discs." Teed changed his name to Koresh, the Hebrew name for Cyrus, and called his new religion Koreshanity. In 1886, he moved his following, consisting of four women, to an apartment in New York City. A year later he relocated to Chicago and opened the College of Life to offer courses on Koreshanity. At the same time he opened the Church Triumphant and the Society Arch-Triumphant, both organizations dedicated to faith healing. He published a periodical, *The Guiding Star,* which was later called *The Flaming Sword*. In 1888, he organized the Koreshan Unity community of 60 members, mostly women. By 1893, the colony had expanded to 123 members. That year he had another revelation that compelled him to move the Koreshan Unity to Florida. He purchased a 300-acre property south of Fort Myers and his followers moved to the site. By 1906, Teed had acquired 7,500 acres and incorporated the community as Estero, with a system of government. In 1908, he died from injuries received in a physical assault in Fort Myers. The community survived his death and continued to have a variety of cultural activities and to run the colony's businesses. In 1961, the members deeded the property to the state of Florida and today it is open to visitors as the Koreshan State Historic Site.

See Also Koreshan Unity

Sources:

Fogarty, Robert S. 1990. *All Things New: American Communes and Utopian Movements 1860–1914.* Chicago: University of Chicago Press.

Miller, Timothy. 1998. *The Quest for Utopia in Twentieth-Century America.* Syracuse, N.Y.: Syracuse University Press.

Rea, Sara Weber. 1994. *The Koreshan Story.* Estero, Fla.: Guiding Star Publishing House.

Sutton, Robert P. 2003. *Communal Utopias and the American Experienced: Religious Communities, 1732–2000.* Westport, Conn. and London: Praeger.

Trahair, Richard C.S. 1999. *Utopias and Utopians: An Historical Dictionary.* Westport, Conn.: Greenwood Press.

TEMPLE OF THE PEOPLE (HALCYON). In 1903, William H Dower, a physician, and Mrs. Frances A. La Due moved the Syracuse faction of the Theosophists to Pismo Beach, California, and organized a cooperative community called Halcyon. They called themselves the Temple of the People and started a construction business and farmed. Members were given half-acre plots on which to plant oats, barley, sugar beets, and vegetables. Families lived in bungalows and sent their children to the public schools in the town of Arroyo Grande. They also founded 22 satellite colonies, called "squares," throughout the United States. The colony published a monthly magazine called the *Temple Artisan.* They were unable to make a profit and in 1912 they abandoned cooperative work and continued as a private enterprise business. In the 1920s, they built a temple-office building that became the headquarters of a small worldwide Halcyon movement.

Sources:

Hine, Robert V. 1983. *California's Utopian Colonies.* Berkeley: University of California Press.

Miller, Timothy. 1998. *The Quest for Utopia in Twentieth-Century America.* Syracuse, N.Y.: Syracuse University Press.

Sutton, Robert P. 2003. *Communal Utopias and the American Experience: Religious Communities, 1732–2000.* Westport, Conn. and London: Praeger.

THE THELEMIC "MAGICK" COMMUNITY. In 1939, Jack Parsons, a founder of the Jet Propulsion Laboratory in Pasadena, and about a dozen followers opened a communal house called the Abbey on Orange Grove Avenue in Pasadena, California. It was modeled on the communal colony founded by British occultist and magician, Aleister Crowley, the Abbey of Thelema, in Sicily, whose members practiced ritual sex, or "sex magick." Most of the members of Parsons's Abbey had already belonged to the Agape

Lodge of Los Angeles, where they practiced the unconventional sexual activities of the Abbey of Thelema. At the Pasadena Abbey, they continued their experiments in ritual sex for about a decade. Membership reached about eight for a while. One member of the colony was L. Ron Hubbard, the founder of the Church of Scientology.

Sources:

Fichter, Joseph H., ed. 1983. *Alternatives to American Mainline Churches.* New York: Rose of Sharon Press/Unification Theological Seminary.
Miller, Timothy. 1998. *The Quest for Utopia in Twentieth-Century America.* Syracuse, N.Y.: Syracuse University Press.

TINGLEY, KATHERINE AUGUSTA WESTCOTT. Tingley (1847– 1929) was born in Newburyport, Massachusetts, the daughter of a shipbuilder, and educated in the public schools. At the age of 40, she went to New York City where she converted to Theosophy. She founded various philanthropic societies such as the Society of Mercy, the Martha Washington Home for the Aged, and the Do-Good Mission. During the Spanish-American War, she opened a hospital for the sick and wounded. She took over the American branch of the Theosophical Society as its "Outer Head" and changed its name to the Universal Brotherhood and Theosophical Society. Under Tingley's leadership, the society moved away from the occult tenets of Helena Petrovna Blavatsky and toward humanitarian causes. In 1896, Tingley founded the Point Loma community near San Diego as the international headquarters of the Universal Brotherhood, and for 27 years she was its uncontested leader. She died from injuries suffered in a car accident in Berlin in 1929.

See Also Point Loma (Universal Brotherhood and Theosophical Society)

Sources:

Fogarty, Robert S. 1980. *All Things New: American Communes and Utopian Movements 1860–1914.* Chicago: University of Chicago Press.
Greenwalt, Emmett A. 1978. *The Point Loma Community in California: 1897– 1942—A Theosophical Experiment.* Berkeley: University of California Press, 1955. Rev. ed. Published as *California Utopia: Point Loma: 1897–1942.* San Diego: Point Loma Publications.
Hine, Robert V. 1983. *California's Utopian Colonies.* Berkeley: University of California Press.
Miller, Timothy. 1998. *The Quest for Utopia in Twentieth-Century America.* Syracuse, N.Y.: Syracuse University Press.
Sutton, Robert P. 2003. *Communal Utopias and the American Experience: Religious Communities, 1732–2000.* Westport, Conn. and London: Praeger.
Trahair, Richard C. S. 1999. *Utopias and Utopians: An Historical Dictionary.* Westport, Conn.: Greenwood Press.

TOLSTOY FARM. In 1962, Hugh "Piper" Williams founded this open land community near his grandparents' farm at Davenport, Washington, after he had participated in a peace activist training center at a 40-acre farm close to Voluntown, Connecticut. There he became involved in peace protest activities directed by the New England Committee for Nonviolent Action (CNVA). Ten members joined the farm in the beginning and by summer's end, 50 communards were living at a subsistence level on a $100 monthly cash expenditure. Only funds donated by Williams's parents and from friends helped them to survive. By 1965, the community had divided into settlements two miles apart from each other. An existing farmhouse served as a communal center. Williams imposed almost no rules on the members, who were freely allowed to experience drugs, mainly marijuana, and open sex. The center burned in 1968 but had little negative impact on the farm because residents where living in simple shacks. The community practiced total economic sharing and decision making by consensus. At its peak in the summer of 1968, there were as many as 200 communards at the farm. Williams taught the children at the colony's alternative school in a structure built by residents, who also developed cottage industries. He and his two children left Tolstoy Farm at his wife's insistence and formed another community 25 miles away, known as the Earth Cyclers, on land owned by his parents. By 1990, permanent residents of this community included 27 adults and 22 children living as families but sharing communal potluck meals every Sunday. In 2000, the *Communities Directory* listed Tolstoy Farms as a "decentralized rural community sharing 240 acres of canyon land in eastern Washington." Its 50 members carry out communal organic gardening and sell the produce in Spokane. Most adults worked outside the community.

See Also Gorda Mountain

Sources:

Communities Directory: A Guide to Intentional Communities and Cooperative Living. 2000. Rutledge, Missouri: Fellowship for Intentional Community.

Miller, Timothy. 1999. *The 60s Communes: Hippies and Beyond.* Syracuse, N.Y.: Syracuse University Press.

TRABUCO COLLEGE. This celibate, meditative community inspired by non-Western religions was founded in 1942 by Gerald Heard, an English-born writer, after he had lived in the Vedanta Society of Hollywood under Swami Prabhavananda. Aldous Huxley also lived there. Hoping to train a group of neo-Brahmin spiritual leaders as a counterforce against fascism, Heard created a small colony to practice meditation and spiritual training. He purchased a 392-acre ranch in Trabuco Canyon, located 60 miles south of Los Angeles. Huxley wrote the prospectus for the community and described it as an "un-denominational" community open to both sexes who would live by a cooperative subsistence economy that combined "manual and household work." There would be classes of teachers, students, and missionaries. Heard dominated the community as its guru, conducting daily seminars and doing six hours of meditation instead of the daily three hours done by the residents. Silence prevailed in the evenings until after breakfast the following morning. At other times during the day, they pursued their own projects. For example, Huxley wrote *The Perennial Philosophy* while at the college and Heard composed lectures. But Heard had his own emotional conflicts and never acknowledged his homosexuality. Problems began to surface and some members came to see themselves in a sort of solitary confinement. Heard gave Trabuco College to the Vedanta Society in 1947 and it reopened as a Vedanta colony called the Ramakrishna Monastery in September 1949. Heard died in Los Angeles in 1971.

See Also Heard, Gerald

Sources:

Fogarty, Robert S. 1980. *Dictionary of American Communal and Utopian History.* Westport, Conn.: Greenwood Press.

Huxley, Aldous. 1945. *The Perennial Philosophy.* New York: Harper and Brothers.

Miller, Timothy. 1998. *The Quest for Utopia in Twentieth-Century America.* Syracuse, N.Y.: Syracuse University Press.

Veysey, Laurence. 1973. *The Communal Experience: Anarchist and Mystical Counter-cultures in America.* Chicago: University of Chicago Press.

TRUNGPA, CHOGYAM. Chogyam Trungpa was a Tibetan guru who fled his country when the Chinese overran it in 1959. He and his disciples founded a spiritual community in Barnet, Vermont, named the Tail of the Tiger. Trungpa, however, eventually moved to Boulder, Colorado, and headed Shambhala International, a spiritual organization. Some of his disciples, called the Pygmies, organized the Rocky Mountain Shambhala Center in northern Colorado as a meditation center. Trungpa's unconventional lifestyle included drinking alcohol, smoking cigarettes, eating meat, and having numerous sexual relations with female followers. His successor, Thomas Rich, had AIDS and continued having sexual partners without their knowledge of his disease. He died in 1989. Trungpa's eldest son, Sawang ösel Rangddrol Mukpo, then assumed leadership of the communal centers.

Sources:

Fields, Rick. 1981. *How the Swans Came to the Lake: A Narrative History of Buddhism in America.* Boulder, Colo.: Shambhala.

Miller, Timothy. 1999. *The 60s Communes: Hippies and Beyond.* Syracuse, N.Y.: Syracuse University Press.

Trungpa, Chogyam. 1985. *Born in Tibet.* Boston: Shambhala.

TWIN OAKS. This community was the second of three *Walden Two-*inspired utopian experiments, the first being a Walden House cooperative experiment in Washington, D.C., that lasted only about a year. In June 1967, some members of this colony purchased 123 acres for $2,000 near Louisa, Virginia, and built a colony modeled partly on B. F. Skinner's book *Walden*

Two. Named after a double oak tree on the property, Twin Oaks had a small farmhouse named "Llano" and a cluster of other buildings that the residents themselves constructed. Adults, whether single or married, lived in private rooms in residential buildings clustered around a central courtyard. Each building housed eight individuals who shared a kitchen, bathroom, living room, and a library. In 2000, 100 people lived on "450 acres of farmland and forestland in rural Virginia" (*Communities Directory*, 2000). Communal work rules and other decisions were made in a planner-manager system under a three-member planning board that met three times a week. The colony's main income was from the sale of rope hammocks, with other money coming from the manufacturing of tofu and the indexing of books. They also had a herd of dairy and beef cattle. Every resident was asked to work about 50 hours of assigned labor for which they received labor credits. Such activities as sculpture, music, painting, and drama were done without any credits. The community provided all basic needs and gave each member a monthly allowance of $50. New members did not have to surrender their personal assets but they could use them while living at Twin Oaks. Equality was stressed in matters of race and gender. Gender neutrality was maintained in communication where members used "co" instead of "he" or "she." Men can wear women's clothing and visa versa. Children were a communal responsibility and were raised on Skinner's theories. The community held conferences every autumn open to outsiders and also offered tours on Saturday afternoons. They had a three-week visitor's program available by request through their Web site: http://www.twinoaks.org. Twin Oaks sponsored two sister communities, East Wind near Tecumseh, Missouri, and Acorn, located seven miles from Twin Oaks.

Sources:

Communities Directory: A Guide to Intentional Communities and Cooperative Living. 2000. Rutledge, Missouri: Fellowship for Intentional Community.

Fogarty, Robert S. 1980. *Dictionary of American Communal and Utopian History*. Westport, Conn.: Greenwood Press.

Kindade, Kat. 1994. *Is It Utopia Yet? An Insider's View of Twin Oaks Community in Its 26th Year*. Louisa, Va.: Twin Oaks Publishing.

Miller, Timothy. 1999. *The 60s Communes: Hippies and Beyond*. Syracuse, N.Y.: Syracuse University Press.

Trahair, Richard C. S. 1999. *Utopias and Utopians: An Historical Dictionary*. Westport, Conn.: Greenwood Press.

V

VOCATIONS FOR SOCIAL CHANGE (VSC). In 1968, ten individuals founded a community in a house at Hayward and then in two houses in Canyon, California. The VSC was dedicated to serving as a clearinghouse to find jobs for people who want to change institutions toward bettering humanitarian goals. It published its monthly magazine in June of that year that listed hundreds of jobs and also offered to provide employers with information on the job-seekers.

Source:
Miller, Timothy. 1999. *The 60s Communes: Hippies and Beyond*. Syracuse, N.Y.: Syracuse University Press.

W

WALTERS, JAMES DONALD (SWAMI KRIYANANDA). Walters (1926–?) was born in Telaejen, Romania, the son of an oil geologist employed by the Esso Company. He was home-educated until he enrolled in an English Quaker School for boys at the age of 11. In 1939, his family came back to the United States and he enrolled in Kent School, Connecticut, and then in the Scarsdale, Connecticut, high school. He attended Haverford College and Brown University. In 1948, he converted to Paramahansa Yogananda's Self-Realization Fellowship (SRF) and became his disciple, taking the name Swami Kriyananda. In 1962, he was expelled from the SRF but five years later founded the Ananda World Brotherhood Village in California. Members built 22 homes on 450 acres, 21 of which were destroyed by a fire in July 1976. Although there were a few defectors after this disaster, most members persevered. In 2000, it claimed to be one of the largest intentional spiritual communities in the world, with 300 individuals living at its present location, Ananda Village, located close to Nevada City, California.

See Also Ananda World Brotherhood Village

Sources:

Communities Directory: A Guide to Intentional Communities and Cooperative Living. 2000. Rutledge, Missouri: Fellowship for Intentional Community.

Fogarty, Robert S. 1980. *Dictionary of American Communal and Utopian History.* Westport, Conn.: Greenwood Press.

Miller, Timothy. 1999. *The 60s Communes: Hippies and Beyond.* Syracuse, N.Y.: Syracuse University Press.

Trahair, Richard C. S. 1999. *Utopias and Utopians: An Historical Dictionary.* Westport, Conn.: Greenwood Press.

Walters, Donald J. 1977. *The Path: Autobiography of a Western Yogi (Swami Kriyananda)*. Nevada City, Calif.: Ananda.

WAYLAND, JULIUS A.

WAYLAND, JULIUS A. Julius A. Wayland (1854–1912) was the leading figure in the founding of Ruskin, near Nashville, Tennessee, in 1894. He was born in Versailles, Indiana. Although coming from a poor family, he became wealthy selling real estate. However, he soon was disillusioned with capitalism and became a socialist. In 1893, he founded the radical periodical *The Coming Nation*. Thereafter, he read widely in socialist works written by Edward Bellamy, Laurence Gronlund, and others. Reacting to the economic bad times of the 1890s, he helped to establish Ruskin, but left because of factional disputes.

See Also Burley Colony (Cooperative Brotherhood); Ruskin

Sources:

Brundage, W. Fitzhugh. 1996. *A Socialist Utopia in the New South: The Ruskin Colonies in Tennessee and Georgia 1894–1901*. Urbana and Chicago: University of Illinois Press.

Miller, Timothy. 1998. *The Quest for Utopia in Twentieth-Century America*. Syracuse, N.Y.: Syracuse University Press.

Oved, Yaacov. 1987. *Two Hundred Years of American Communes*. New Brunswick, N.J. and Oxford: Transaction.

Sutton, Robert P. 2004. *Communal Utopias and the American Experience: Secular Communities, 1824–2000*. Westport, Conn. and London: Praeger.

THE WAYNE PRODUCE ASSOCIATION

THE WAYNE PRODUCE ASSOCIATION. In 1924, a group of 75 adult males, some with families, emigrated from Finland and, under the leadership of Isaac Ahlborg, started a communal utopia on 800 acres near McKinnon, Georgia. The colony was a land trust, whereby each resident had a half-acre plot on which he would build a house. All members were able-bodied adult men between the ages of 18 and 45 who received $2.50 daily for work in the colony. The Wayne Produce Association was profitable, selling crops such as cabbage, cauliflower, and potatoes. The community soon gained a reputation for political radicalism since most of the residents were either Communist or members of the Wobblies (Industrial Workers of the World); some of the members even wanted to abolish the communal equal wage system. The colony lasted at least until 1936.

Sources:

Albertson, Ralph. 1936. "A Survey of Mutualistic Communities in America." *Iowa Journal of History and Politics* 34: 4 (Oct.): 375–444.

Miller, Timothy. 1998. *The Quest for Utopia in Twentieth-Century America*. Syracuse, N.Y.: Syracuse University Press.

Wooster, Ernest S. 1924. *Communities of the Past and Present*. Newllano, La.: Llano Colonist.

WHEELER'S RANCH. Bill Wheeler, the financial benefactor who underwrote Morning Star Ranch, also founded Wheeler's Ranch, the second free land community in Sonoma County, California. In 1965, Wheeler, who had money as an inheritance from a family fortune, bought 360 acres several miles from the Morning Star colony and opened Wheeler's Ranch. Three years later, after authorities arrested members of Morning Star Ranch, many of them moved to Wheeler's property. Numbering more than 200, they lived in shacks scattered over the land, planted a community garden, and raised chickens. Communal life included a Sunday dinner, sweat baths, and the use of psychedelic drugs. Like Morning Star Ranch, nudity was prevalent. Wheeler, whom one resident labeled the "benevolent king of the land," insisted on some basic rules such as prohibiting open fires at certain times of the year, not allowing dogs, and requiring members to bury their feces. Within a year, federal authorities searched the community for draft evaders and local police carried out drug busts, as they had done at Morning Star Ranch. In 1969, county officials began a concerted effort to shut down Wheeler's Ranch and Wheeler contested these moves in the Sonoma County Court, but to no avail. In 1973, the bulldozers appeared to demolish the community structures but before they could begin their work, Wheeler burned most of the buildings. Afterwards he rebuilt his home and in 1999 was living there with a few friends selling creative paintings.

See Also Crashpads; Diggers; Drop City; Hog Farm; Morning Star Ranch

Sources:

Davidson, Sara. 1977. *Loose Change*. Garden City, N.Y.: Doubleday.

Gardner, Hugh. 1978. *The Children of Prosperity: Thirteen Modern American Communes*. New York: St. Martin's.

Miller, Timothy. 1999. *The 60s Communes: Hippies and Beyond*. Syracuse, N.Y.: Syracuse University Press.

WHITEHEAD, RALPH RADCLIFFE. Whitehead (1854–1929) was born into a wealthy English family and educated at Oxford, where he came under the influence of John Ruskin. He was infatuated with Ruskin's efforts to establish utopian colonies called the Guild of St. George and experimented in organizing similar collective communities in Europe before he came to the United States in 1899. The artist Bolton Coit Brown bought 1,200 acres close to the town of Woodstock, New York. In 1902, he and Harvey White, a novelist, were joined by other artists and they built the Byrdcliffe colony consisting of craftworkers living in 29 buildings. The colony had a communal school and shops for various craftsmen and writers. The community's main income came from the manufacture of William Morris–style furniture made of heavy oak. But income from the sale of the furniture was not enough to support Byrdcliffe and within a few years morale declined. When Whitehead died, his son Peter continued as director of the arts and crafts colony.

After Peter Whitehead's death in 1976, the local Woodstock Guild of Craftsmen purchased the property.

See Also Byrdcliffe

Sources:

Evers, Alf. 1987. *Woodstock: History of an American Town.* Woodstock: Overlook Press.

Miller, Timothy. 1998. *The Quest for Utopia in Twentieth-Century America.* Syracuse, N.Y.: Syracuse University Press.

Smith, Anita M. 1959. *Woodstock: History and Hearsay.* Saugerties, N.Y.: Catskill Mountains Publishing Corp.

WILLARD, CYRUS FIELD. Cyrus Field Willard (1858–1935) was one of six children of a wealthy Lynn, Massachusetts, family. He was a founder of the socialist cooperative in the Puget Sound known as the Burley Colony. Before founding the colony, he was a Theosophist and a follower of Edward Bellamy and a significant figure in organizing the first Nationalist Clubs. These were organizations founded in 27 states to support Bellamy's ideas of national ownership of production and distribution. He earned a living as a reporter on the *Boston Globe* and as a columnist for the *Nationalist* from 1889 to 1891. Six years later, he became the secretary for the colonization committee of Eugene Debs's Social Democracy Party of America (SDA). In that capacity, he located land for sale at the southern corner of Puget Sound and, in October 1898, purchased 260 acres for $5,917, funded by the SDA, and thus began the Burley Colony. He and his wife moved there and he edited the colony's newspaper, *The Co-operator.* He also started a school in the face of opposition by some members of Burley who discounted the importance of education. He and his wife left the community in 1900 and joined the Theosophical Society. He died in Los Angeles.

See Also Burley Colony

Sources:

LeWarne, Charles P. 1975. *Utopias on Puget Sound 1885–1915.* Seattle: University of Washington Press.

Oved, Yaacov. 1987. *Two Hundred Years of American Communes.* New Brunswick, N.J. and Oxford: Transaction.

Sutton, Robert P. 2004. *Communal Utopias and the American Experience: Secular Communities, 1824–2000.* Westport, Conn. and London: Praeger.

Trahair, Richard C. S. 1999. *Utopias and Utopians: An Historical Dictionary.* Westport, Conn.: Greenwood Press.

WKFL FOUNTAIN OF THE WORLD. Francis H. Pencovic, who was born in San Francisco in 1911, was a petty criminal and mental patient before he claimed that he was a messiah come to save humanity. He took the name Krishna Venta and preached a message of total unity, according to which his disciples would live communally in wisdom, knowledge, faith, and love—

hence the acronym WKFL. In the late 1940s, they lived in Box Canyon in Southern California, wore biblical robes, and went barefoot. In the 1950s, they founded another community at Homer, Alaska. By that time, Krishna Venta had attracted about 200 followers. Pencovic practiced polygamy, and in December 1958 some male members charged him with having systematic sex with their wives and underage girls. They murdered him by bombing the central colony building in which he and some disciples were meeting. His wife, Ruth, kept the community together until the 1980s by inviting hippies into the colony as visitors, one of whom was Charles Manson and his family.

Sources:
Beam, Maurice. 1964. *Cults of America*. New York: Macfadden.

Lewis, James R. 1991. *Religious Leaders of America*. Detroit: Gale.

Mathison, Richard. 1960. *Faiths, Cults, and Sects of America*. Indianapolis: Bobbs-Merrill.

Miller, Timothy. 1998. *The Quest for Utopia in Twentieth-Century America*. Syracuse, N.Y.: Syracuse University Press.

THE WOMAN'S COMMONWEALTH. This colony was one of the Protestant evangelical communities founded during the last quarter of the nineteenth century. In 1874, Martha McWhirter formed the group, otherwise known as the Sanctificationists, as a celibate community that lived in the Central Hotel in Belton, Texas, where they offered outsiders meals and rented rooms. In 1898, with the profits made from running the hotel, they purchased a large boardinghouse in Washington, D.C., and later, in Maryland, a 120-acre farm. The community included 32 women and four men. Under McWhirter's leadership, they stressed moral reform, voluntary associations to promote sanctification, and Bible study. After McWhirter's death in 1904, membership fell from 36 to 17 within three years. Not encouraging new members to join, the Woman's Commonwealth steadily eroded over the following decades and by 1946, there were only two members still living at the Maryland farm.

See Also New House of Israel; The Olive Branch Mission; Shiloh: Church of the Living God

Sources:
Fogarty, Robert S. 1980. *Dictionary of American Communal and Utopian History*. Westport, Conn.: Greenwood Press.

Kitch, Sally. 1989. *Chaste Liberation: Celibacy and Female Cultural Status*. Urbana: University of Illinois Press.

Miller, Timothy. 1998. *The Quest for Utopia in Twentieth-Century America*. Syracuse, N.Y.: Syracuse University Press.

Trahair, Richard C. S. 1999. *Utopias and Utopians: An Historical Dictionary*. Westport, Conn.: Greenwood Press.

WOMANSHARE FEMINIST WOMEN'S LAND. In 2000, this commune advertised itself in the *Communities Directory* as being "a home and family of lesbians on 232 acres near Grants Pass in southern Oregon." Three lesbians founded WomanShare in 1974 and its five members, in addition to farming the land, worked toward self-sufficiency by becoming skilled at traditionally male tasks, such as car repair. It was a feminist retreat center made up entirely of women. They built a main house, open to visitors, and members lived in separate cabins, some of which were set aside for the visitors. The commune had hot water, electricity, a composting toilet, and hot tub. They asked a sliding-scale fee for women visitors, who were asked to make advance reservations, of $15 to $35 per night for accommodations in a private cabin.

Sources:

Communities Directory: A Guide to Intentional Communities and Cooperative Living. 2000. Rutledge, Mo.: Fellowship for Intentional Community.

Miller, Timothy. 1999. *The 60s Communes: Hippies and Beyond.* Syracuse, N.Y.: Syracuse University Press.

Sue, Nelly, Dian, Carol, and Billie. 1976. *Country Lesbians: The Story of WomanShare Collective.* Grants Pass, Ore.: WomanShare.

WOODBINE. In 1891, the Hirsch Fund, a Jewish philanthropic agency that promoted communal farm communities, appointed Julius Goldman as head of a Committee on Agricultural and Industrial Settlements. He purchased 5,300 acres in Dennis Township in South New Jersey, about 50 miles from Philadelphia, as the site for the Woodbine Land and Improvement Company. He designated 800 acres for a communal square and divided the rest into 15-acre family parcels. Families had to pay an admission fee of $200 and purchase stock in the company. Initially, 60 families joined Woodbine. They constructed houses, a hotel, railway station, school, and synagogue. Woodbine's main source of income was a factory that made Jonasson cloaks, and members planned other factories to make cigars, cutlery, and knitted items. In addition, Woodbine advertised itself as an agricultural school that would give young Jewish men training in farming. By 1929, Woodbine had become predominantly a colony of farmers and 12 years later, the trustees of the Hirsch Fund permitted the residents to purchase their farms. The town exists in the year 2004 as an incorporated borough, although both Jews and non-Jews live there.

See Also Carmel

Sources:

Brandes, Joseph. 1971. *Immigrants to Freedom: Jewish Communities in Rural New Jersey since 1882.* Philadelphia: University of Pennsylvania Press.

Eisenberg, Ellen. 1995. *Jewish Agricultural Colonies in New Jersey 1882–1920.* Syracuse, N.Y.: Syracuse University Press.

Herscher, Uri D. 1981. *Jewish Agricultural Utopias in America, 1880–1910.* Detroit: Wayne State University Press.

Sutton, Robert P. 2003. *Communal Utopias and the American Experience: Religious Communities, 1732–2000.* Westport, Conn. and London: Praeger.

Y

YADDO. This arts colony was founded in 1926 at Saratoga Springs, New York, on 500 acres that contained a Victorian mansion built by Spencer Trask. After his death in 1909, his wife, Katrina, remarried and in 1926 she and her second husband turned the estate into an arts colony. By 1946, an average of 20 artists, along with their nonartistic mates, lived at Yaddo and worked in studios scattered about the colony. Some of its residents over the years included Katherine Anne Porter, Aaron Copland, and Truman Capote.

Source:
Miller, Timothy. 1998. *The Quest for Utopia in Twentieth-Century America*. Syracuse, N.Y.: Syracuse University Press.

Z

ZEN CENTER OF LOS ANGELES. Taizan Maezumi and several students opened the Zen Center of Los Angeles (ZCLA) in 1967 in a rented house. The next year, they purchased a permanent home and by the 1980s the several hundred members of ZCLA occupied an entire city block. The center required hours of daily meditation, plus "full-time intensives." After they purchased land outside the city in 1980, the community opened a rural retreat to provided training in Zen. Unfortunately, Maezumi's alcoholism and sexual relations with female followers brought about a crisis in the 1980s and he had to undergo therapy to reestablish his control before he died in 1995.

See Also Kwan Um Zen School; San Francisco Zen Center

Source:
Miller, Timothy. 1999. *The 60s Communes: Hippies and Beyond*. Syracuse, N.Y.: Syracuse University Press.

ZION CITY. In January 1900, John Alexander Dowie, a Chicago faith healer and founder of the Christian Catholic Church, founded Zion City on 6,500 acres 40 miles north of Chicago on Lake Michigan. Dowie prepared his followers, who at the start numbered over 1,000, for the millennium while they lived according to the Bible and total acceptance of his power of divine healing. He claimed that Satan caused all diseases. Dowie forbade the use of tobacco and alcohol and the consumption of pork and oysters. His followers built an elaborate, well-planned city that ultimately housed 8,000 people. Dowie, however, owned all basic operations—such as the bank, retail stores, and factories. He demanded daily religious ceremonies where everyone, on the blowing of a city whistle, would stop and pray. Family life was patriarchal, dominated by the father, and Dowie arranged all marriages. City laws prohibited drunkenness, smoking, swearing, gambling, fighting, spitting, and the riding of bicycles on sidewalks. In 1903, when Dowie faced bankruptcy proceedings because he did not pay the city's bills, he temporarily left Zion City for Australia, then for Mexico, to gather new disciples. In his absence, a series of Overseers ran the community, but morale declined. In April 1906, one of the Overseers, Wilber Glenn Voliva, led a revolt against Dowie and deposed him. Dowie died on March 9, 1907. Over the next four years, more than 1,500 members left Zion City and outsiders purchased some of its businesses and factories. After Voliva's death in 1942, the theocratic utopia dissolved and Zion (the name City had been dropped by then) became just another American town, although the Christian Catholic Church was still predominant there at the end of the twentieth century.

See Also Dowie, John Alexander

Sources:

Cook, Philip L. 1996. *Zion City, Illinois: Twentieth-Century Utopia.* Syracuse, N.Y.: Syracuse University Press.

Fogarty, Robert S. 1980. *Dictionary of American Communal and Utopian History.* Westport, Conn.: Greenwood Press.

Miller, Timothy. 1998. *The Quest for Utopia in Twentieth-Century America.* Syracuse, N.Y.: Syracuse University Press.

Sutton, Robert P. 2003. *Communal Utopias and the American Experience: Religious Communities, 1732–2000.* Westport, Conn. and London: Praeger.

APPENDIX: LOCATIONS AND DATES OF ORGANIZATIONS

Abode of the Message. New Lebanon, New York 1875–ongoing.

The Alamo Christian Foundation. Hollywood and Saugus, California; Alma, Arkansas, 1969–1994.

Alpha Farm. Deadwood, Oregon, 1972–ongoing.

The Altruist Community. Sulphur Springs, Missouri, 1895–1917.

Amana. Amana, Iowa, 1854–1932.

The American Woman's Republic. Rancho Atascadero, California, 1913–1921.

Amity Colony. Fort Amity, Colorado 1898–1910.

Ananda Ashram. Monroe, New York, 1964–ongoing.

Ananda Ashrama. La Crescenta, California, 1923–ongoing.

Ananda World Brotherhood Village. Nevada City, California, 1968–ongoing.

Arcosanti. Mayer, Arizona, 1970–ongoing.

The Army of Industry. Auburn, California, 1914–1920.

Arpin. Arpin, Wisconsin, 1904–1958.

Beaux Arts Village. Seattle, Washington, 1909–?

Berea. Berea, Kentucky, 1866–1908.

Bethany Fellowship. Bloomington, Minnesota, 1945–ongoing.

Bethel Home. Brooklyn, New York, 1904–ongoing.

Black Bear Ranch. Forks of Salmon, California, 1968–ongoing.

Black Mountain College. Bloomington, Minnesota, 1933–ongoing.

The Bohemian Cooperative Farming Company. Maryland, Tennessee, 1913–1916.

Branch Davidians (Davidian Seventh-Day Adventists). Waco, Texas, and other locations, 1934–1993.

Bruderhof. Germany, England, Paraguay, Rifton, New York and other locations, 1920s–ongoing.

Bryn Athyn. South Strafford, Vermont, 1967–1969.

Burley Colony (Cooperative Brotherhood). Puget Sound, Washington. 1898–1924.

Burning Bush. Waukesha, Wisconsin, 1912–1919.

Byrdcliffe. Washington, New York, 1902–1906.

Carmel. Carmel, New Jersey, 1889–1932.

Catholic Worker Movement. Various locations, 1933–ongoing.

Celo Community. Burnsville, North Carolina, 1937–ongoing.

Cerro Gordo. Cottage Grove, Oregon, 1973–ongoing.

Cheeseboard. San Francisco, California, 1967–ongoing.

Children of God (The Family). Many locations, 1969–ongoing.

Children of Light. Dateland, Arizona, 1949–ongoing.

Church of God and Saints of Christ. Belleville, Virginia, 1901–ongoing.

Church of the Savior. Washington, D.C., 1946–ongoing.

Clarion. Gunnison, Utah, 1911–1915.

Cold Mountain Farm. Hobart, New York, 1967–1968.

The Colony. Hawkins Bay, California 1940–ongoing.

Colorado Co-operative Company. Tabegauche Park, Colorado, 1894–1906.

Commonwealth College. Mena, Arkansas, 1923–1940.

Community for Creative Nonviolence (CCNV). Washington, D.C., 1970–ongoing.

Crashpads. Various places, 1967–1968.

Davidian Seventh-Day Adventists. Waco, Texas, 1934–1993.

Delta and Providence. Hillhouse and Cruger, Mississippi, 1933–1956.

The Des Moines University of Lawsonomy. Des Moines, Iowa, 1943–1954.

Diga. San Antonio, Texas, 1932–1936.

Diggers. San Francisco, California, 1966–?

The Divine Light Mission. Denver, Colorado and other locations, early 1970s–1980s.

Drop City. Trinidad, Colorado, 1965–1973.

Drummond Island. Lake Huron, 1905–1914.

Durham and Delhi. Chico, California, 1917–1932.

Ellicott City. Ellicott City, Maryland, 1900–after 1908.

The Emissary Communities. 1939–ongoing

Equality. Puget Sound, Washington, 1897–1907.

Esalen Institute. Big Sur California, 1962–ongoing.

Fairhope. Fairhope, Alabama, 1895–ongoing.

The Family (Taos). Taos, New Mexico, 1967–?

The Farm. Summertown, Tennessee, branches in Missouri, New York, Michigan, Wisconsin, Texas and Florida. 1971–ongoing. (All the branches have closed.)

Fellowship Farm. Puente, California, 1912–1927.

Fellowship Farm. Westwood, Massachusetts, 1908–1920s.

Fellowship for Intentional Communities (FIC). Yellow Springs, Ohio and elsewhere. 1940–ongoing.

Ferrer Colony. Shelton, New Jersey, 1915–1946.

Freedom Colony. Fulton, Kansas, 1898–1905.

Freedom Hill. Roscoe, California, 1908–1940.

Freeland. Whidbey Island, Washington, 1899–1906.

Gesundheit Institute. Hillsboro, West Virginia, 1971–ongoing.

Glendenning: The Levites/Order of Aaron. EskDale, Utah, 1956–ongoing.

Gorda Mountain. Gorda, California, 1962–1968.

Gould Farm. Great Barrington, Massachusetts, 1913–ongoing.

Grateful Dead. 710 Ashbury, San Francisco, California, 1960s.

Happyville. Aiken, South Carolina, 1905–1908.

Havurat Shalom. Somerville, Massachusetts, 1968.

The Healthy-Happy-Holy Organization. Santa Fe, New Mexico, 1969–ongoing.

Helicon Hall Colony. Fort Lee, New Jersey, 1906–1908.

Heaven City. Harvard, Illinois, 1923–1927.

High Ridge Farm. Southern Oregon, 1968–?

The Himalayan Academy. Virginia, Nevada and Kapaa, Hawaii, 1962–ongoing.

Hoedads. Eugene, Oregon, 1970–?

Hog Farm and Friends (Black Oak Ranch). Sunland, California; Llano, New Mexico; Berkeley, California, 1965–ongoing.

Holy City. San Jose, California, 1919–1952.

Home Colony. Puget Sound, Washington, 1898–1909.

The House of David. Benton Harbor, Michigan, 1903–ongoing.

Hutterites. South Dakota and elsewhere, 1874–ongoing.

International Society for Krishna Consciousness (ISKCON). New York City and elsewhere, 1965–ongoing.

Jesus People USA. Milwaukee, Wisconsin, Chicago, Illinois, 1972–ongoing.

Kerista. San Francisco, California, 1971–ongoing.

Kilgore: Zion's Order. Mansfield, Missouri, 1951–ongoing.

Koinonia. Baltimore, Maryland, 1951–1981.

Koinonia Farm. Americus, Georgia, 1941–ongoing.

Koreshan Unity. Estero, Florida, 1894–1961.

Krishna Venta. Box Canyon, California and Homer, Alaska, late 1930s–ongoing.

Kristenstaet. Fort Worth, Texas, 1928–late 1930s.

Krotona. Hollywood and Ojai, California, 1911–ongoing.

Kwan Um Zen School. Providence, Rhode Island and elsewhere, 1972–ongoing.

Lama Foundation. San Cristobal, New Mexico, 1967–ongoing.

The Land of Shalam. Dona Ana, New Mexico, 1884–1907.

Lemurian Fellowship. Romona, California, 1941–ongoing.

Libre. Gardner, Colorodo, 1968–ongoing.

Lila. El Rito, New Mexico, 1969.

Lily Dale and Cassadaga. Southwestern New York and Cassadaga, Florida, 1897–ongoing

The Little Landers Colony. Tijuana River Valley, California, 1909–1918.

Llano del Rio/Newllano. Palmdale, California and Staples, Louisiana, 1914–1938.

Lopez Island. Lopez Island, Washington, 1912–1920

The Lord's Farm. Woodcliff, New Jersey, 1889–1910.

Love Israel Family. Seattle and Arlington, Washington, 1968–ongoing.

MacDowell Colony. Petersborough, New Hampshire, 1907–ongoing.

Macedonia Cooperative Community. Clarksville, Georgia, 1937–1958.

Ma-Na-Har Cooperative Fellowship and the Bhoodan Center of Inquiry. Oakhurst, California, 1953–1990s.

Mankind United. Scattered locations in California after 1942 until they gathered at Willits, California, in the early 1960s.

The Maverick. Woodstock, New York, 1904–ongoing

Melbourne Village. Melbourne, Florida, 1947–ongoing.

Merry Pranksters. La Honda, California and Pleasant Hill, Oregon, 1963–1969.

The Messianic Communities (Twelve Tribes). Island Pond, Vermont, 1972–ongoing.

Millbrook. Millbrook, New York, 1962–1967.

The Molokan Communities. Los Angeles, San Francisco and other locations, 1904–ongoing.

Montague Farm. Montague, Massachusetts, 1968–?

Moonies (Unification Church). Oregon, San Francisco, California, Washington D.C. and elsewhere, 1960–ongoing.

The Morehouses. California and other locations, 1967–?

Morning Star East. Taos, New Mexico, 1969–1972.

Morning Star Ranch. Occidental, California, 1966–1973.

MOVE. Philadelphia, Pennsylvania, 1971–ongoing.

Movement for a New Society (MNS). Philadelphia, Pennsylvania, 1970–ongoing.

New Buffalo. Arroyo Hondo, New Mexico, 1967–1996.

New Clairvaux. Montague, Massachusetts, 1900–1909.

New Deal Cooperatives. Suffern, New York; Elida, New Mexico; San Antonia, Texas; Alicia, Michigan; Hightown, New Jersey; Woodlake, Texas; Dyess, Arkansas; Pine Mountain, Georgia; Cherry Lake, Florida; Lake Dick, Arkansas; Casa Grande, Arizona; Terrebonne Parish, Louisiana; Greenbelt, Maryland; Greendale, Wisconsin; Greenhills, Cincinnati, Ohio, 1932–1957.

Nevada Colony. Nevada City, Nevada, 1916–1919.

New House of Israel. Livingston and Leggett, Texas, 1895–1920.

The Olive Branch Mission. Chicago, Illinois, 1876–ongoing.

Olompali Ranch. Novato, California, 1967–1969.

Packer Corner/Total Loss Farm. Guilford, Vermont, 1968–ongoing.

Padanaram Settlement. Williams, Indiana, 1966–ongoing.

Peace Mission (Father Divine). Various places, 1929–1965.

Penn-Craft. Uniontown, Pennsylvania, 1937–?

Peoples Temple. Redwood Valley, California; Jonestown, Guyana, early 1970s–1978.

Pisgah Grande. Santa Susana, California, Pikesville, Tennessee, 1914–1990s.

Point Loma (Universal Brotherhood and Theosophical Society). San Diego and Covina, California, 1898–1942.

Preston. Cloverdale, California, 1869–1988.

Projects One, Two, and Artaud. San Francisco, California, 1971–late 1980s.

Quarry Hill. Rochester, Vermont, 1946–ongoing.

Rancho Rajneesh. Antelope, Oregon, 1981–1985.

Reality Construction Company. Taos, New Mexico, 1969–1972

Reba Place Fellowship. Evanston, Illinois, 1957–ongoing.

Red Rockers. Farisita, Colorado, 1969–early 1970s.

Renaissance Community/Brotherhood of the Spirit. Leyden and Gill, Massachusetts; Guilford, Vermont, 1968–ongoing.

The Rochester Folk Art Guild (East Hill Farm). Naples, New York, 1967–ongoing.

Rose Valley. Philadelphia, Pennsylvania, 1901–1921.

Roycroft. East Aurora, New York, 1895–ongoing.

Ruskin. Ruskin, Ware County, Georgia. 1894–1902.

San Francisco Zen Center. San Francisco, California, 1959–1983.

Sandhill Farm. Rutledge, Missouri, 1974–ongoing.

School of Living. Suffern, New York, 1936–45.

Shaker Communities. Mount Lebanon, New York, and other locations 1774–ongoing.

Shiloh: Church of the Living God. Bowdoinham, Maine, 1893–1920.

Shiloh Communities. Chautauqua County, New York, and Sulphur Springs, Arkansas, 1941–ongoing.

Shiloh Youth Revival Center. Costa Mesa, California, Eugene, Oregon, and other locations, 1969–1989.

Short Creek (Colorado City). Colorado City, Utah, 1928–53.

The Societas Fraternia. Fullerton, California, 1876–1921

Spirit Fruit Society. Lisbon, Ohio, Chicago, Illinois, and Santa Cruz, California, 1901–1928.

Sojourners Community. Washington, D.C., 1972–ongoing.

Southern Co-operative Association of Apalachicola. Apalachicola, Florida, 1900–1904.

Stelle. Stelle, Illinois, 1973–ongoing.

Straight Edge Industrial Settlement. New York City and Alpine, New Jersey, 1899–1918.

Sunrise Community. Alicia, Michigan, 1933–1936.

Sunrise Cooperative Farms. Hightstown, New Jersey, 1933–1936.

Sunrise Hill. Conway, Massachusetts, 1966–1967.

Sunrise Ranch. Loveland, Colorado, 1945–ongoing.

Synanon. Santa Monica, California and other locations, 1958–1991.

Table Mountain Ranch. Albion, California, 1968–ongoing.

Temple of the People (Halcyon). Pismo Beach, California, 1903–1912.

The Thelemic "Magick" Community. Pasadena, California, 1939–1949.

Tolstoy Farm. Davenport, Washington, 1962–ongoing.

Trabuco College. Trabuco Canyon, California, 1942–1947.

Twin Oaks. Louisa, Virginia, 1967–ongoing.

Vocations for Social Change (VSC). Oakland, Hayward, and Canyon, California, 1968–?.

The Wayne Produce Association. McKinnon, Georgia, 1924–1936.

Wheeler's Ranch. Sonoma County, California, 1967–ongoing.

WKFL Fountain of the World. Box Canyon, California and Homer, Alaska, 1940–1980s.

The Woman's Commonwealth. Belton, Texas and Washington, D.C., 1874–1946.

Womanshare Feminist Women's Land. Grants Pass, Oregon, 1974–ongoing.

Woodbine. Woodbine, New Jersey, 1891–1941.

Yaddo. Saratoga Springs, New York, 1926–ongoing.

Zen Center of Los Angeles (ZCLA). Los Angeles, California, 1968–ongoing.

Zion City. Zion City, Illinois, 1901–1942.

LIST OF WEB SITES

FELLOWSHIP FOR INTENTIONAL COMMUNITY

http://www.ic.org This is the metasite of the Fellowship for Intentional Community, as listed on page four of *Communities Directory: A Guide to Intentional Communities and Cooperative Living,* Rutledge, Missouri: Fellowship for Intentional Community, 2000. It has a long listing of communities at the top of the left sidebar.

H-COMMUNAL SOCIETIES: AN H-NET NETWORK

http://www.h-net.org/~commsoc/ This is concerned with topics related to intentional communities, including the academic study of communities, participation and membership in them, and curatorship and other activities related to the preservation of historic communal sites and artifacts.

THE COHOUSING ASSOCIATION OF THE UNITED STATES (COHO/US)

http://www.cohousing.org/cmty/groups.html The Cohousing Association of the United States (Coho/US) is an organization whose purpose is to promote and encourage the cohousing concept, support both individuals and groups in creating communities, provide assistance to completed groups for improving their systems for living together in community, and provide networking opportunities for those involved or interested in cohousing.

THE COHOUSING ASSOCIATION OF CANADA
(CANADIAN)

http://www.cohousing.ca/ (Canadian) Cohousing as defined by the Cohousing Network is a concept that came to North America in 1988 from Denmark, where it emerged over 25 years ago. It describes neighborhoods that combine the autonomy of private dwellings with the advantages of shared resources and community living.

OPEN DIRECTORY PROJECTS

http://dmoz.org/Society/Lifefstyle_Choices/Intentional_*Communities*/ This web site is for the Open Directory Projects listings for intentional communities. Dmoz.org., aka Open Directory Project, is similar to Yahoo! and its directory, but it is open source, meaning that anyone can participate in it.

SELECTED READINGS

Adams, Patch, with Maureen Mylander. 1993. *Gesundheit! Bringing Good Health to You, the Medical System, and Society through Physician Service, Complementary Therapies, Humor, and Joy.* Rochester, Vt.: Healing Arts.

Adkin, Clare. 1990. *Brother Benjamin: A History of the Israelite House of David.* Berrien Springs, Mich.: Andrews University Press.

Aidala, Angela A., and Benjamin D. Zablocki. 1991. "The Communes of the 1970s: Who Joined and Why?" *Marriage and Family Review* 17: 87–116.

Alyea, Paul E., and Blanche Alyea. 1956. *Fairhope 1894–1954: The Story of a Single Tax Colony.* Tuscaloosa: University of Alabama Press.

Andelson, Jonathan G. 1997. "The Community of True Inspiration from Germany to the Amana Colonies." In *America's Communal Utopias,* Donald E. Pitzer, ed. Chapel Hill and London: University of North Carolina Press.

Andrews, Edward D. 1963. *The People Called Shakers: A Search for the Perfect Society.* New York: Dover.

Arndt, Karl J. R. 1971. *George Rapp's Successors and Material Heirs, 1846–1916.* Rutherford, N.J.: Farleigh Dickinson University Press.

Arnold, Joseph L. 1971. *The New Deal in the Suburbs: A History of the Greenbelt Town Program 1935–1945.* Columbus, Ohio: Ohio State University Press.

Arrington, Leonard J., Feramorz Y. Fox, and Dean L. May. 1976. *Building the City of God: Community and Cooperation among the Mormons.* Salt Lake City: Desert Book Co.

Ayers, William, ed. 1983. *A Poor Sort of Heaven, a Good Sort of Earth: The Rose Valley Arts and Crafts Experiment.* Chadds Ford, Pa.: Brandywine River Museum.

Baer, Hans A. 1988. *Recreating Utopia in the Desert: A Sectarian Challenge to Modern Mormonism.* Albany: State University of New York Press.

Baldwin, Sidney. 1968. *Poverty and Politics: The Rise and Decline of the Farm Security Administration.* Chapel Hill: University of North Carolina Press.

Bammer, Angelika. 1991. *Partial Visions: Feminism and Utopianism in the 1970s.* London: Routledge and Keagan.

Barkun, Michael. 1984. "Communal Societies a Cyclical Phenomena." *Communal Societies* 4: 35–48.

Bartelt, Pearl W. 1997. "American Jewish Agricultural Colonies." In *America's Communal Utopias,* Donald E. Pitzer, ed., 352–74. Chapel Hill and London: University of North Carolina Press.

Barthel, Diane L. 1984. *Amana: From Pietist Sect to American Community.* Lincoln: University of Nebraska Press.

Berger, Bennett M. 1981. *The Survival of a Counterculture: Ideological Work and Everyday Life among Rural Communards.* Berkeley: University of California Press.

Berry, Brian J.L. 1992. *America's Utopian Experiments: Communal Havens from Long-Wave Crises.* Hanover, N.H. and London: University Press of New England.

Boris, Eileen. 1986. *Art and Labor: Ruskin, Morris, and the Craftsman Ideal in America.* Philadelphia: Temple University Press.

Borowski, Karol. 1984. *Attempting an Alternative Society: A Sociological Study of a Selected Communal-Revitalization Movement in the United States.* Norwood, Pa.: Norwood Editions.

Bouvard, Marguerite. 1975. *The Intentional Community Movement.* Port Washington, N.Y.: National University Publications, Kennikat Press.

Bradley, Martha Sonntag. 1993. *Kidnapped from That Land: The Government Raids on the Short Creek Polygamists.* Salt Lake City: University of Utah Press.

Brandes, Joseph. 1972. *Immigrants to Freedom: Jewish Communities in Rural New Jersey since 1882.* Philadelphia: University of Pennsylvania Press.

Brewer, Priscilla J. 1986. *Shaker Communities, Shaker Lives.* Hanover, N.H. and London: University Press of New England.

Brundage, W. Fitzhugh. 1996. *A Socialist Utopia in the New South: The Ruskin Colonies in Tennessee and Georgia1894–1901.* Urbana and Chicago: University of Illinois Press.

Champney, Freeman. 1968. *Art and Glory: The Story of Elbert Hubbard.* New York: Crown.

Cohen, David Steven. 1977. "'The Angel Dancers': The Folklore of Religious Communitarianism." *New Jersey History* 95 (spring 1977): 5–20.

Cohen, Joseph J. 1975. *In Quest of Heaven: The Story of the Sunrise Co-operative Community.* New York: Sunrise History Publishing Committee, 1957; reprint, Philadelphia: Porcupine Press.

Communities Directory: A Guide to Cooperative Living. 1995. Langley, Washington: Fellowship for Intentional Community.

Communities Directory: A Guide to Intentional Communities and Cooperative Living. 2000. Rutledge, Mo.: Fellowship for Intentional Community.

Conkin, Paul K. 1959. *Tomorrow a New World: The New Deal Community Program.* Ithaca, N.Y.: Cornell University Press.

———. 1964. *Two Paths to Utopia: The Hutterites and the Llano Colony.* Lincoln: University of Nebraska Press.

Cook, Philip L. 1996. *Zion City, Illinois: Twentieth Century Utopia.* Syracuse, N.Y.: Syracuse University Press.

Coyote, Peter. 1998. *Sleeping Where I Fall: A Chronicle.* Washington, D.C.: Counterpoint.

Crepeau, Richard C. 1988. *Melbourne Village: The First Twenty-five Years (1946–1971).* Orlando: University of Central Florida Press.

Cutler, Phoebe. 1985. *The Public Landscape of the New Deal.* New Haven, Conn.: Yale University Press.

Dallas, Jerry W. 1987. "The Delta and Providence Farms: A Mississippi Experiment in Co-operative Farming and Racial Cooperation, 1936–1956." *Mississippi Quarterly* 40 (3): 283–308.

Day, Dorothy. 1952. *The Long Loneliness: An Autobiography.* New York: Harper.

Desroche, Henri. 1971. *The American Shakers: From Neo-Christianity to Presocialism.* Trans. John K. Savocoo. Boston: University of Massachusetts Press.

Diamond, Stephen. 1971. *What the Trees Said: Life on a New Age Farm.* New York: Dell.

Dohrman, H. T. 1958. *California Cult: The Story of "Mankind United."* Boston: Beacon.

Duberman, Martin. 1973. *Black Mountain: An Experiment in Community.* Garden City, N.Y.: Doubleday/Anchor.

Dubrovsky, Gertrude Wishnick. 1992. *This Land Was Theirs: Jewish Farmers in the Garden State.* Tuscaloosa: University of Alabama Press.

Egerton, John. 1977. *Visions of Utopia: Nashoba, Rugby, Ruskin and the "New Communities" in Tennessee's Past.* Knoxville: University of Tennessee Press.

Eisenberg, Ellen. 1995. *Jewish Agricultural Colonies in New Jersey, 1882–1920.* Syracuse, N.Y.: Syracuse University Press.

Evers, Alf. 1987. *Woodstock: History of an American Town.* Woodstock: Overlook Press.

Fairfield, Richard [Dick]. 1972. *Communes USA: A Personal Tour.* Baltimore: Penguin.

———. 1971. *The Modern Utopian: Communes, U.S.A.* San Francisco: Alternatives Foundation.

Fields, Rick. 1981. *How the Swans Came to the Lake: A Narrative History of Buddhism in America.* Boulder, Colo.: Shambhala.

Fike, Rupert, ed. 1998. *Voices from The Farm: Adventures in Community Living.* Summertown, Tenn.: Book Publishing Co.

Fogarty, Robert. 1990. *All Things New: American Communes and Utopian Movements 1860–1914.* Chicago: University of Chicago Press.

———. 1980. *Dictionary of American Communal and Utopian History.* Westport, Conn.: Greenwood Press.

———. 1981. *The Righteous Remnant: The House of David.* Kent, Ohio: Kent State University Press.

Gardner, Hugh. 1978. *The Children of Prosperity: Thirteen Modern American Communes.* New York: St. Martin's.

Gardner, Joyce. 1970. *Cold Mountain Farm: An Attempt at Community.* n.p.

Gaskin, Stephen. 1999. *Amazing Dope Tales.* Berkeley, Calif.: Ronnin.

———. 1972. *The Caravan.* New York: Random House.

———. 1974. *Hey Beatnik! This Is the Farm Book.* Summertown, Tenn.: Book Publishing Co.

———. 1980. *Mind at Play.* Summertown, Tenn.: Book Publishing Co.

Gaston, Paul M. 1993. *Man and Mission: E. B. Gaston and the Origins of the Fairhope Single Tax Colony.* Montgomery, Ala.: The Black Belt Press.

_____. 1984. *Women of Fair Hope.* Athens: University of Georgia Press.

Goldberg, Robert A. 1986. *Back to the Soil: The Jewish Farmers of Clarion, Utah, and Their World.* Salt Lake City: University of Utah Press.

Grant, H. Roger. 1971. "Missouri's Utopian Communities." *Missouri Historical Review* 66 (Oct.): 20–48.

———. 1977. "Portrait of a Workers' Utopia: The Labor Exchange and the Freedom, Kan., Colony." *Kansas Historical Quarterly* 43(Oct. 1971): 56–66.

———. 1988. *Spirit Fruit: A Gentle Utopia.* DeKalb: Northern Illinois University Press.

Gravy, Wavy. 1974. *The Hog Farm and Friends.* New York: Links.

———. 1974. *Something Good for a Change: Random Notes on Peace through Living.* New York: St. Martin's.

Greenstein, Paul, Nigey Lennon, and Lionel Rolf. 1992. *Bread and Hyacinths: The Rise and Fall of Utopian Los Angeles.* Los Angeles: California Classics Books.

Greenwalt, Emmett A. 1978. *The Point Loma Community in California: 1897–1942—A Theosophical Experiment.* Berkeley: University of California Press, 1955. Rev. ed. Published as *California Utopia: Point Loma: 1897–1942.* San Diego: Point Loma Publications.

Gustaitis, Rasa. 1969. *Turning On.* London: Weidenfeld and Nicolson.

Hall, John R. 1978. *The Ways Out: Utopian Communal Groups in an Age of Babylon.* London: Routledge and Kegan Paul.

Hayden, Dolores. 1976. *Seven American Utopias: The Architecture of Communitarian Socialism, 1790–1975.* Cambridge, Mass.: MIT Press.

Hedgepeth, William, and Dennis Stock. 1970. *The Alternative: Communal Life in New America.* New York: Macmillan.

Henry, Lyell D., Jr. 1991. *Zig-Zag-and-Swirl: Alfred W. Lawson's Quest for Greatness.* Iowa City: University of Iowa Press.

Herscher, Uri D. 1981. *Jewish Agricultural Utopias in America, 1880–1910.* Detroit: Wayne State University Press.

Hinds, William A. 1908. *American Communities and Co-operative Colonies.* Chicago: Kerr, 3d ed.

Hine, Robert V. 1997. "California's Socialist Utopias." In *America's Communal Utopias,* Donald E. Pitzer, ed. Chapel Hill and London: University of North Carolina Press.

———.1983. *California's Utopian Colonies.* Berkeley: University of California Press.

Hoagland, Alison K., and Margaret M. Mulrooney. 1991. *Norvelt and Penn-Craft, Pennsylvania: Subsistence-Homestead Communities of the 1930s.* Washington, D.C.: Historic American Buildings Survey/Historic American Engineering Record, America's Industrial Heritage Project, National Park Service.

Holley, Donald. 1975. *Uncle Sam's Farmers: The New Deal Communities in the Lower Mississippi Valley.* Champaign: University of Illinois Press.

Horsch, John. 1977. *The Hutterite Brethren 1528–1931.* Cayley, Alberta, Canada: Macmillan.

Hostetler, John A. 1974. *Hutterite Society.* Baltimore: Johns Hopkins University Press.

Hostetler, John A., and Gertrude Enders Huntington. 1967. *The Hutterites in North America.* New York: Holt, Rinehart and Winston.

Houriet, Robert. 1971. *Getting Back Together.* New York: Avon.

Huntington, Gertrude E. "Living the Ark: Four Centuries of Hutterite Faith and Community." 1997. In *America's Communal Utopias,* Donald E. Pitzer, ed. Chapel Hill and London: University of North Carolina Press.

Inscoe, John C., ed. 1994. *Georgia in Black and White: Explorations in the Race Relations of a Southern State, 1865–1950.* Athens and London: University of Georgia Press.

Jackson, Carl T. 1994. *Vedanta for the West: The Ramakrishna Movement in the United States.* Bloomington: Indiana University Press.

Jackson, David, and Neta Jackson. 1987. *Glimpses of Glory: Thirty Years of Community: The Story of Reba Place Fellowship.* Elgin, Ill.: Brethren Press.

———. 1974. *Living Together in a World Falling Apart.* Carol Stream, Ill.: Creation House.

Janzen, Rod A. 1999. *The Prairie People: Forgotten Anabaptists.* Hanover, N.H.: University Press of New England.

Jerome, Judson. 1974. *Families of Eden: Communes and the New Anarchism.* New York: Seabury.

Jones, Libby F., and Sarah W. Goodwin, eds. 1990. *Feminism, Utopia and Narrative.* Knoxville: University of Tennessee Press.

Kagan, Paul. 1975. *New World Utopias: A Photographic History of the Search for Community.* New York: Penguin.

Kanter, Rosabeth Moss. 1972. *Commitment and Community: Communes and Utopias in Sociological Perspective.* Cambridge, Mass.: Harvard University Press.

———. 1974. "Communes in Cities." *Working Papers for a New Society* (summer): 36–44.

———, ed. 1973. *Communes: Creating and Managing the Collective Life.* New York: Harper and Row.

Katz, Elia. 1971. *Armed Love.* New York: Bantam.

Kinkade, Kat. 1994. *Is It Utopia Yet? An Insider's View of Twin Oaks Community in Its 26th Year.* [Louisa, Va.]: Twin Oaks Publishing.

———.1973. *A Walden Two Experiment: The First Five Years of Twin Oaks Community.* Norwood, Pa.: Norwood Editions.

Kitch, Sally. 1989. *Chaste Liberation: Celibacy and Female Cultural Status.* Urbana: University of Illinois Press.

Klelps, Art. 1977. *Millbrook: The True Story of the Early Years of the Psychedelic Revolution.* Oakland, Calif.: Bench Press.

Koch, Raymond, and Charlotte Koch. 1972. *Educational Commune: The Story of Commonwealth College.* New York: Schocken.

Komar, Ingrid. 1983. *Living the Dream: A Documentary Study of Twin Oaks Community.* Norwood, Pa.: Norwood Editions.

Kopkind, Andrew. 1973. "Up the Country: Five Communes in Vermont." *Working Papers for a New Society* 1 (1973): 44–49.

Kumar, Krishan. 1987. *Utopia and Anti-Utopia in Modern Times.* Oxford: Basil Blackwell.

Laffan, Barry. 1997. *Communal Organizations and Social Transition: A Case Study from the Counterculture of the Sixties and Seventies.* New York: Peter Lang.

Landing, James E. 1981. "Cyrus R. Teed, Koreshanity and Cellular Cosmogony." *Communal Societies* 1 (3): 1–17.

Laurel, Alicia Bay. 1971. *Living on the Earth*. New York: Random House.

Leder, Kit. 1970. "Women in Communes." *WIN* 6 (Mar. 15): 14–16. Originally published in *Women: A Journal of Liberation*.

Lee, Dallas. 1971. *The Cotton Patch Evidence*. New York: Harper and Row.

Lee, Martin A., and Bruce Shlain. 1985. *Acid Dreams: The CIA, LSD and the Sixties Rebellion*. New York: Grove.

Lemieux, Christina M. 1990. "The Sunrise Cooperative Farm Community: A Collectivist Utopian Experiment." *Communal Societies* 10 (1990): 9–67.

Levine, Saul V., Robert P. Carr, and Wendy Horenblas. 1973. "The Urban Commune: Fact or Fad, Promise or Pipedream?" *American Journal of Orthopsychiatry* 43 (Jan.): 149–63.

LeWarne, Charles P. 1975. *Utopias on Puget Sound, 1885–1915*. Seattle: University of Washington Press.

Lewis, Betty. 1992. *Holy City: Riker's Roadside Attraction in the Santa Cruz Mountains*. Santa Cruz: Otter B. Books.

Loomis, Mildred J. 1982. *Alternative Americas*. New York: Universe Books.

Marling, Karal Ann. 1977. *Woodstock: An American Art Colony, 1902–1977*. Exhibition Catalog, Vassar College Art Gallery.

McKee, Rose. 1963. *"Brother Will" and the Founding of Gould Farm*. Great Barrington, Mass.: William J. Gould Associates.

McLaughlin, Corinne, and Gordon Davidson. 1985. *Builders of the Dawn: Community Lifestyles in a Changing World*. Walpole, N.H.: Stillpoint Publishing.

Melcher, M. Fellows. 1975. *The Shaker Adventure*. New York: The Shaker Museum.

Melton, J. Gordon. 1994. *Encyclopedia of American Religions*. 4th ed. Detroit: Gale Research.

Melville, Keith. 1972. *Communes in the Counter Culture: Origins, Theories, Styles of Life*. New York: Morrow.

Mercer, Duane D. 1967. "The Colorado Co-operative Company, 1894–1904." *Colorado Magazine* 44 (fall): 293–306.

Metcalf, Bill, ed. 1996. *Shared Visions, Shared Lives*. Forres, Scotland: Findhorn.

Meyer, Pauline. 1980. *Keep Your Face to the Sunshine: A Lost Chapter in the History of Woman Suffrage*. Edwardsville, Ill.: Alcott Press.

Meyers, Mary Ann. 1983. *A New World Jerusalem: The Swedenborgian Experience in Community Construction*. Westport, Conn.: Greenwood Press.

Miller, Ernest I. 1942. *Some Tennessee Utopias* (Monograph No. 2, Special Studies in Sociology). Knoxville: Department of Sociology, University of Tennessee.

Miller, Timothy. 1998. *The Quest for Utopia in Twentieth-Century America*. Syracuse, N.Y.: Syracuse University Press.

———. 1999. *The 60s Communes: Hippies and Beyond*. Syracuse, N.Y.: Syracuse University Press.

Morse, Flo. 1980. *The Shakers and the World's People*. New York: Dodd Mead.

Mungo, Raymond. 1970. *Famous Long Ago: My Life and Hard Times with Liberation News Service*. Boston: Beacon.

———. 1971. *Total Loss Farm: A Year in the Life*. New York: Bantam.

Murphy, James L. 1989. *The Reluctant Radical: Jacob L. Beilhart and the Spirit Fruit Society*. Lanham, Md.: University Press of America.

Negley, Glenn Roberts. 1977. *Utopian Literature: A Bibliography with a Supplementary Listing of Work Influential in Utopian Thought.* Lawrence: Regents Press of Kansas.

Nelson, Shirley. 1989. *Fair Clear and Terrible: The Story of Shiloh, Maine.* Latham, N.Y.: British American Publishing.

Neusner, Jacob, ed. 1972. *Contemporary Judaic Fellowship in Theory and Practice.* New York: Ktav.

Nursey-Bray, Paul F., ed. 1992. *Anarchist Thinkers and Thought: An Annotated Bibliography.* Westport, Conn.: Greenwood Press.

Oliphant, John. 1991. *Brother Twelve: The Incredible Story of Canada's False Prophet and His Doomed Cult of Gold, Sex, and Black Magic.* Toronto: McClelland and Stewart.

Orser, W. Edward. 1981. *Searching for a Viable Alternative: The Macedonia Cooperative Community, 1937–1958.* New York: Burt Franklin and Co.

Oved, Yaacov. 1988. *Two Hundred Years of American Communes.* New Brunswick, N.J. and Oxford: Transaction.

———. 1996. *The Witness of the Brothers: A History of the Bruderhof.* New Brunswick, N.J.: Transaction.

Padanaram Settlement. 1994. Williams, Ind.: Padanaram Press.

Perkins, David. 1996. "Commune." *Spirit Magazine: Rocky Mountain Southwest* 9 (spring/summer): 12–15, 36–39.

Perry, Paul. 1990. *On the Bus: The Complete Guide to the Legendary Trip of Ken Kesey and the Merry Pranksters and the Birth of the Counterculture.* New York: Thunder's Mouth.

Peters, Victor. 1965. *All Things Common: The Hutterian Way of Life.* Minneapolis: University of Minnesota Press.

Piehl, Mel. 1982. *Breaking Bread:The Catholic Worker and the Origin of Catholic Radicalism in America.* Philadelphia: Temple University Press.

Pitts, William L. 1995. "Davidians and Branch Davidians: 1929–1987." In *Armageddon in Waco: Critical Perspectives on the Branch Davidian Conflict,* Stuart A. Wright, ed., 20–42. Chicago: University of Chicago Press.

Pitzer, Donald E., ed. 1997. *America's Communal Utopias.* Chapel Hill and London: University of North Carolina Press.

Popenoe, Cris, and Oliver Popenoe. 1984. *Seeds of Tomorrow: New Age Communities That Work.* San Francisco: Harper and Row.

Raimy, Eric. 1979. *Shared Houses, Shared Lives: The New Extended Families and How They Work.* Los Angeles: Tarcher.

Rainard, R. Lyn. 1981. "Conflict inside the Earth: The Koreshan Unity in Lee County." *Tampa Bay History* 3 (1981): 5–16.

Rawlinson, Andrew. 1997. *The Book of Enlightened Masters: Western Teachers in Eastern Traditions.* Chicago: Open Court.

Rettig, Lawrence L. 1975. *Amana Today: A History of the Amana Colonies from 1932 to the Present.* Amana, Iowa: Amana Society.

Richard, Jerry, ed. 1973. *The Good Life.* New York: New American Library.

Roberts, Ron E. 1971. *The New Communes: Coming Together in America.* Englewood Cliffs, N.J.: Prentice-Hall.

Ross, Joseph. 1989. *Krotona of Old Hollywood*. Montecito, Calif.: El Montecito Oaks Press.

Rothchild, John, and Susan Berns Wolf. 1976. *The Children of the Counterculture*. Garden City, N.Y.: Doubleday.

Sears, Hal D. 1969. "Alcander Longley, Missouri Communist: A History of Reunion Community and a Study of the Constitutions of Reunion and Friendship." *Bulletin of the Missouri Historical Society* 25 (Jan.): 123–37.

Shambaugh, Bertha. 1971. *Amana: The Community of True Inspiration*. New York: B. Blom.

Shankman, Arnold. 1978. "Happyville, the Forgotten Colony." *American Jewish Archives* 30 (Apr.): 3–19.

Shepperson, Wilbur S. 1996. *Retreat to Nevada: A Socialist Colony of World War I*. Reno: University of Nevada Press.

Shi, David. 1985. *The Simple Life: Plain Living and High Thinking in American Culture*. New York: Oxford University Press.

Shields, Steven L. 1982. *Divergent Paths of the Restoration: A History of the Latter Day Saint Movement*. Bountiful, Utah: author.

Sor, Francis. 1987. "The Utopian Project in a Communal Experiment of the 1930's: The Sunrise Colony in Historical and Comparative Perspective." *Communal Societies* 7 (1987): 82–94.

Spann, Edward K. 1989. *Brotherly Tomorrows: Movement for a Cooperative Society in America 1820–1920*. New York: Columbia University Press.

Spence, Clark C. 1985. *The Salvation Army Farm Colonies*. Tucson: University of Arizona Press.

Sperber, Mae T. 1976. *Search for Utopia: A Study of Twentieth Century Communes in America*. Middleboro, Mass.: The Country Press.

Stein, Stephen J. 1992. *The Shaker Experience in American History: A History of the United Society of Believers*. New Haven, Conn.: Yale University Press.

Sternsher, Bernard. 1964. *Rexford Tugwell and the New Deal*. New Brunswick, N.J.: Rutgers University Press.

Stevens, Jay. 1987. *Storming Heaven: LSD and the American Dream*. New York: Harper and Row.

Sundancer, Elaine [Elaine Zablocki]. 1973. *Celery Wine: The Story of a Country Commune*. Yellow Springs, Ohio: Community Publications Cooperative.

Sutton, Robert P. 2003. *Communal Utopias and the American Experience: Religious Communities, 1732–2000*. Westport, Conn. and London: Praeger.

———. 2004. *Communal Utopias and the American Experience: Secular Communities, 1824–2000*. Westport, Conn. and London: Praeger.

Swichkow, Louis J. 1964–65. "The Jewish Colony of Arpin, Wisconsin." *American Jewish Historical Quarterly*. 54 (1964–65): 82–91.

Tabor, James D., and Eugene V. Gallagher. 1995. *Why Waco? Cults and the Battle for Religious Freedom in America*. Berkeley: University of California Press.

Taylor, R. James. 1996. *Mary's City of David*. Benton Harbor, Mich.: Mary's City of David.

Trahair, Richard C. 1999. *Utopias and Utopians: An Historical Dictionary*. Westport, Conn.: Greenwood Press.

Traugot, Michael. 1994. *A Short History of The Farm*. Summertown, Tenn.: the author.

Veysey, Laurence. 1973. *The Communal Experience: Anarchists and Mystical Countercultures in America*. New York: Harper and Row.

Wagner, Jon, ed. 1982. *Sex Roles in Contemporary American Communes*. Bloomington: Indiana University Press.

Ward, Hiley H. 1972. *The Far-Out Saints of the Jesus Communes*. New York: Association Press.

Watts, Jill. 1992. *God, Harlem, U.S.A.: The Father Divine Story*. Berkeley: University of California Press.

Webber, Everett. 1959. *Escape to Utopia: The Communal Movement in America*. New York: Hastings House.

Weisbrot, Robert. 1997. "Father Divine and the Peace Mission. In *America's Communal Utopias,* Donald E. Pitzer, ed. Chapel Hill and London: University of North Carolina Press.

———. 1983. *Father Divine and the Struggle for Racial Equality*. Urbana: University of Illinois Press.

Whisenhut, Donald W. 1983. "Utopians, Communalism, and the Great Depression." *Utopian Societies* 3(1983): 101–9.

Wizansky, Richard, ed. 1973. *Home Comfort: Stories and Scenes of Life on Total Loss Farm*. New York: Saturday Review Press.

Wooster, Ernest S. 1924. *Communities of the Past and Present*. Newllano, La.: Llano Colonist.

Zablocki, Benjamin. 1971. *The Joyful Community*. Chicago: University of Chicago Press.

———. 1980. *Alienation and Charisma: A Study of Contemporary American Communes*. New York: Free Press.

Zicklin, Gilbert. 1983. *Countercultural Communes: A Sociological Perspective*. Westport, Conn.: Greenwood Press.

INDEX

ROBERT P. SUTTON was a Professor of History at Western Illinois University until his retirement in January 2005. His fields of expertise include communal utopias and American legal history on which he has published 13 books and numerous articles.